The Big House Anthology

The Big House Anthology
Diverse Plays for Diverse Casts

Phoenix Rising
Knife Edge
Bullet Tongue (Reloaded)
The Ballad of Corona V (The Remix)
Redemption

Edited by
BEL PARKER

methuen | drama
LONDON • NEW YORK • OXFORD • NEW DELHI • SYDNEY

METHUEN DRAMA
Bloomsbury Publishing Plc
50 Bedford Square, London, WC1B 3DP, UK
1385 Broadway, New York, NY 10018, USA
29 Earlsfort Terrace, Dublin 2, Ireland

BLOOMSBURY, METHUEN DRAMA and the Methuen Drama logo are trademarks of
Bloomsbury Publishing Plc

First published in Great Britain 2023

Copyright © The Big House, 2023
Phoenix Rising © Andrew Day, 2023
Knife Edge © David Watson, 2023
Bullet Tongue (Reloaded) © Andrew Day, 2023
The Ballad of Corona V (The Remix) © David Watson, 2023
Redemption © James Meteyard, 2023

The Big House have asserted their right under the Copyright, Designs and Patents Act, 1988,
to be identified as author of this work.

Cover image © Nia Visser

All rights reserved. No part of this publication may be reproduced or transmitted in any form or by any means, electronic or mechanical, including photocopying, recording, or any information storage or retrieval system, without prior permission in writing from the publishers.

Bloomsbury Publishing Plc does not have any control over, or responsibility for, any third-party websites referred to or in this book. All internet addresses given in this book were correct at the time of going to press. The author and publisher regret any inconvenience caused if addresses have changed or sites have ceased to exist, but can accept no responsibility for any such changes.

No rights in incidental music or songs contained in the work are hereby granted and performance rights for any performance/presentation whatsoever must be obtained from the respective copyright owners.

For *Phoenix Rising* and *Bullet Tongue* (*Reloaded*):
All rights whatsoever in this play are strictly reserved and application for performance etc. should be made before rehearsals to Permissions Department, Bloomsbury Publishing Plc, 50 Bedford Square, London, WC1B 3DP, UK. No performance may be given unless a licence has been obtained. No rights in incidental music or songs contained in the Work are hereby granted and performance rights for any performance/presentation whatsoever must be obtained from the respective copyright owners.

For *Knife Edge* and *The Ballad of Corona V (The Remix)*:
All rights whatsoever in this play are strictly reserved and application for performance etc. should be made before rehearsals by professionals and by amateurs to Casarotto Ramsay & Associates Ltd, Waverley House, 7–12 Noel Street, London W1F 8GQ Mail to: agents@casarotto.co.uk.
No performance may be given unless a licence has been obtained.

For *Redemption*:
All rights whatsoever in this play are strictly reserved and application for performance etc. should be made before rehearsals by professionals and by amateurs to United Agents LLP of 12–26 Lexington Street, London, W1F 0LE. No performance may be given unless a licence has been obtained.

A catalogue record for this book is available from the British Library.

Library of Congress Cataloging-in-Publication Data
Names: Big house (Theater company) editor.
Title: The Big House anthology : diverse plays for diverse casts : Phoenix rising, Knife edge, Bullet tongue (reloaded), The ballad of corona v, Redemption / edited by The Big House.
Description: London ; New York : Methuen Drama, 2023. |
Identifiers: LCCN 2022049368 | ISBN 9781350359741 (paperback) | ISBN 9781350359758 (epub) | ISBN 9781350359765 (pdf)
Subjects: LCSH: English drama--21st century. | LCGFT: Drama.
Classification: LCC PR1272.2 .B54 2023 | DDC 822.9205—dc23/eng/2022/1213
LC record available at https://lccn.loc.gov/2022049368

ISBN: PB: 978-1-3503-5974-1
ePDF: 978-1-3503-5976-5
eBook: 978-1-3503-5975-8

Series: Methuen Drama Play Collections

Typeset by RefineCatch Limited, Bungay, Suffolk

To find out more about our authors and books visit www.bloomsbury.com
and sign up for our newsletters.

In memory of Dwayne Kieran Nero, Sonya Hale and Rapheal Addai.

*And for all members of The Big House.
Past, present, and future.*

Contents

Foreword by Jez Butterworth ix

Introduction by Maggie Norris 1

Phoenix Rising by Andrew Day 5
Interview with writer Andrew Day 6
Production information 8
Play 10
In conversation with director Maggie Norris 67

Knife Edge by David Watson 71
Interview with writer David Watson 72
Production information 74
Play 76
In conversation with director Maggie Norris 138

Bullet Tongue (Reloaded) by Andrew Day 141
How it was written 142
Interview with writer Andrew Day 143
Production information 145
Play 147
In conversation with director Maggie Norris 208

The Ballad of Corona V (The Remix) by David Watson 211
Interview with writer David Watson 212
Production information 214
Play 216
In conversation with director Maggie Norris 277

Redemption by James Meteyard 279
Interview with writer James Meteyard 280
Production information 283
Play 287
In conversation with director Maggie Norris 349

Foreword by Jez Butterworth

At school I lived for the one drama class per week. It was the only lesson where I felt alive, connected to the world. Everything began to make sense.

And when the lesson was over, I'd simply wait for the next week.

I feel The Big House provides the same for the young people involved. Many of them need their lives to make sense much more urgently than a white boy growing up in the 1980s in Watford with a mum and dad to come home to. It goes beyond passion. It's a necessity.

But that's not why I admire The Big House. It's not because what they're doing is worthy or honourable. Most theatre is mind-crushingly boring chiefly *because* it's worthy or honourable.

It's the work.

'Phoenix' and 'Bullet Tongue' are two of the top three shows I've seen anywhere in the past decade. (Shonagh Marie was so good in 'Bullet Tongue' I cast her in a central role in my Sky Atlantic show *Britannia*. And she absolutely smashed it.)

The work is as powerful, as visceral, funny, and inspired as the best theatre I've seen. It's immediate, present, blisteringly committed and real. It certainly wipes the floor with anything I've seen at The Royal Court over the same period!

I know that putting on the shows is not always an easy task. But creating excellent theatre never is. Theatre folk are traditionally as wild, difficult and unruly as Theatre itself. As the song says, there's no people like show people. They used to bury us outside the church walls!

Long Live The Big House! Your work is not just necessary, rare, alive, authentic, compelling, scary and important . . .

It's world class.

Jez Butterworth
13 September 2022

Introduction by Maggie Norris
Founder and Artistic Director of The Big House

I have spent most of my working life in the theatre, originally as an actress, then as a writer and latterly as a director. It is an exciting place to be. Anything is possible. Everything is imaginable.

I didn't imagine, however, that at the peak of my career I would set up a charity called The Big House (a slang term for prison) and work with young people leaving the care system. I am so glad that I did. Using drama combined with long-term support to transform lives, we have developed a programme that breaks entrenched, debilitating and self-destructive patterns of behaviour with a combination of nurture, discipline and creativity which in turn generates resilience, self-belief and capability in our young people.

You may be wondering why I chose this path. It certainly wasn't planned. It really emerged as a result of some research I did initially to direct *Bad Girls The Musical* (set in prison) at West Yorkshire Playhouse and then at The Garrick Theatre in the West End. This was followed by time spent talking to inmates in Wormwood Scrubs and Pentonville Prison. I realised then that many of those people should not have been there and that a disproportionate number of those inmates were care leavers.

I decided to do some voluntary work in prisons to explore the problem further. I used drama as a tool to inspire some of the most hard-to-reach inside and found myself in a rehearsal room in Wormwood Scrubs with twenty-eight prisoners and only one prison guard. Steve, on day three, was slouched in a side room with a tabloid and a cup of tea. I had been told initially that I would need eight prison guards in rehearsal in this Category B prison. The guards got bored however and left pretty swiftly when they realised that I was having no problem with the 'bad behaviour' which had been predicted. I have found that if you treat people with respect and don't judge them, it is rare not to have that reciprocated. Every single prisoner from that production (except a Lifer who remains inside) has found me on 'the outside' to express what the project meant to them.

The great majority of children in care do not commit criminal offences, yet there is a consistent over-representation of care leavers in the criminal justice system. Less than 1 per cent of the population have been in the care system, but a recent review chaired by Lord Laming reports that approximately 50 per cent of children in custody have been in care. This figure becomes truly disturbing when you consider that just 2 per cent of children are in care because of 'socially unacceptable behaviour' and 60 per cent are there because of traumatic abuse and neglect. It is easy for those young people's lives to spiral out of control when they emerge from care, bruised and depressed. They have few life skills and are ill equipped to navigate the complex transition from adolescence to adulthood. For those readers with children, you know how much guidance a teenager needs leaving home, finding a job, going to university or managing a budget. The Big House provides wraparound long-term support.

Most arrive at The Big House feeling isolated, misunderstood and angry. They have been treated like a dangerous parcel by clumsy systems that have mislabelled them, as they are passed from one agency to another. They are lost and wary as a result, distrustful and fragile. The Big House helps them see that they deserve better and should expect more: from themselves, from their corporate parents and from their community. We have created a loving family at The Big House for those who lack one and we are committed to inspiring the incredible young people who walk through our doors. This is a reciprocal, self-generating process. The more confident our young people become, in turn they are more able to pay back the love, by nurturing our new recruits.

The scripts that you will read in this anthology are a collaboration between the writer, the young people and the director on each project. The bond formed between all parties is strong and hopefully gives the plays an authenticity that is unique. Most of the young people that we work with have never been to the theatre before and many have never left their postcode. None are auditioned. We give them a platform to speak about issues they care deeply about. The parts are created to showcase the talent of the young people and we make sure that they are playing to their natural strengths. We eschew conventional theatre techniques which can often make our young people feel confused or left out. We develop their acting skills through fun game-based improvisation sessions and build their confidence to such a level that they become fearless. We have discovered some incredible talent at The Big House and are proud to have launched the careers of some extraordinary actors.

We never put our young people on stages, as that creates a barrier between performer and audience. Instead we abolish the separation between the audience's space and the performance space, either in an immersive or promenade setting or a space that allows the audience and cast to intermingle, whether that be in a restaurant, a cinema or a car park. This adds to the power of the performance as you are in the midst of it. It is not unusual at The Big House for the performances to be so real, so believable that audiences are too emotional and immersed to applaud. But let me introduce the work with the words of an audience member who wrote to me after seeing *Phoenix Rising* in the car park underneath Smithfield Meat Market . . .

> The world of the play, transported me back. Back to a world in which I lived. A world I'd managed to 'escape' in some ways. I use that term lightly because I'm not ashamed of my past, nor embarrassed to tell people where I'm from. The friends, the parties, the social workers, the drugs, sex, all of it. The scene where the Mum said 'take my teeth, take my bones, but don't take my kids', threw me right back to the moment my mum threw a table at the social workers as they took us all away. The skanky bedsit, shitty walls and crappy little sofa. The frustration when the social workers tell you to calm down. When you've watched your family be broken into tiny little pieces and you feel worthless. The loss, at losing everyone but also losing a sister for years to the system. All of these things . . . this world you created. This world that made me cry because I felt like a character in this play instead of a bystander watching in. I lived it with the cast, moment to moment, because it was ACCURATE. The feelings of just wanting to go home, really just wanting your Mum. Just wanting a chance and never understanding why it always has to be soo much harder for us. Those feelings and realities that this show had and felt were real. More real than I've ever felt from any performance I've ever seen. Between the direction, the writing and the passion of the cast, you portrayed real life in front of me. Yes,

there were abstract moments, but in all, it was life as we know it. And that's why I cried, I cried because I felt like a ten year old watching her past and present in front of her. Watching her family and friends. I find this amazing, because that means that what you are showing people who don't come from that world is honest work. An honest portrayal of a difficult life. A hard world to be born into and this is needed and so important. Even if 10 per cent of the audience walk away with a better understanding of what that life is like then great. If next time at least 5 per cent of them stop before they judge the 'trouble maker' or brand the young Mum a waste of space . . . great! Because every step is a step towards a future where people stop to understand instead of stop to judge. (Laura Thompson)

Phoenix Rising

Andrew Day

Interview with writer Andrew Day

Phoenix Rising *is an evolution of* Phoenix, *the first show that The Big House ever put on and that you wrote back in 2013. What sparked the initial idea?*

The story was inspired by Kieran Nero, who sadly passed away between the first and second productions. Kieran had Multiple Sclerosis. He had been a promising runner in his youth. Maggie suggested I talk to him. He emailed some thoughts in a document called 'Dream' and we had a long chat. He talked about how he had dreams where he was actually OK and the whole MS thing was a nightmare he'd woken up from.

I hear that the male lead Callum was originally a female character . . .?

For the first version of the show, we had an obvious lead in the teenage Jasmine Jobson. So I wrote it around her because she could carry it on her own. Kieran played her brother, beautifully. After Kieran died, Maggie wanted to do a tribute to him. So we re-staged the show with a male lead character. That was fascinating because then you have to ask yourself: what changes if the gender changes? I came up with my own answers to that but it is an interesting case study!

How involved were the cast in developing the material for Phoenix Rising*?*

There were so many workshops and improvisations. The cast were amazing. Two things I remember coming out of the cast were: anger brimming under the surface all the time and being needed as a defence mechanism – a gun to draw at the slightest hint of trouble; the bewildering and impersonal experience of being moved around by care workers and social workers. I also read through one care leaver's local authority file with her. It was so disjointed. Normally, when you write a play, you write it then look for a cast. With TBH it flows both ways, which is a nightmare in one sense, but leads to some magical outcomes.

When was the decision taken for the disease to be played by an actor?

It was because we had this fantastic dancer for the first show, Osman Enver. So I was trying to find a way to showcase that. I don't think I explained the idea very well and it was dropped. Then, he was working on the revival of the show so we resurrected the idea. MS is a creeping spectre of a disease.

What were some of the issues you wanted to raise about the care system?

Users of the care system are not usually able to understand why it fails them. They're also not able to appreciate how they are making it so hard for the system to help them. That's not a criticism of the young people – it's the inevitable consequence of their experiences: they are young and have prolonged experience of chaos, betrayal and injustice – otherwise they wouldn't have got anywhere near the care system in the first place. So they see those evils repeated in the everyday failings of an under-resourced, undermined service that is propped up by the dedication of the underpaid people in it. And even a half-decent care system is a shit parent.

    The other point for me is that when a young person is vulnerable, they are vulnerable to all the things that hurt everyone, but more so: illness, rudeness, cruelty, every kind of loss – even someone eating their food . . . they have less resilience but are often then blamed for that lack. People say 'Well that happens to everyone and he just needs to learn to be more . . . blah, blah'. Callum's outburst about his 'anger solution' and the 'brokenness in the window' – that's the key.

You were worried about writing a 'bad girlfriend' character – why was that?

This comes back to the gender switch. In the earlier version, the girl had an awful boyfriend who ridiculed her, stole from her and manipulated her. Nobody ever asked 'Mm, why is he like that?'. Then, when the main character switched to a male I could have still given him a boyfriend but the dynamic is obviously different between two males. So I gave him a girlfriend. There was some discomfort about portraying her as a real piece of work with no background explanation – no redeeming excuse. Nina's cruelty is more gratuitous and sadistic than the boyfriend's was. Maybe that was the problem . . . or maybe we see evil differently in boys than girls.

Tell us about the extraordinary events that happen on the running track when it morphs out of reality and into Callum's head.

In the play, the running track is the one place where Callum is inviolable, so for the nightmares to take place on the track, that's important.

The dream/hallucination part came from Kieran's idea about the dream.

By the way, it's very difficult for a playwright to determine exactly how a scene like that should be staged just through stage directions. So anyone producing should just focus on trying to show a fractured, tortured mind. In the TBH rehearsals, it was heavily worked and its success was down to the director and the ensemble.

Phoenix Rising was first performed in the Car Park under Smithfield Meat Market, London, on 8 November 2017, with the following cast:

Bready	Daniel Akilimali
Callum	Aston McAuley
Diane	Lou Mussington
Disease	Osman Enver
Dr Bernard	Anthony Brown
Hannah	Rebecca Farinre
Josiah	Charmel Koloko
Judge	Rowan Fornah
Julie	Rebecca Oldfield
Lauren/Adembambo	Shakira Robertson
Linda	Jade Sullivan
Nina	Perrina Allen
Omar	Jordan Bangura
Receptionist/Adebola	Melissa Madden
Shauna	Atlantia Sami
Slyvester/Denzel	Jay Scott
Suzanne	Ishara Bilson-Graham

Creative Team

Writer	Andy Day
Director	Maggie Norris
Dramaturgy	Maggie Norris
Production Manager	Nick Slater
Associate Director	Sammy Glover
Stage Manager	Sophie Stoddart
Set and Costume Design	Emma Bailey
Lighting designer	Zoe Spurr
Sound Designer	Ed Clarke
Assistant Director	Francisca Olivares
Movement Directors	Maggie Norris and Osman Enver
Fight Director	Kate Waters
Costume Assistant	Kyle Davies

Characters

Callum
Interviewer
Sylvester
Frankie
Guard
The Disease
Josiah
Suzanne
Hannah
Bready
Omar
Diane
Denzel
Charlie
Lauren
Shauna
Nina
Linda
Julie
Adebola
Adebambo
Judge
Receptionist
Patient
Foreign Woman
Security
PA System
Nurse
Dr Bernand

Race Track

Athletics meeting. Young athletes milling on the track. Some are warming up, some walking from track to changing room or back. An official with a clipboard on his way somewhere . . . A coach calling to someone impatiently . . . A **PA System** *echoes around the field, distantly:*

PA System   Runners for the 100m to the starting line . . . Runners for the 200m relay to the starting line . . . Competitor 103 Samantha Coombe-Brown to Registration . . . Competitor 103 Samantha Coombe-Brown to Registration . . . Could Mr (*hesitates*) Fenoulli make your way to the long jump pit . . .

As we get closer to the start of the show, athletes assemble at the starting line, stretching, eyeing each other or ignoring each other, tension building . . .

Track

The final stages of the warm-up. The starter has a walkie-talkie and a clipboard.

PA System   Could Competitor 77 Callum Connor report to the starting line for the 100m. This race is about to begin. That's Competitor 77 Callum Connor to the starting line immediately . . . (*More impatient tone.*) Message to all competitors and spectators, there is no smoking allowed anywhere within the stadium. No smoking anywhere in the stadium – thank you.

Callum *enters, walks fast down the track to the starting line, wearing hoody – smoking. We can't see his face. He flicks the lit cigarette towards the other runners. They part, can't help being intimidated. Takes off his hoody and his track trousers – he is number 77 – casts them behind him, and drops to his mark. All one long continuous entrance to here.*

The other runners take their marks . . .

The starter raises the gun into the air . . . Runners get set . . . Bang! The sound of the gun is slowed down . . . **Callum** *goes into slow motion – everything goes into slow motion, sound too. Sounds of the crowd and PA mix in and the sound of a deep breath – all slowed down . . . The runners burst from their marks in slow motion, make their way down their lanes . . .* **Callum** *pulls ahead, focused straight ahead . . . Then we return to normal speed and the athletes disappear down the track,* **Callum** *breaking the tape.* **Callum** *turns and walks straight back the way he came, hyped, but without looking left or right. Picks ups his clothes. An interviewer approaches* **Callum** *with a microphone. The voice goes out over the PA.*

Interviewer   Callum. What do you have to say?

Callum   Nothing.

Interviewer   No message to anyone in the stand?

Callum I'd like to thank everyone that believed in me. Which is no-one. I'd like to NOT thank my mum, 'cos she was never that into me, and I'd like to NOT thank my dad wherever he is, and I'd like to NOT thank all the teachers and coaches and . . . wait a minute . . . I would like to say thank you . . . to my legs. Thank you, legs, for all your support. Without you two, I would never have won that race.

Callum *hands the microphone back. Walks away . . .*

Changing Room

Changing room: pegs, a bench. **Callum** *wanders over and picks up a bottle of water – takes huge gulps . . .* **Frankie** *and* **Sylvester**, *two of the other runners in his race appear, surrounding him. He doesn't seem to notice at first, now sloshing it over his head. Then sees that eyes are on him.*

Sylvester Frankie's crucifix has gone.

Callum (*swishes his mouth out*) His what?

Frankie Crucifix. On a chain.

Callum First thing, there's a fucking great sign up there saying Beware Of Thieves, Do Not Leave Valuables, so why would you leave jewellery lying around in here?

Frankie I put it in –

Callum I don't think you did. I think you're making shit up, 'cos you just got owned out there on the track and you don't like my kind.

Frankie You were the last one out.

Callum (*laughing, but dripping with malice*) You think you can step to me and call me a thief? Huh? You think you can do that?

Callum *grabs* **Frankie** *by the throat, pushing him backwards.*

Dialogue overlapping and confused through next section.

Sylvester (*panicking*) Ah, shit, look . . . Oi! Oi!

Frankie Get the fuck off . . .

Callum You think you're gonna walk away now?

Callum *throws* **Frankie** *to the floor,* **Sylvester** *puts his arms round* **Callum** *from behind in a bear hug.*

Sylvester Hey, cool it, cuz . . .

Frankie Jesus Christ . . .

Callum *leans forward then throws his head back, headbutting* **Sylvester**, *who crumples to the floor.*

Frankie Hey, hey, hey!

Callum *kicks* **Sylvester** *in the ribs. A* **Security Guard** *bursts in. Takes* **Callum***'s arm. Commotion.*

Callum (*to the guard*) Get the fuck out of here – you? Get out of here and get your mates. Get your whole fucking firm – come on!!!

Guard Come on . . . Out! . . . Out! . . . Hey! . . . Calm down! . . . Christ's sake . . . What's the matter with this kid?! Oi! . . . Easy . . .

Guard *drags* **Callum** *away, but he keeps pulling back and to the side. Several people now filming on phones, grinning.* **Callum** *and the* **Guard** *stagger in a zig zag, backwards, forwards. On the edge of the track,* **Callum** *bursts out of his grip. Sees the* **Interviewer***. Grabs the mic –*

Callum Here's a message for you. Fuck you for coming, fuck you for organizing this, and fuck every single person who gave up their time to help out today. That's you I'm talking about. Fuck you . . . and fuck you . . . and fuck you . . .

The **Guard** *grabs him again. Again they wrestle.* **Callum** *allows himself to be thrown out. He stumbles forward, cracking his head on a pillar . . . He slides to the ground . . . Everything goes haywire . . . Dreamlike. Voices in the distance call '***Callum***' . . . '***Callum***'.* **Callum** *pulls himself unsteadily to his feet.*

'**The Disease**'*, A wraith-like figure appears, out of the haze.* **Callum** *sees him, looks puzzled, but walks away . . . But he's dizzy, disorientated . . . He staggers and falls onto the track.*

The runners assemble, slow motion, dreamy, just like the start of the play all over again, but weird. The voice over the pa system is distorted but saying the same things as before. **Callum***, still puzzled, in a dream . . .*

Callum Wait . . . Wait . . . I'm coming . . . Don't start it. . . .

Callum *stumbles towards the starting line. He's not going to make it. The disease is the starter. He raises his gun. The other runners hear the starter's orders, distorted (recorded) and drop to all fours.* **Callum** *is just in front of the starting line, confused. The disease raises his gun. But instead of firing into the air, he turns, lowers the weapon and fires at* **Callum***'s leg. The other runners sprint away in slow motion as* **Callum** *collapses in agony. They crash into him, Trampling and kicking him. Sounds rise to a crescendo and then fall as the runners disappear, and the disease backs away, disappearing into the crowd.*

Lighting change – back in the real world.

Track

Josiah *is standing over* **Callum***, looking curious.*

Callum Say it. What d'you want?

Josiah I wanna coach you.

Callum (*dismissive*) I ain't never had a coach.

Josiah It shows.

Callum What do I want a coach for?

Josiah You're out of control.

Callum I don't believe in control.

Josiah What about success – you believe in that? There's tons of guys like you on the scrapheap, alright? They didn't train, they didn't eat right, they didn't master themselves. They have dreams now where they can run like they used to . . . Then they wake up, and they cough, and they slap their bellies, and wonder how they're gonna fill up one more day. That's your future, right there.

Callum What's in it for you though? Who's gonna pay you?

Josiah No-one else is gonna help you, OK? You can't set foot in that club again, not after that. What you got to lose?

Callum What's in it for you? Unless you're a paedophile . . . *Are* you a paedophile?

Josiah No.

Callum How do I know that?

Josiah You need to trust me.

Callum Wait. Do you trust me?

Josiah Well, what I'm prepared to do is to place my –

Callum Do you trust me? No. You'd be fucking stupid if you did.

Walks away.

Josiah I know some people at Nike.

Callum *stops.*

Josiah Every year they sponsor a few youngsters. If you show promise, they give you all the kit.

Callum What?

Josiah Free Nike gear.

Callum OK . . . You come up with the gear, then we talk. Starting with spikes. Size 9.

Josiah First, you gotta produce on the track. That's the way it works.

Callum You wanna own me for the price of a few clothes you ain't even gonna pay for!

Josiah I ain't gonna own shit. You can fire your coach any time you like.

Callum Serious? I can? Ah, now you're talking my language . . . I hereby appoint you as my official coach. I'll fire you later, some day when I really feel I gotta fire someone. Cool.

Josiah Monday. Out on the field. 8am.

Callum I reach when I reach, man.

Josiah 8am

Callum I ain't got a watch or nothing.

Josiah Phone? (**Callum** *shakes his head.*) Alright. If you're there 8am Monday, I'll give you a phone.

Callum What kind of phone? I don't want –

Josiah A phone that you can use to talk to people who are too far away to hear you shouting. If you want something nice-nice, get a job.

Callum How do you know I ain't got a job?

Josiah Lucky guess. Your name's Callum, right?

Callum *nods.*

Josiah You wanna know my name?

Josiah *starts to walk away.*

Callum (*watching* **Josiah** *leave*) Nah. You just Coach, innit? Until I fire you, then you're nobody again.

Callum's Bedsit

Callum*'s bedsit.* **Suzanne** *waits. A little impatient. She takes out her phone.*

Suzanne Hello, is that Mr Telford? This is Suzanne Tambo. Yes. Yes, I'm inside the property now and I'm sorry but it's not up to standard. Well, I'm sorry but . . . I'm sorry but . . . (*She is getting interrupted.*) It's not clean, OK? Or in a satisfactory state of repair. No, that's not the case . . . The Local Authority is paying you a market rent for – yes it is – you are being paid to provide – (**Mr Telford** *hangs up. She dials again.*) Hi Diane? It's Suzanne. Yeah, the landlord's done it again. It hasn't been cleaned and everything's just . . . How far away are you? OK see you in a minute. Callum? He hasn't turned up yet. Hopefully he won't. It might give us time to –

Callum *ambles in.*

Suzanne I'll call you back . . . (*Hangs up.*) Callum!

Callum *looks around the room. He takes it all in.*

Callum Where's my stuff?

Suzanne My colleague Diane is bringing it.

Callum This is an insult.

Suzanne I could try to get you a temporary bed and breakfast until he sorts –

Callum Fuck those places. Smell of piss, bleach and breakfast. (*Considers, sighs.*) Alright this is what you got me. What happens now?

Suzanne This is the start of your adult life.

Callum How long am I here?

Suzanne This is your home now.

Callum Something weird's going on with my legs.

Suzanne OK, well registering with a GP is one of your first jobs. I've put the address in here. And here are the numbers to call if you need things. And I'll be visiting regularly. Now that I've had a chance to get to know you, I'm very hopeful.

Callum Ain't you read my file?

Suzanne I'm not judging you by your past.

Callum You should. You seen the 200 metres?

Suzanne The what?

Callum The 200 metres. It's a staggered start. The runner on the inside track has to start further back. To make it fair, see? In real life, it's the other way round. The people on the inside track get to start further forward. And the people on the outside track . . . That's people like me . . . We start way back. And that's where we stay.

Suzanne Do you run the 200 – I mean in real life?

Callum 100. All on the same line.

Suzanne What we'll do now is make a plan for the first six months after local authority care.

Callum I want you to find my sister.

Suzanne We can look into that.

Callum That's the only thing I want you to do.

Suzanne Let's get some objectives written down.

Callum Ah, just write whatever they want you to say.

Suzanne I want to know what you want to achieve.

Callum Why?

Suzanne So I can help.

Callum I wanna win the 100 metre trials and get on the British team.

Suzanne   We can't exactly help you with that.

Callum   Get me some spikes.

Suzanne   Sorry, is that street slang – you're not talking about knives?!

Callum   Running shoes. I need new spikes.

Suzanne   Can't you make do with trainers – for now? Keep going to the club?

Callum   No! You can't even wear a baggy t-shirt. They got bare rules about everything.

Suzanne   How much are spikes?

Callum   Two hundred.

Suzanne   There must be cheaper ones!

Callum   Second best for me, right? Whatever no-one else wants. (*He gestures around him at the bedsit.*)

Suzanne   We don't have the budget for top of the range running shoes.

Callum   OK. So write down that you wanted to help me BUT you didn't have the budget. Write it down. Go on. You can't, can you? 'Cos there's no box for the truth.

Suzanne   There's a fund I can try for. I think your involvement at the athletics club has been a lifeline. You're making friends, right?

Callum   Yeah. My peer group is a positive influence and we've really bonded.

Suzanne   If there was a gold medal for bullshit, you'd win it.

Callum   Not if any social workers went in for it.

Suzanne   See? Sense of humour. That's a vital life skill. (**Suzanne**'s *phone goes.*) One moment. (*Into phone.*) Hi Diane. He's here. Yeah, you can park outside Tesco. I'll meet you there. (*To* **Callum**.) Diane's brought your belongings. I'll go down and meet her.

Callum *takes his phone out immediately. Dials.*

Outside on the Step

Hannah *sits, vacant, dejected. Sound of child crying incessantly.* **Suzanne** *leaving (Coming from* **Callum**'s *place). Stops as she sees* **Hannah**.

Suzanne   Hi . . . Is that your little one?

Hannan *nods slightly.*

Suzanne   Boy or girl?

Hannah (*inaudible*)   Girl.

Suzanne   What's her name?

Hannah (*inaudible*)   Paradise.

Suzanne   Sorry?

Hannah   Paradise.

Suzanne   You on your own with her? I wonder what she's up to . . . Up there, eh?

Hannah *shrugs.*

Suzanne   She's alright, is she?

Hannah   I just needed a break.

Suzanne   Yeah. It can really get on top of you when they're that age. Maybe . . . give someone a call?

Hannah (*inaudible*)   What?

Suzanne   Call someone? Someone to come and help out for a bit. Who could you call . . . do you think?

Hannah (*inaudible*)   I don't know.

Suzanne   Grandparents? Neighbours? Who can we think of? (*Silence.*) Tell you what, I'm just going over to Tesco to meet my friend, what shall I get, save you the journey?

Hannah (*inaudible*)   No thanks.

Suzanne   Loaf of bread? . . . Nappies? . . . Packet of biscuits?

Hannah   Nothing.

Suzanne *exits.* **Hannah** *remains.*

Callum's Bedsit

Bready *and* **Omar** *looking around.*

Bready   So this is Callum's new crib.

Bready *takes out rizlas.* **Omar** *a bag of weed.*

Omar   If social services gave me this, I'd be like 'Is this what you think I'm worth?'

Bready   Well they ain't gave me nothing so what does that say?

Omar   I thought you was going to live with your dad.

Bready   He's sick.

Omar   How does that stop you living in his house?

Bready   Just ain't easy right now. He ain't easy anyway and this thing he's got . . .

Callum Social worker's coming back. So let's do it.

Bready Woah. Can we get a chilled vibe here?

Callum She'll be back in, like, five minutes.

Bready How long's she gonna stay?

Callum Not long, if I don't argue with her.

Omar Yeah but you will argue with her . . .

Callum Just roll that thing.

Bready You can't rush these things. They require care and consideration, and – oh, shit.

Suzanne *enters with* **Dianne**, *carrying two black bin liners.*

Suzanne Ah.

Callum That was quick.

Diane Hello.

Suzanne (*looking at* **Omar**) Is that weed?

Callum (*faking horror*) Ah, for Christ's sake, you two! I don't want any of that going on here.

Bready (*playing along*) Sorry, Callum. We forgot you don't agree with illegal shit.

Callum If you come round here again carrying drugs, I'll flush it straight down the toilet.

Omar *pockets the joint.*

Suzanne The point is, Callum. You're breaking the terms of your lease.

Diane And you're putting us in a very difficult position.

Suzanne Now guys . . . I have a few things I have to go through with Callum.

Bready *and* **Omar** *just nod, don't move.* **Callum** *has spotted the bin bags, starting to get tense again. Turns away.*

Bready Cool.

Suzanne It's confidential.

Omar We're kind of like his next of kin, so . . .

Diane Sure.

Suzanne Seriously. Callum?

Callum Bruv . . . Fam . . . I'm gonna have to talk to her.

Bready Seen.

Omar Call us when you're done.

As they leave . . .

Bready (*confidential, indicating* **Suzanne**) That one's into you, man. (**Callum** *gestures – WTF?*) Just saying.

They're gone. **Callum** *has his back to them – and the bags.*

Diane So it took a while, but here are your . . .

Callum D'you ever think of getting a suitcase?

Diane Sorry?

Callum Or, like, a proper bag? Instead of a bin liner. What does that say? Chucking people's property in a bin liner.

Diane Whenever I move house my clothes are in bin liners.

Suzanne Is it all there? Do you want to check?

Callum It's not all there. My duvet ain't there. I told you about it.

Diane Ah. They said it was theirs.

Suzanne The foster family?

Callum It's mine.

Diane They said they paid for it.

Callum Yeah, with the money they got from you.

Diane (*slowly, trying to manage his anger*) I can tell you're angry.

Callum Course you can fucking tell I'm angry. I'm making it very clear.

Suzanne OK, OK . . .

Callum Why d'you make it about me being angry? Why d'you always put it on us? You watch us lose every single thing we've got and say 'Oh, he has a sense of loss'. You shut us out of everything and say 'He has an outsider mentality'. You see us get treated like shit and say 'This one suffers from low self-esteem'. You know we're getting cheated and lied to and ripped off and you say 'I sense anger', 'You seem angry', 'I'm detecting a lot of anger' – that's like throwing a brick at a window and saying 'Hmm I sense a lot of brokenness in the window'.

Suzanne So you don't think you have an anger problem?

Callum No I do not. I have an anger solution. If I wasn't angry then that would be a problem. That would be me accepting it. When I feel anger I know there's one person fighting for me. So don't try to take my anger away.

Diane I'm sorry about the duvet. I'll look into it.

Suzanne Is there anything else you need for tonight?

Callum *takes the two bags and empties them on the floor. Not much in there: A few clothes, an ashtray, a couple of toiletries. He gives an amused shrug. Points at the pathetic heap.*

Callum   Nothing else I need . . . for tonight. Go on, go.

Reluctantly, exchanging looks, the two leave. **Callum** *is alone for a few seconds. A whistle from the yard.* **Callum** *looks down, sees* **Omar** *and* **Bready**, *he beckons them up.*

Omar *and* **Bready** *enter.*

Callum   Finally.

Bready   I think they're both into you, man.

The joint is now fully rolled. They sit. **Omar** *lights and passes the joint.*

Omar   Now . . . Times like this . . . You gotta sit back, you gotta assess the situation . . . Think about how you're gonna attack it.

Bready   That's right. You need a plan.

Callum   Go on.

Omar   So let's look at what we got. OK? So, Thing Number One is . . . The place they've given you to live is a shithole. Correct?

Callum   Correct.

Omar *takes a deep contemplative mouthful. Breathes out. Very long silence. Seems to be contemplating this thought.*

Callum   And?

Omar   Er . . . That's about it really. Yeah.

Omar *passes joint to* **Callum**. *Another pause.*

Callum   Thanks, Omar. It was all a bit fuzzy before but now it's crystal clear.

Bready   You guys are missing something. And you don't even know it. You live in a shithole, but . . . There's a yard. Out there. A big yard.

Callum   What can I do with a yard?

Bready   I'll tell you what you can do. You can let me call a few of my peeps. They call up dem peeps and dem peeps' peeps. We cook up a party!

Omar   In that yard?

Bready   Yard party na yard party.

Omar *leaps like a lightning bolt to his feet, throws his arms wide as he realises it's a brilliant idea.*

Omar   Yard party na yard parteeeeeee!!!!!!!

The Yard

Party is full on. **Callum** *enters. Stands and takes it all in. Everyone dancing apart from* **Denzel**, *who is standing looking edgy, and* **Charlie**, *who moves from group to group (including the audience) offering drugs.*

Charlie *acts more like a waiter or magician. Jazzily dressed. Continually moving to the rhythm. He doesn't speak, just mime and gesture.*

(Note: When there is dialogue the music goes low to accomodate but the characters shout just as if the music was still loud)

Denzel What you got?

Charlie *pulls a gas canister half out of his pocket.*

Denzel What's that?

Charlie *mimes inhaling gas and laughing.* **Denzel** *shakes his head.*

Denzel What else?

Charlie *mimes a big sniff.*

Denzel How much?

On his hands, **Charlie** *shows ten . . . Twenty . . . Thirty . . . Still going . . .* **Denzel** *waves him away.* **Charlie** *moves on.*

Music back up loud.

Denzel *changes his mind. Walks round the other side of* **Charlie** *to stop him.*

Denzel *pays for the laughing gas.*

Callum *enters. Looks around approvingly. Clocks* **Denzel** *just as* **Charlie** *finishes with* **Denzel**. *Grabs him.*

Callum (*referring to the drugs he's taken*)   I ain't come up yet.

Charlie *shrugs.*

Callum When am I gonna come up on this?

Charlie *shrugs again.*

Callum You better be for real . . .

Charlie *gives him a hurt 'who me?' Expression and jogs on . . . Towards a huddle of girls who are catching his eye. They start to negotiate discreetly.* **Callum** *joins* **Bready** *and* **Omar**, *who has a bottle of whisky.* **Omar** *shouts into* **Callum**'s *ear, pointing at the huddle of girls.*

Omar Do you know them?

Callum No.

Omar What?

Callum *grabs the whisky bottle.*

Omar That chick at the back is –

Omar *takes a breath to emphasise the next word, but the music returns, drowning it out. At the same time,* **Callum** *steps away, across to the huddle of girls, just as* **Charlie** *leaves them.*

Hannah *enters. She is alone, remote, dazed. Walks across* **Callum***'s path.*

Callum You live upstairs?

Hannah *nods.*

Did we wake your kid up?

Hannah *smiles.*

You want a drink?

She takes the whisky he offers. Closes her eyes. Takes a mouthful. Eyes don't open. **Callum** *accepts that the conversation is over, takes the bottle back and moves away . . .*

. . . Straight into **Denzel***, who now finds everything funny and wants to make everyone happy . . .* **Callum** *steps around him . . .*

Suddenly . . . the music changes, becomes washy, slowed down . . . something **Callum** *has taken has hit his brain. Everything goes into slow motion. He floats over to the huddle of girls who are all in slow motion. Everyone's speech is slowed down, like a slow motion video.*

Callum (*to* **Lauren**) You want some?

Lauren Yeah, I'll have some.

She takes a slow motion swig. Always the gentleman, **Callum** *wipes the neck.*

Callum (*to* **Shauna**) And you'll have one?

Shauna (*taking the bottle*) Nice. (*Swig.*) What's your name?

Callum (*as if it took a while to work out the answer*) . . . Callum. (*To* **Nina**.) And one for you?

Callum Nina *shakes her head.*

Callum Don't you drink?

Callum Nina *shakes her head.*

Callum Do you smoke?

Callum Nina *shakes her head.*

Callum Do you do anything?

Nina *shakes her head.*

Callum   Do you dance?

Nina *gives him a slightly weary look.*

Callum   I dance.

Callum *spins away and loses himself in the music. He shuts his eyes – the music and the people go back to normal speed. After a while he opens them again – everything is slow motion. This happens several times. As if he changes existence with his eyelids. Next time he opens his eyes there is a strobe, combining slow motion and normal speed.*

Nina *starts to shake.* **Shauna** *catches her as she starts to fall. Then* **Nina** *is on the ground in a full epileptic fit. The strobe ends, everything normal speed as people around* **Nina** *notice what's happened, panic, take pictures.* **Charlie** *sees and runs. People are yelling for an ambulance, disagreeing. Through all this,* **Callum** *is slow to realise . . .*

A siren is heard over the music. Everyone starts to run off. The music stops abruptly. **Callum** *opens his eyes. Sees the exodus. Sees* **Nina**. *It's just him and her.*

The siren continues . . . away into the distance . . . only sound is **Nina**'s *jewellery against the floor as her body shakes.* **Callum** *looks around, doesn't know what to do. Kneels. Holds her hand. It's not stopping.* **Callum** *looks over his shoulder . . . All around . . . Trying to think what he can do . . .*

Finally the fit stops. **Nina** *pushes herself up off the floor.*

Nina   Did I fit?

Callum *nods.*

Nina   Shit . . .

She's frustrated and disappointed, covers her face with her hands, then looks at him again.

Nina   Who saw?

Callum   I dunno.

Nina   Everyone saw.

Callum   You wanna call your friends?

Nina   What friends?

Relieved that it's all over, **Callum** *lights a cigarette.*

Callum   Where d'you live?

Nina   Why?

Callum   I could walk you home.

Nina   I need to run.

Callum   Run?

Nina   Just run. Just make everything go past fast.

Callum   Run then.

She climbs to her feet.

Nina   I'm too tired.

Callum   Someone better be with you, innit?

Nina   It won't happen again. It doesn't.

She walks away.

Street

Callum *catches up with* **Nina**, *still has cigarette and bottle.*

Callum   I wanna walk with you.

Nina   Why?

Callum   I wanna know you.

Nina   Why?

Callum   Do I need a reason?

Nina   Why would I want to know you?

Callum   I didn't think about that.

Nina   Think about it now. Make yourself interesting.

Callum   What do you wanna know about me?

Nina   Nothing. I want you to do something. To fill up the emptiness. Make something happen.

Callum   I made that party happen.

Nina   Nothing was happening. You'd have to take a load of drugs to think it was.

Callum   Well yeah. That's kind of the point of the drugs.

Nina   I'm real. Are you? Are you real?

Callum (*laughing*)   I dunno, what's real?

Nina   You want me to show you?

Callum   Yeah.

Nina *takes the cigarette and the bottle. Points up above them somewhere.*

Nina   See that camera up there. It sees me, sees you.

Callum *turns and presents himself to the camera.*

Nina   Run.

Callum *turns back, gives her a puzzled look. Deliberately,* **Nina** *drops the cigarette into the bottle. It flames, then she flings the bottle at something unseen. We hear it smash. We hear a car alarm go off.*

Nina   Run!

Callum   Shit . . .

The two of them run off laughing.

Park, Tree. Moonlight

Nina *and* **Callum** *run in, out of breath.*

Nina   Why did you run here?

Callum   This is my spiritual home.

Nina   The park . . . is your spiritual home?

Callum   It's what's IN the park. The track. You see it? Down there.

Nina   A running track, that's what we're looking at?

Callum   What's your name?

Nina   Nina.

Callum   Nina . . . I want you to come here when I run.

Nina   You're a runner . . .

Callum   I never have anyone come and watch me. If you come I can look in the crowd and think, 'Where's Nina?'

Nina   You gonna tell me your name?

Callum   Right now it feels like I ain't got one. That's good.

Nina   I don't get that.

Callum (*pointing, his head next to hers*)   Look at them lines – perfect, clean, white. And that space between, when I'm there, in the lane, I got no name, no history, nothing – all I am is what I'm doing that moment. Nothing follows me onto the track. I leave it back there. (*He gestures to the outside world.*)

Nina   What if you lose?

Callum   I don't. Something happens. Soon as I get into the starting position, it's like I gather together all the energy in the universe. It's all going through me. What is that? Where does it come from? D'you ever get that?

Nina   No.

Callum   I live for it. I feel it now.

Nina   What?

Callum   I just knew. When I saw you – I knew.

Nina   Maybe that was a drug epiphany.

Callum   What's a drug . . . Whatever-it-is

Nina   You take drugs, and suddenly the whole world makes perfect sense, and then the drugs wear off, and the world doesn't make sense anymore, because it, like, actually doesn't.

Callum   You think I'm all about the drugs? Drugs is second best. Third best.

Nina   What's first best?

Callum   The race.

Nina   Second best?

Callum   You.

Nina   You don't know me.

Callum   I see you.

Nina   If you think I'm second best to anything, you don't understand the first thing about me.

Callum   You're better than the race? (*She nods.*) Can you prove that to me?

Nina   Uh-huh. But you haven't proved yourself to me, yet.

Callum   Nothing to prove. I told you everything about me. All that I am.

Nina   You haven't told me your name.

Callum   Why don't you give me a name? I'll start again right here. I don't need to keep a single thing from the last eighteen years. Except my legs. To carry me.

Nina   It's not your legs I want. It's your heart.

They kiss. Sound of white noise, Growing and growing . . .

Callum's Mum's House, Ten years ago

Callum *is eight and* **Linda** *is twelve.* **Julie** *their mum is asleep, with a can of irn bru in one hand and a screwdriver in the other. TV on, white noise.* **Linda** *creeps in and pulls the plug and it dies. She throws a sheet over it, starts trying to lift the TV.*

Callum   Linda?

Linda   Shhhh . . . Whisper, Little Bear, whisper.

Callum   If we chuck it away we won't have no telly.

Linda   We just need to hide it for a bit.

Callum   How long?

Linda   Till Mum's feeling better.

Callum   When's Mum gonna feel –

Linda   Just shut up and help me with this telly . . . OK . . . That's it . . .

But **Julie** *wakes up.*

Julie   What you doing with my window?

Linda   We're taking it for a rest.

Julie   What about the devils?

Linda   That's why. To stop the devils coming out the telly.

Julie   It's a window, I told you! How the devils gonna climb back through the window if you take it away? You don't think about that do you? You don't think about the dangers . . .

Linda   We can be alright if we can –

Julie (*seeing a devil*)   There's one!

Linda   That's Callum, Mum.

Julie   It's a boy devil. They're the worst.

Linda   It's your son.

Julie   I ain't got a son. I got that in my house and I want it out.

Linda   Mum . . .

Julie   Kill it.

Linda   Mum you're making him cry . . .

Julie   It's trying to look into me. Get its eyes!

Julie *brandishes the screwdriver.* **Linda** *throws the sheet over* **Callum***'s head.*

Linda   It's gone. Must have gone back through the window.

Julie   You love it. You let it in your bed. I seen you.

Linda   He gets scared, Mum, you keep scaring him.

Julie   They burrow in. Into your body. They give you diseases and babies and you're just gonna let him . . .

Linda (*can't take it anymore*)   Shut up! Shut your crazy mouth. Now! Shut it!

She pushes **Julie** *back and drags the TV out.* **Julie** *sobs pathetically.* **Callum** *sticks his head out from under the sheet. She doesn't see him. Silence. In the distance the echo of an ice cream van on the estate.*

Callum   Mum? . . . Mum? Listen, it's the ice cream van. You want me to get you an ice cream?

Linda   Yeah. Some money in my skirt.

Callum *picks up her discarded skirt off the floor. Turns out the pockets. There is nothng there.*

Callum   I don't need no money for it. I'll wait till he gives me it then run away. Don't cry. What do you want? Magnum? Flake?

Julie   My throat's all dry.

Callum   Lolly then. Orange lolly?

Julie *just stares into space. Eyelids droop.*

Callum   Just tell me what you want. Mum . . . Mum! . . . Mum . . . Mum?

Track

Josiah *stands waiting. Looks at his watch.* **Callum** *arrives.*

Josiah   You're five minutes late.

Callum   Yeah?

Josiah (*claps his hands twice in* **Callum***'s face*)   That's three quarters of a second. That's how far you are from the British team. If you think five minutes is nothing, how you gonna shave three quarters of a second off your time?

Callum   Alright, alright . . .

Josiah   What's your dream?

Callum   I told you before, why d'you keep –

Josiah (*interrupting*)   Say it out loud every day. What's your dream?

Callum   To be a champion.

Josiah   Now listen. Everyone's got a 'dream'. And for most people it's just an illusion – a thing to cheer them up, like thinking about how they'd spend the money if they won the lottery. Turning a dream into reality is long, slow, shitty work. I don't know if you got that in you.

Callum   Man, I've been on time nearly every day for the past three weeks.

Josiah   Nearly?! Nearly?! Is you a nearly man? 'Cos if you is . . .

Callum   Let's just fucking train, Josiah!

Josiah   Yeah? You wanna train?

Callum   Yeah!

Josiah   Jog to the end and back.

Callum *jogs away.* **Josiah** *shouts down the track to him.*

Josiah   Every drop of beer, Callum . . . Every crumb of fried chicken . . . Every molecule of marijuana . . . that enters your bloodstream, it leaves its trace in your body . . . and when you call on that body to perform, it will fall short. You feel pressure? Good! Pressure is your new best friend. It's with you all the time, 24/7, it's your guardian angel.

Callum *arrives back. Jogs on the spot.*

Callum   Can you stop talking?

Josiah   You mean stop coaching?

Callum   I don't think the way you think.

Josiah   That's your problem. It ain't your fault. The minute you hit a challenge, you're like 'Ah, that's long!' and you're done with it. But if you wanna get anywhere you gotta fail and fail and –

Callum   Can you do your other speech – about the gold medals? I like that one better.

Josiah   This is exactly what I mean.

Callum   All that downbeat shit's not motivating. I wanna hear about the glory.

Callum *speeds away.*

Josiah   Don't sprint till you're warmed up! . . . (*To himself.*) Fuck's sake . . .

Callum *slows to a jog. Then stutters. He tries to shake the sleepiness out of his leg . . . start, stop, start, stop. Stop. The disease is coming the other way, walking towards him like a robot, a skeleton, a bag of bones.*

Callum's Bedsit

Door buzzer. **Bready** *is asleep on the floor, snoring. Buzzer again. And again.* **Bready** *wakes up, sits up, irritated. The buzzing stops. He lies down, relieved. Buzzes again.* **Adebola** *enters.* **Bready** *leaps up.*

Adebola   Someone downstairs let me in. Callum?

Bready (*thinks about it for a second*)   Yeah.

Adebola   I'm Adebola. Your temporary social worker.

Bready   Cool. What you got for me?

Adebola We need to continue the assessment you started with . . . (*Searches file for name.*) Diane?

Bready (*cutting in*) Listen I got a job interview so I can't give you long.

Adebola Job interview, that's great! What for?

Bready Bodyguard. Nikki Minaj is over from America. They need extra bodyguards 'cos she's, like, got extra body.

Adebola Right.

Bready But that's a week away. And I need scrilla. Cash.

Adebola Are you having trouble managing your finances?

Bready No. It's just that most of my money goes on weed. And I need to help out my two boys, Bready and Omar.

Adebola You have children?

Bready They're like family to me but they're skint. It would break your heart. Madam.

Adebola Callum, have you done the 'Money Matters' course?

Bready Another thing, I've turned gay.

Adebola OK . . .

Bready Can you write that in my file? And I might want a sex change, so can you apply for the money for that.

Adebola OK, there's a few things all together there . . .

Callum *enters.*

Adebola Hello, I'm Callum's social worker.

Callum What?

Adebola I'm Adebola. Callum's social worker. We're having a meeting.

Callum *realises what's going on.*

Bready *and* **Callum** *both laugh, point at each other etc.*

Adebola (*to* **Bready**) Callum, could you explain?

Callum That's Bready. I'm Callum.

Adebola You're Callum?

Callum Let him do it though. Put whatever he says.

Bready I said you turned gay. And you want a sex change.

Callum *now totally helpless with silent laughter.*

Adebola (*to* **Bready**) I think you'd better leave.

Bready Nice to meet you.

Bready *high-fives* **Callum**, *leaves.*

Callum Where's Suzanne?

Adebola She's on indefinite sick leave.

Callum Definite sick leave?

Adebola Indefinite sick leave.

Callum So it ain't definite . . . that she's sick?

Adebola It means we don't know how long.

Callum What's wrong with her?

Adebola That's confidential.

Callum Right, right. Course, if I was sick, that goes straight in the file for anyone to read.

Adebola Your file is confidential.

Callum Yeah, and whoever's doing the job this week gets to read it. Nothing in my life is private, believe. If I had something wrong with my dick, some stupid teacher would have told the whole class. They'd probably have read it out in assembly – 'Callum Connor, the care boy, has got a sore dick. But don't bully him'.

Adebola Could I sit down?

Callum Sure

Callum *points vaguely at the sofa.* **Adebola** *sits down. She sits on* **Omar**, *who was under a pile of blankets and pizza boxes. She shrieks, he sits up, aggrieved.*

Omar Jesus! Who's this?

Callum A social worker.

Omar Don't they, like, train you to not sit on man when he's sleeping?

Adebola Maybe that is something they should include in the university degree! Callum, please can we get on with the assessment.

Callum Sure. Omar? Can you go out and . . .

Omar *gets up.*

Callum (*to* **Omar**) Later.

Omar *leaves.*

Adebola Are those two living here? (**Callum** *shakes his head.*) How often do they sleep here?

Callum Thing is . . . Omar there . . . Like . . . This crib's shitty, but his crib is actually shittier, so he sleeps here. And Bready, he's homeless.

Adebola So he lives here?

Callum No, he don't live nowhere. His dad's sick and got evicted and there's all bedroom tax, anyway, he's homeless.

Adebola You're not really looking after this place, it's . . .

Callum Wait, wait, did you see this place when I got here?

Adebola If the place isn't well maintained, people are –

Callum You must've seen needles in that corridor. There's used condoms in the yard.

Adebola You have to keep this room clean.

Callum I have to do this, I have to do that. What are you gonna do about the state of this place?

Adebola We can take it up with the landlord.

Callum 'Take it up' – what does that mean? You have this whole language – Take it up, look into it, bring it to our attention, make them aware. Ten hundred ways to say nothing, do nothing. In that file, what does it say I asked Suzanne for? Look!

Adebola I still have fourteen questions.

Callum I ain't answering till you answer my ONE question.

Adebola *consults another page of the file.*

Adebola It says . . . You raised the idea of us looking into the possibility of re-establishing contact with your sister.

Callum Have you done it?

Adebola Well I'll find out how far Suzanne managed to progress that request.

Callum I wrote her a letter. I want you to see she gets it.

Passes over a letter. **Adebola** *takes it.*

Callum Find my sister.

Adebola How's your running?

Callum It's none of your business.

Adebola It's good if I can put down positive steps you're –

Callum I got rights. I don't have to earn them with good behaviour.

Adebola I work within a system. If you won't co-operate . . .

Callum Prove you can get me something I want. Then we talk.

Adebola I can't get what you want if we don't complete the assessment.

Callum No comment.

Adebola   I see how it is.

Callum   You people. You think you're so fucking great, you're so caring, you're idiots. You ARE the system and you don't even know it. They just brainwash you into thinking you're helping us. Fuck off. Go on. Get out of here. Why is your fat arse still in my chair, I told you to go!

Adebola *stands.*

Adebola   Yes, I do this job to help people. If you behave in this way it's much harder. (*No reply.*) Good bye, Callum.

Callum *leaps up and past her, blocking her path to the door. (Next section of dialogue they talk over each other).*

Callum   Where you going? You can't leave.

Adebola   Callum . . .

Callum   You can't just give up and walk out.

Adebola   You told me to leave in no uncertain terms –

Callum (*warning tone*)   No . . . No . . . No . . . (*Sudden burst of energy.*) Get away from that door!

He shoves her back into the room, onto the chair. For a second, his dominance is absolute, and she's scared. But his anger is already turning in on himself.

Callum   I fucking told you. Shit . . . Shit . . . Shit . . . Shit-shit-shit-shit-shit-shit-shit-shit . . .

Adebola   The next appointment is in three weeks. I won't report what you said today. But I won't accept it a second time. You understand me, Callum?

Callum (*as she leaves*)   Won't be you next time anyway.

Adebola *exits. We hear the baby crying upstairs.* **Callum** *looks up.*

Callum   Shut up! . . . Will you shut that fucking kid up?

Burnt-Out Car

Nina *and* **Shauna** *sitting on top of a burnt-out car. Listening to music on phone.*

Shauna *throws her head back.*

Shauna   Here comes your man.

Nina   Don't.

Callum *arrives.*

Callum   Last night, I had a loaf of bread.

Shauna   What?!

Nina   It's all gone.

Callum   Where?

Shauna   I ate it. There weren't nothing else.

Callum   That was my lunch.

Shauna   What, just bread on its own?

Callum   If bread on its own is so bad why d'you eat all of it?

Nina   Easy, babe.

Callum   I gotta train, right? I need energy.

Shauna   So . . . (*Points to her temple to indicate thought.*) Yah no haffi burn up wollah yah energy if yah got no food fi nyam.

Shauna *laughs, teasing.* **Nina** *smiles.* **Omar** *and* **Bready** *arrive (***Bready** *in a bright coloured hoody). Each has a sandwich.*

Shauna   Come on Nina, let's go.

Omar (*to* **Shauna**)   Go where? Why?

Shauna   Find something to do. Someone to do it with.

Omar (*flirty*)   You're looking at someone to do it with.

Callum (*meaning the sandwich*)   You could have got me one.

Bready   We didn't know you would be here. Thought you was out training.

Callum   I gotta be there in ten minutes, all my food's ate by people squatting in my flat.

Bready   We ain't welcome?

Callum   I didn't say that. You could just . . .

Nina   Go back and get one for Callum.

Omar   Can't. I can't get nothing from that shop for another month.

Nina   Why not?

Omar   'Cos I didn't pay for it.

Bready (*to* **Callum**)   You can have some of this.

Bready *carefully pulls out the lettuce and tomato from his sandwich and gives it to* **Callum**.

Don't know why they put that shit in a BLT. Ruins it.

Omar   They have to put lettuce and tomato in a BLT.

Bready   What for?

Omar   Or else it wouldn't be a BLT.

Bready   What would it be?

Omar   A 'B'.

Callum   Sometimes, you two really do my head in.

Omar   Tell you what. We'll get you one from another shop. What flavour?

Callum   Can you get a loaf?

Bready   What about that loaf in the –

Nina   Shauna ate it.

Bready   The whole fucking loaf?! That ain't natural.

Shauna   I was hungry. I didn't have no dinner.

Omar   Chill! That ain't the vibe. Listen, everyone, the vibe we need to be feeling is the vibe from Callum. This man here. Callum is hungry.

Nina   So get him a sandwich.

Omar   That won't solve it. It's about do we, the five of us, feel his feeling, his hunger?

Bready   Well SHE don't, she just scoffed a whole loaf of bread.

Callum   Omar, the vibe don't buy shit. I step out that door onto the pavement and what do I see? Turkish shops all in a line next to each other all selling food, food, food. But I ain't got paper and metal to hand over.

Shauna   Seriously is that what's bothering you, getting P?

Callum   Yeah it is.

Shauna   'Cos there's this guy . . . I don't know him . . . He says you can make ten grand in one day.

Callum   How?

Shauna   You gotta move a body.

Omar   Say what?

Shauna   Some guy got killed, yeah? And there's these people don't want the police to find the body, but it's in a bad place where it might get found. So they need someone to take the body, drive it up North, to Cornwall or something, and just throw it on a golf course.

Bready   A golf course?

Shauna   Somewhere green. Countryside. The sheep'll just eat it.

Callum   Jesus Christ.

Bready   Truth is, to get by, you gotta do a bit of shotting. Or rob some phones or something.

Nina   Really?

Callum   Omar, if you could go get me a loaf of bread, just like the one I had here this morning, that makes you top man in my eyes.

Omar   Alright, alright.

Shauna   Can you get me a Rubicon?

Omar   If you come with me.

She sighs and gets up. The two of them leave. Silence.

Nina   Fuck's sake, Callum.

Callum   What?

Nina   'What?'

Callum   What?!

Nina   How you think that makes me feel? You talking like that. Like some wino on the street.

Callum   Telling the truth.

Nina   How does that make me feel? To listen to that?

Callum   I don't know. Tell me.

Nina   If that's who you are, who am I?

Callum   Stop asking me questions like it's all obvious.

Nina   It would be obvious to anyone who had a brain, or like, one little drop of class.

Callum *kicks the car. Goes to kick it again, but something isn't right. He bends and holds his thigh.*

Nina   Kick it again. Go on. Let's see what damage you can do. Why you stopping?

Callum   What d'you want me to do?

Nina   Hold your head up. Get out of that pigsty. Earn some money. Be a man.

Callum   How? Where?

Nina   You ain't supposed to ask your girl for the answers. At least Bready's got a system going.

Callum   I don't roll like that no more.

Nina   What do you do?

Callum   Run.

Nina   You get paid for that?

Callum   No but . . . If I'm doing that . . . properly . . . I can't be thieving and shotting.

Nina   Running. Even the word is stupid.

Callum   What d'you mean?

Nina   Up and down on a bit of earth every day on your own. Going nowhere, no reason. No-one cares. No-one pays you. No-one watches. You should have grown out of sports day.

Callum   Tell that to Mo Farrah, Usain Bolt . . .

Nina   They're millionaires. When you make your first million, give me a call, I'll come crawling back on my hands and knees. And stay there.

Nina *wanders off.*

Bready   She just don't get it. She needs to see you run, and then she'll . . .

Callum (*interrupting*)   I gotta train.

Bready *goes the opposite way.* **Nina** *comes back unexpectedly.* **Bready** *is uncomfortable, hopes to just walk past but she is right in front of him.*

Bready   Hey.

Nina   I probably shouldn't talk to you. Callum wouldn't like that.

Bready   I think he was a bit pissed off about the bread.

Nina   Why does he think he's better than you?

Bready   What?

Nina   Do you ever wonder that? Him and Omar, they treat you like you're thick.

Bready (*uncomfortable*)   What you talking about?

Nina   It's like you're there just for them to laugh at. I asked him, you know. I said why do you hang round with Bready. You don't respect him. He said he didn't know why. Then he started laughing. Sorry, it's none of my business, but . . . It's the same with Shauna, Omar thinks she's stupid. But he's all nice with her 'cos he thinks one of these days she might just get drunk and give him a blow job.

Bready *sniggers – there's some truth in it.*

Bready   Shauna ain't so stupid.

Nina   Neither are you. Difference is, she don't let no-one take advantage of her.

Silence. Lights down.

Track

Josiah *with a stopwatch. Waiting.*

Callum *finishes a run.*

Callum   What does it say?

Josiah   You ain't hitting the times you hit two weeks ago.

Callum   I hit the heights on race day. That's my style.

Josiah   Why you getting worse not better?

Callum   Who says I'm getting worse?

Josiah   The numbers are the numbers, Callum. I'm asking you why?

Pause.

Callum   What's wrong with my legs?

Josiah   What?

Callum   There's something wrong with them. Swear down. I fell over last night.

Josiah   Had a large one did you?

Callum   I fell over when I stood up.

Josiah   Couple drinks? Pill? Joint at the end of the night to come down?

Callum   Where's that Nike gear you were talking about? Where's my spikes?

Josiah   That's what's important to you?

Callum   Yeah. I want Nike trousers. I want Nike hoody. I want Nike water bottle, and Nike phone, and Nike car and Nike condoms and Nike job for my new girlfriend . . .

Pause.

Josiah (*hesitating to say it*)   I used to be in care.

Callum   What?

Josiah   I know what it's like. They used to move me from foster home to foster home. I couldn't get to the club. No-one thought running was important. But it was the ONLY thing that was important. That day I saw you, it brought back memories. That's why I wanted to take you on.

Callum   Don't use the word 'care' when you talk about me.

Josiah   Ain't nothing to be ashamed of.

Callum   Did I say I was ashamed? Did I say that?

Josiah   Forget it. The care thing. (*Pause.*) I'll see you tomorrow.

Callum *starts. The disease suddenly appears and knocks* **Callum** *off balance.*

Callum   Wait.

Josiah   Work by yourself.

Callum *takes up the starting position. The disease grips his ankle.* **Callum** *lifts his foot. The disease lets go. But as* **Callum** *starts, the disease knocks the foot away, tripping him.*

Callum *tries again and again to run. The disease drags him back and pulls him down. He growls with frustration, walks along the lane towards . . .*

A Pavement, Somewhere. Rain. (Played out on the running track)

In the distance, **Charlie** *is there, on a street corner, bobbing, pacing, looking for business.*

Callum *walks to him, the disease walks alongside, mocking, but then falls behind, left behind.*

Callum *does fast business with* **Charlie**. **Charlie** *exits.* **Callum** *turns. His body is not doing what he wants it to do. His legs seem stuck to the track.*

Callum   Woooah. What am I on? It's not acid . . . But it's something weird. I must be very, very, very, very stoned. Hello, legs? (*Pretending each leg is answering.*) 'Yes, Callum?', 'Yes Callum?'. I need you two to walk. 'Cos I'm in the middle of the street, and I need to get back to my yard. 'But we can't!' . . . Why not? 'Because we're stoned.' *I'm* stoned. I'm relying on you.' (*He sees the figure.*) Huh?

In the distance, a figure in **Bready**'s *hoody – hood up – is on the ground. Rolling and flailing like a stricken animal that doesn't know how to get up.*

Callum *is drawn to it. He staggers towards it. It moves less, as an animal often does when you approach.*

Callum *is close now. The figure makes another effort to get up. Shoulders on the ground, it walks like a crippled breakdancer.*

Callum   What you doing? Bready??

The figure is facing away but throws its arm back, out straight, like it wants help.
Callum *hesitates.*

Callum   Bready, that you? What's wrong?

The arm writhes and strains, reaches towards **Callum**. **Callum** *gingerly extends his arm to meet it. They lock on – palm to wrist – and* **Callum** *leans back, the figure is about to be lifted but then hauls* **Callum** *down to the ground and rises in his stead.* **Callum** *is wasted, flounders. The hooded figure walks away, light on its feet. Turns back to pull back the hood and reveal the face we've seen before, of the disease. It smiles at* **Callum** *and walks away.*

Bready (*off*)   Callum!

Bready *and* **Omar** *are looking for* **Callum**. *Each walks along a different running lane. They look straight ahead, not at* **Callum**, *not at each other. This is the beginning of a stylised physical sequence on the track.*

Omar   He's gone, man.

Bready   He was here!

Omar Callum!

Bready Callum?

As they go past, **Adebola** *is heard, and she approaches – in her lane.*

Adebola Callum. This is very disappointing.

Callum Who are you?

Adebola I'm Adebola.

Omar (*as they exit, to* **Bready**) Forget him.

Callum Who?

Adebola Adebola. Your case worker.

Callum (*to* **Adebola**) You're not meant to be here.

Adebola This is a dream. Anyone can be here.

Callum A dream? A dream . . . All of it? So my legs are fine?

Adebola No, you have a serious problem with your legs.

Suzanne *and* **Diane** *approach from opposite ends of the track.*

Suzanne You want this file?

Diane No, you keep it.

Suzanne I don't want it.

Suzanne *throws the file to* **Diane**. *As they reach level with each other,* **Diane** *hands it straight back.*

Diane Just give it to Adebola.

Suzanne Who?!

Diane Adebambo!

Callum Who?!

Callum *tries to get to his feet, but it's too hard.*

Callum Wait . . . I'm just talking to – which one are you?

Adebambo *approaches.*

Adebambo Adebambo. I am your acting case worker.

Callum Where's Ade-what's-it who was just –

Adebambo Adebola? She left.

Callum When?

Adebambo Four months ago.

Callum She was just here.

Adebambo That was me.

Callum This dream is so . . .

Adebambo This is not a dream.

Callum You said it was.

Adebambo That was Adebola.

Callum Nina! Wake me up, I'm dreaming!

Adebambo Have you been smoking cannabis?

Callum That's what I'm trying to work out. Either that, or I'm mental, or I hope it's just a dream, 'cos –

Linda Callum? Stay there, don't move. Mum's not well, OK?

Callum Wait!

Callum *struggles to his feet but then sees* **Linda** *wheeling* **Julie** *in a wheelchair, fag in her mouth.*

He covers his head, trying to hide from her.

Callum Mum?

Julie *is wheeled past. Didn't see him, but now he's upset. Has to call out . . .*

Callum Mum – I'm here!

She stops. Stands up out of the wheelchair. Sheds her dressing gown to reveal a demure party frock. Puts on a santa hat. She is suddenly the perfect postcard mum. She still has the london accent but none of the harshness in her voice.

Julie Right . . . crackers, turkey, balloons, stockings, pudding, Quality Street, lights for the tree, carrot for the reindeer, what have I forgotten?

Callum Mum?

Julie *turns round, beams at* **Callum**.

Julie Now, who've we got here?

Callum It's Callum.

Linda (*to* **Callum**) Don't talk to her!

Julie That's a nice name. Where's your mum?

Callum You're my mum.

Linda That's not Mum.

Callum Course it is, look at her.

Linda   How can that be Mum?

Adebambo *speaks from behind* **Callum**, *making him turn.*

Adebambo   That is not your real mother!

Callum   Real? Shit . . . It's Mum, but she's fine.

As he turns back once more towards **Julie**, *she laughs, cackles, she is turning back into the same old* **Julie**, *hunched and spiteful, laughing at him. The old voice is back. She's drunk.*

Julie   You're so stupid, I love it.

Laughs, coughs, seizes the hat off her head, coughs/retches into it.

Linda *spins the chair around,* **Julie** *falls into it.*

Linda   She went court. She's an unfit mother.

Linda *spins the chair away again.*

A **Judge** *suddenly appears.*

Judge   Callum Connor, I declare you an unfit child. You are clearly not able to keep up a relationship with a parent or to be looked after adequately. You do not inspire love, loyalty or commitment in other people. For this reason you must be cut loose from other human beings so that you do not burden them with your worthless existence. This order is effective immediately. You may appeal against this judgement . . . repeatedly, but every person you ever meet will, eventually, come to the same conclusion.

The **Judge** *bangs a gavel.*

At the other end of the track, the disease picks up the banging. He bangs a nail into a miniature coffin. Finished, he picks it up and cradles it like a baby. The disease retreats.

Bready *comes back, and we are back in reality.* **Bready** *grabs* **Callum**'*s shoulder.*

Bready   Hey. Come on.

Callum *sees* **Bready** *and laughs – overwhelmed with relief.*

Callum   Bready!

Bready   What's so funny?

Callum   You came back. Or did I just . . .

Bready   You gotta get off the ground, man.

Callum   Why d'you come back?

Bready   'Cos you're my friend. Anything could happen to you like this.

Bready *pulls* **Callum** *to his feet.*

Callum   You're the best, man. You . . .

Bready Shut up and walk.

Callum No, listen . . .

Bready Walk!

Bready *helps him walk . . .*

They walk back to **Callum**'s *bedsit, under this dialogue.*

Callum Where's Nina?

Bready I don't know.

Callum Where's Omar?

Bready I don't know.

Callum Where's that chick he keeps trying to bang?

Bready I don't know, man.

Callum Where's Bready?

Bready I'm Bready.

Callum I mean where's the real Bready, the one with a sense of humour.

Bready Come on, in here . . .

Callum's Bedsit

Callum Fuck it . . .

Bready You gotta look after yourself, man.

Callum *starts giggling.*

Bready What?

Callum You.

Bready Me? What?!

Callum You're just funny.

Bready Yeah? Fucking funny . . .

Bready *starts to move towards the door.* **Callum** *pulls at his arm.*

Callum Come on, man.

Bready *flings* **Callum**'s *arm away.*

Bready Don't fucking laugh at me, boy!

Callum Where you going, you fool? You're homeless?!

Bready What do you know about me? My dad been in Intensive Care for two weeks and you never ask me about it.

Callum   What did he ever do for you?

Bready   You don't give a shit about me.

Callum   I don't give a shit about your dad. You're cool.

Bready *decks* **Callum** *in one punch.* **Callum** *falls behind the sofa.*

Bready   Fuck you talking about 'cool'?! Huh?!

Bready *kicks* **Callum** *four or five times. Heads for the door.*

Bready *is gone.* **Callum** *struggles to his feet, groans and gasps with the effort and frustration.*

We hear groans and gasps from elsewhere . . . The next scene.

Callum's Mum's House, six years ago

Groans and gasps. Two people are having sex somewhere.

Julie *is watching a porn film, and we have been hearing it. Twelve-year-old* **Callum** *enters slowly, school uniform on.* **Julie** *is in an 'up' mood. Flirty with him to start with.*

Julie   Look who it is! Why ain't you at school?

Callum   Finished three hours ago.

Julie (*short laugh*)   Huh.

Callum   Why you watching that?

Julie (*suggestively*)   I think you can see why I'm watching it.

Callum   Yeah but . . . In front of me?

Julie   You boys, you got worse than this on your phones.

Callum   I ain't got a phone, have I? 'Cos you sold it.

Julie   It got nicked. Why you still going on about that?

Callum   It pisses me off. You let people come round here, people you don't even know, and they take my stuff. So you say.

Julie   What's the matter? Cheer up! Chill out! Sit down, will you?

Callum   If you watch something else.

Julie (*picks up the remote*)   Maybe if you watched this you wouldn't be such a moody little shit.

Callum *doesn't answer.* **Julie** *sighs and switches channel* – Teletubbies. *Sniggers.*

Julie   There. Happy?

Callum *takes the remote, switches it off.*

Callum   Christ's sake.

Callum *sees some jeans on the sofa.*

Callum   Mum . . . Mum . . . What's this?

Julie *looks at the jeans, puzzled.*

Julie   Eh? Oh. They're Tyler's.

Callum   What you talking about?

Julie   They're Tyler's. He must've . . . Wait a minute . . . How did he leave without his trousers? . . . That's weird! Wait . . .

She gets up, goes over to look into the bedroom. Gives a startled laugh.

Julie   Oh My God . . . He's still there. (*Starts to really laugh.*) . . . Can you believe that? . . . He's still asleep! That's funny . . . Innit, though? I thought he'd gone.

She has a thought. Tiptoes back to the jeans. With a cheeky expression she turns out the pockets of the jeans: Keys . . . Lottery ticket . . . £20 note.

Julie   Here we go. That's dinner and a bottle of wine, eh? Quick, take it.

Callum (*knocks her hand away*)   What's the matter with you?

Julie   Why you being like this?

Callum   I don't want that guy's money.

Julie   Callum, don't be an idiot.

Callum   I am an idiot. Alright? 'Cos I stand up for you. For our name. For our honour. You know I've had a line of twenty kids chanting 'Your mum is a . . ., Your mum is a . . .' (*He can't bring himself to say the insults.*) and I fight the whole lot of them till the teachers come! What for? It's a joke. I'm a joke 'cos everything they say is true.

Julie   Why you always gotta ruin everything? Look at you. With your sour face.

Callum   You know my fantasy . . . My wish . . . Is that I come home one time and find you hanging from the ceiling.

Julie *hits* **Callum** *across the head with the jeans.*

Callum   You think you can HURT me?! You?!

Heads for the door.

Julie (*calling into the bedroom*)   Tyler? Tyler!

Callum   I ain't coming back, Mum . . . (*No answer.*) I ain't coming back.

Callum *leaves.*

Julie   Tyler, wake up! Get in here!

Julie *looks into the bedroom again.*

Julie   Get up! . . . GET UP! . . . G-E-E-E-E-T U-U-U-U-UP!

Callum's Bedsit

Dark. **Callum** *is asleep on the sofa. Someone is in the room watching him.* **Callum** *wakes, hits the light. It's* **Hannah**. *It's almost like she's sleepwalking.*

Callum   What you doing?

Hannah   Looking for you. Why d'you leave the door open?

Callum   It was shut.

Hannah   It wasn't locked. I thought maybe you moved out. I don't see you. It's getting light. You used to get up when it was getting light.

Callum   How d'you know?

Hannah   Out my window, I used to see you run off down the street. To the park.

Callum   I gave that shit up.

Hannah   I don't hear you anymore. I don't hear your friends.

Callum   I gave that shit up too.

Hannah *nods. This makes sense to her.*

Callum   I ain't got nothing here. I don't think you should leave Paradise.

Hannah   I always wait till she's sleeping.

Callum   What if she wakes up and . . . wonders what's going on?

Hannah   Like you?

Callum   What?

Hannah   You wondered what was going on. You thought, 'Who's that in my room?'

Callum   You shouldn't be here.

Hannah   Why not?

Callum   It's not your house, is it?

He stands, shows her to the door, she doesn't move.

Callum   Come on . . . Hannah . . . Let's go . . .

Gently, he steers her out. She complies.

Burnt-Out Car

Omar *pushes a shopping trolley up to the burnt-out car. Waits.* **Callum** *wanders along. Stops. Difficult for them to talk.*

Callum Ain't seen you lately.

Omar What you been doing?

Callum What you here for?

Omar (*shrugs*) I saw Nina . . .

Callum Nina?

Omar When I said I was coming over she asked me to pick up some stuff.

He indicates the trolley.

I got a whip over the car park.

Callum What stuff?

Omar She said she left stuff at yours?

Callum She tell you what it was?

Omar She said you'd know.

Callum Why was you coming over?

Omar What?

Callum The story you're giving me is that you was ALREADY coming over here, and THEN you saw Nina and just dropped that you was on your way and then she asked you to blah-blah – I'm asking what you was coming over here for. Or maybe that ain't your story.

Pause.

Omar She said she wasn't seeing you no more. (*No answer.*) You alright about that?

Callum Why wouldn't I be alright about that?

Omar Dunno. You might like her or something. (**Callum** *starts to walk away.*) You going training?

Callum Fuck you care. If you, like, run into Nina again . . . Tell her she can come anytime she like.

Omar Shall I just go up and . . .

Callum No. She can come herself, innit?

Omar I think . . . She don't want to come if you're here.

Callum I'm going out. Call her, tell her.

Omar Is it locked?

Callum Ain't never locked, Omar, you know that.

Callum's Bedsit

Nina *enters,* **Adebambo** *following hesitantly.* **Nina** *is playing sweet and naive.*

Adebambo   I'm not sure about this . . .

Nina   It's fine. I come here whenever I want. I'm his girlfriend. Welcome.

Adebambo   Do you . . . live with Callum?

Nina   No. (*Abruptly changing the subject.*) Social Worker – how do you get to be one?

Adebambo   Do a degree. Do your practice. Get a job. Then they chuck you in.

Nina   Give you a head case like Callum. He scares me sometimes. (**Adebambo** *looks awkward.*) It must be difficult to help him. Smokes so much gear. Quitting the athletics club . . .

Adebambo   Did he?

Nina   Oh yeah. Sorry I shouldn't tell you that.

Adebambo   No, it's probably better if you don't.

Nina   No, right. Sorry. Still . . . it's quieter round here now. His friends don't hang out since Callum beat Bready up. (*No answer.*) Have you met Bready, he's really sweet?

Adebambo   I haven't had Callum's case very long.

Nina   Sorry, I thought you knew all this. Never mind. I suppose I just wanted your advice.

Adebambo   It's hard to advise people on their personal lives.

Nina   I know but . . . Isn't that your job?

Adebambo   Nnnnno.

Nina   I'm stupid. Sorry.

Adebambo   Not at all.

Nina   I wish I had your education, your knowledge. Maybe I wouldn't get into relationships with losers. Which I keep doing. Not that I should be telling you, why would you care?

Adebambo (*cutting in*)   I'm going to go to my next appointment then come back.

Nina   Sorry Callum wasn't here.

Adebambo   Thanks for letting me in.

Nina *pulls out a black bin liner and puts a few things into it. No hurry.*

Callum *enters.*

Nina   Did you see your social worker? She just left.

Callum   I hid.

Nina   I mean, who has a social worker? What are you a kid, or a retard, or what? I don't mean that. I just . . .

The buzzer goes. **Callum** *turns back towards the entrance.* **Josiah** *enters, talking.*

Josiah   Three days. Three days I stood out there waiting for you to show and then three weeks to track you down here . . .

Josiah *trails off as he sees* **Nina**. *Feels embarrassed.*

Nina (*to* **Josiah**)   Hello.

Callum   Nina . . .

Nina   I'm Callum's girlfriend.

Callum   Why you saying that?

Nina   Sorry . . . Is he your boyfriend?

Callum   Don't be pathetic.

Nina   Oh my God . . .

Callum   You think this is funny or something?

Nina   Look at his face . . . Look!

Callum   I ain't got nothing to say to you, I don't want nothing from you . . .

Nina   Alright, I'll, er . . . Leave you to it. (*Moving closer to* **Callum**.) You do know he's gay? Tell me you do know that? Oh my God . . . Is that what you've been doing, running up and down the track while he watches your tush go boom-boom, boom-boom . . . That's your 'training'?

Josiah   You ain't nice.

Nina   You are gay though, innit?

Callum   Just go, Nina.

Nina   Callum, he ain't denying it. Look at his face. (*Walks over to* **Josiah**.) Gay, gay, gay. (*She takes his hand and puts it on her body.*) Go on! Teach me a lesson . . . Plug up my nasty mouth. Hmmm. (*Point proved. She changes tone. Thinking out loud.*) Hiding it's weird, but . . . Batty Man is worse than dirt. Better to be drowned at birth. I'm not saying that's what I think, it's just what people say.

She moves towards the door.

Nina   I'm not really good for you, am I Callum? I think I just thought you were someone different.

She exits. Silence. **Josiah** *doesn't know what to say.*

Callum   Don't worry about it.

Josiah This was never about –

Callum Why did you come looking for me? I can't win races no more. I can't walk proper. Find some kid who can.

Josiah I care about you.

Callum No. You think that, but you . . .

Josiah I care what happens to you.

Callum You just made me into something.

Josiah Callum . . .

Callum Whatever you think I am . . . I'm not that. So whatever you felt walking in that door – I don't know if it's a gay thing, or a coach thing, or some fucked up trying to be my dad thing – Anything good you felt, if it was about me, that all came from you and it goes with you.

Josiah You're not a bad person.

Callum Why don't you get that I don't care? Now leave.

Josiah No.

Callum Get out. I'll just beat the shit out of you.

Josiah leaves. **Callum** *breathes hard. Sinks to his knees, groaning. Fists clenched . . . Breaks down.*

Callum (*soft, at first, hissing*)   I can't do it. I don't know how to do it. Pleeeeease. I don't. Understand. Why. You can't. Just. Look after me . . . Why can't you look after me? Look after me! Please. Mum!

Door buzzer goes. Again. After a while, the disease emerges, lifts him back upright by the shoulders, then helps him to his feet . . . Then back to the sofa. Turns his head towards the door. Door buzzes until . . .

Callum's Bedsit (continuous with last scene)

Adebambo *enters. She comes to the centre of the room.*

Adebambo Hello.

Callum Hello.

Adebambo I'm Adebambo.

Callum No shit.

Adebambo Sorry? I'm taking over your case. I was buzzing for fifteen minutes – were you asleep?

Callum Kind of.

Adebambo Shall we get started?

Callum Have they posted my letter?

Adebambo Sorry?

Callum The letter to my sister that I gave the other woman, have they posted it?

Adebambo Let me see.

She starts to look in the file. Flicks backwards and forwards. The letter falls out. **Callum** *picks it up.*

Adebambo Oh is that it? (**Callum** *sighs, nods*.) The process has been initiated.

Callum Ain't no process to posting a letter. Write the address, put a stamp on it, put it in the post box.

Adebambo We have to just check that contact is appropriate and how best to facilitate that.

Callum In case my sister reading this letter might be a bad thing.

Adebambo I wouldn't say that.

Callum It's from me, so yeah, bad.

Callum *slowly tears up the letter.*

Adebambo Callum . . .

Callum I'm like a virus. Whatever I touch . . . I should stay away from people.

Adebambo I can see that you are not in the best place right now. Let's make a list of the problems you'd like help with.

Callum I'm the problem. I'm a problem 'cos I exist.

Adebambo You need to see a counsellor.

Callum (*bitter laugh*) What's a counsellor gonna do?

Adebambo Listen.

Callum Why can't you do that?

Adebambo I don't have that specific . . .

Callum You're not allowed to listen to me without training?

Adebambo Well . . .

Callum It's my legs. Something's done something to my legs.

Adebambo Does it hurt?

Callum No. It's like they're disappearing.

Adebambo Have you seen a doctor? (**Callum** *shakes his head.*) See a doctor, as soon as you can.

Callum   Maybe they can't fix it.

Adebambo   You're young and healthy.

Callum   Is that what it looks like to you? I'm finished. I was finished before I started. Kind of makes sense that my body's falling apart.

Adebambo   With some help, the world won't look so bleak.

Callum   Help? Ah, you mean medication. What's the point in taking medication just so you can't see what's staring you in the face?

Adebambo   Go to a doctor, Callum.

Callum   I don't wanna look at shit and think it's chocolate.

Adebambo   Go now. Today.

Callum   Tomorrow maybe.

Adebambo   Now. They'll still be open. I'll take you.

Callum   I ain't moving.

Pause. **Adebambo** *changes tack.*

Adebambo   I'll buy you fried chicken if you get in my car.

Callum   You sound like a paedophile.

Adebambo   I'll be outside in five minutes. Wait down there.

Adebambo *exits.* **Callum** *waits a few moments, sighing. Uses his hands to unfold each leg, looking down at them like someone who's just had them fitted. Stands. Walks to the door and out through the yard . . .*

Street

Callum *steps out onto the street, still looking down at his creaky legs. A car starts up down at the other end. Headlights on.* **Callum** *looks up. The car moves, swings round, lights raking the dark . . . Faces* **Callum**. **Callum** *starts to hobble towards it. It revs slightly. He tries to pick up speed. It revs more . . . The revs scream.* **Callum** *stands stock still. Out of the headlights steps the disease, grinning. Points towards the car.*

Callum   Wait! What are you?! What d'you want with me?

The sound of a loud phone conversation in a foreign language.

GP Reception. Merging to Consulting Room

The **Receptionist** *is on the phone. The* **Foreign Woman** *is talking away on her mobile. A* **Patient** *is at the desk trying to get attention. He is at the front of a long queue.*

Receptionist (*to foreign woman*)   Excuse me? Excuse me? No mobile phones? (*Into the phone.*) Sorry, now . . . Have you filled in the form . . . Yes . . .

Patient   Excuse me.

Receptionist (*ignoring the* **Patient**)   Yes . . . Have you filled in the form though? No, the one the nurse gave you . . .

Patient (*deliberately, sarcastically, using the same tone*)   Excuse me.

Receptionist (*ignoring the* **Patient**)   You need to bring that form in . . . On Monday at 11 . . . Yes . . . Yes, I know . . .

Patient   Excuse me.

Receptionist (*into the phone*)   Excuse me a moment. (*To the* **Patient**.) Just a moment. (*Into the phone again.*) 11 o'clock, Monday . . . That's right . . . I know . . . I know . . . You just need to tell the doctor when you get here. . . .

Patient   Excuse me.

Receptionist (*ignoring the* **Patient**)   On Monday. Monday. Yes, Goodbye.

Callum *enters as the* **Receptionist** *puts the phone down.*

Callum   Is this the GP?

Receptionist   Yes.

Callum   Something's wrong with my legs.

Receptionist (*to the* **Patient**)   Yes?

The **Patient** *hands her a form. She takes it. The* **Patient** *stands there.*

Receptionist   Are you registered here?

Callum   Er, yeah.

Receptionist   What's your name?

Callum   Callum Connor.

She taps the keyboard. Scans the screen.

Receptionist   I can't find you. When did you register?

Callum   My social worker registered me.

Receptionist   No she didn't. You have to register yourself, if you're over eighteen.

Callum   Maybe when I was seventeen, I'm eighteen now –

Receptionist (*interrupting*)   Then it would have to be a parent.

Callum   I doubt it. My mum's sectioned under the mental health act and no-one knows who my dad is. So . . .

Receptionist   Then you're not registered here, I'm afraid. What you can do . . .

Callum Can't you register me now?

Receptionist We're not taking any more patients.

Callum What if it's an emergency?

Receptionist Then you go to the hospital.

Callum Hospital told me to go GP!

Receptionist There are other GPs . . .

Callum You fucking love it, don't you? Getting sick people to beg you . . .

Growing sound . . . **Callum** *is losing his grip on reality.*

Receptionist I'm sorry but if you're abusive I won't –

Callum The moment I walked in here you looked at me –

Receptionist Abusive behaviour will not be –

Callum You thought 'I'm not helping him'

Receptionist I have been trying to –

Callum Call Security. What you waiting for? I need to be removed. That's how you deal with people like me.

Everything is weird now . . . But the foreign woman is still jabbering away.

Callum (*to foreign woman*) You! Shut up. I was born in that. . . . That hospital . . . I was born . . . Fucking big fuck up that was, well you brought me into this shitty world and now you can deal with me. Come on!

The characters in the queue are morphing into a horror movie, zombies and the walking dead. A heavily pregnant woman on a chair gives birth and when her baby emerges, it is the disease. **Callum***'s hold on reality slips. The disease offers a pill in one hand and plastic cup half full of water in the other to* **Callum***. All the characters spill back on to the race track.*

Security I'm sorry you can't sleepwalk in this area.

Callum I gotta see a doctor . . . Wait a minute, I got his name here . . .

Receptionist This is A&E, Neurology is down the corridor.

Callum Mum?

Security I'm sorry you can't smoke in this area.

Callum I just wanna see what's happening in there. My mum's in there.

Security Get into the car. Emergency foster care has been arranged for you.

Callum Let me through! Mum?

Security Callum Connor?

Julie *is some way off.*

Julie   Don't worry sweetheart! (*To someone we can't see.*) I'm taking my meds. You can't come in here. You can't do nothing, 'cos I'm taking my meds now. They told me, if I take my meds they won't take my children. Don't take my children. Wait. Wait! Just wait. Stand there a minute. You got to go back and check and they'll tell you, 'cos someone's told you wrong, 'cos they can't . . . 'Cos they promised . . . I swear I was promised . . . I . . . They . . . (*Drops to her knees.*) I'm begging you . . . Please . . . Look at me . . . Take my eyes, take my teeth, take my heart right out through my ribs, but don't take – (*She stands again, brandishing her screwdriver.*) No! I see you the whole time, writing and talking, and lying and promising . . . Your smile is the most evil thing I could ever see in hell. Don't you laugh, bitch, I'll put this right through your skull!

Linda *calls from the other direction.*

Linda   Hey . . . Little Bear, take my hand . . . Quick!

Callum   You're not Nina.

Julie   Nina's sorry. She's waiting for you.

Receptionist   Callum Connor?

Callum   They're calling me.

Receptionist   You're running in the 100 metres at 11.40. Take this.

She offers a pill and a glass of water.

Callum   What is it?

Linda   It's alright, Callum. Everything's alright.

Callum   I tore up the letter.

Linda   I read it. I understand. We all understand.

PA announcement . . .

PA System   Callum Connor . . . To the starting line.

Callum   Shit . . . I can't run.

PA System   Callum Connor to Doctor Bernard.

Linda   Callum, it's got to be now!

Nurse   Callum Connor?

Callum (*to* **Linda**)   They're calling my name now.

Linda   It's a dream.

Nurse   We just need to take some blood.

Linda   Give me your hand.

Callum   It's my legs.

Linda   Your legs are fine. That was just a dream . . .

Nurse   We need to take some spinal fluid.

Callum   I fucked it up with everyone. Bready, Josiah, Nina . . .

Linda   None of that happened. Just wake up.

Callum   I got this appointment . . .

Linda   No, that's a bad dream.

Callum   With this doctor.

Linda   Come out. Wake up! Callum!

Nurse   Callum? Wake up! Callum?

Dr Bernard   Callum. Hi, I'm Dan Bernard. Come this way . . .

Abruptly **Callum** *is back in reality.*

A Doctor's Consulting Room. The Disease is tied to a crucifix on the wall of the room between the Doctor and Callum and watches the scene

Callum *sits on a chair.*

Dr Bernard   Right, so . . . There were two things we thought it could be. We've got it down to one. Unfortunately, it's the one I was hoping it wouldn't be. It's a very serious condition. I wonder if you know what Multiple Sclerosis is?

Callum   Yeah.

Dr Bernard   Ah, OK.

Callum   Why?

Dr Bernard   What? Oh. That's . . . what this is.

Callum   How long have I had it?

Dr Bernard   A year, maybe.

Callum   How old will I be when I die?

Dr Bernard   I don't know.

Callum   Like twenty? thirty?

Dr Bernard   Is there someone we can call? Someone who can come and meet you and take you home? (**Callum** *shakes his head.*) Like parents? . . . Brother or sister? . . . Friend? . . . Neighbour? Well, we'll contact your GP and take it from there. And we have some literature.

Callum   Literature?

Dr Bernard   I'll get it. (*Starts to get up.*) Oh, here it is. (*He sees some leaflets right in front of him, gives them to* **Callum**.) Any questions?

Callum   If I was a dog . . . Would you put me down?

Dr Bernard   We . . . don't do that with people.

Callum   Lately, nothing's been feeling real and now it's, like, true . . . nothing was.

Dr Bernard   If there's anything else you need . . .

Callum *catches himself, starts to laugh.*

Dr Bernard   Why are you laughing?

Callum   'Cos, like . . . You finished, innit? I'm still talking about what's real or not . . . And you got patients and work and . . . What am I even on about, right?

Dr Bernard   I'm sorry. I'm not sure . . .

Callum   Nah, it's good man, it's cool.

Callum *reaches for a handshake.* **Dr Bernard** *tries to shake his hand but* **Callum** *is going for a big street-style handshake. Teaches the embarrassed doctor.*

Here . . . Like this . . . Yeah . . . No . . . There you go. You got it.

Callum *spins and come face to face with the disease, pause for a moment. In the same curious spaced-out mood,* **Callum** *has an inkling of what this figure is.*

The disease steps off the crucifix and leads the way. **Callum** *struggles to walk.*

Callum's Bedsit

Bready *sits. Disease leads* **Callum** *close, then lets him walk alone towards* **Bready**.

Bready   I shouldn't have listened to that gyal, man.

Callum   Forget it, man. You just stupid, innit?

Bready   Why would she do that though? Women though. I dunno. They ain't like normal people.

Callum   No-one's like normal people. Not even normal people.

Bready   I'm just here, 'cos I got hold of these.

Bready *gives* **Callum** *a box.*

Bready   We get a discount.

Callum   You got a job?!

Callum *opens the box. A pair of running spikes.*

Bready They probably fit. They're pretty good ones, they said. And I had some cash 'cos I'm staying at my dad's and working.

Callum Thought your dad was in hospital.

Bready He's out. And he don't mind me being there these days 'cos he can't do stuff for himself.

Callum Why not?

Bready They chopped his leg off.

Callum That's harsh.

Bready They'll probably chop the other one off next year. It's a diabetes thing.

Callum I can't run.

Bready What? You gotta run.

Callum I got Multiple Sclerosis. MS. You know?

Bready Shit? Really? For definite? Ah, that's shit.

He reaches for the box.

Well, might as well take these back.

Callum You're kidding, right?

Bready Exchange them, innit?

Callum I want them.

Bready What for?

Callum I like them. I want them here.

Callum *lifts up the sofa. Pulls out a sock. Inside the sock is a paper bag. Inside the bag is a crucifix.*

Callum Take this.

Bready What is it?

Callum A crucifix.

Bready I'm a Muslim bruv.

Callum You ain't shit.

Bready You can't say that to a Muslim.

Callum Keep it. Give it to someone else if you like. I can't give it back to the person I got it from. And I don't want anyone to find it here when I'm dead. Let's get some cans, eh, fam?

Bready Dunno if we should call Omar. I dunno if he's still with Nina. I don't think HE knows if he's still with her.

Callum Whatever. Cans! You know those guys who sit in the park, on the benches, with cans? I think I might do that for a bit.

Bready Why would you wanna do that? We can sit and drink cans in here.

Callum Working from home, I think they call it.

Bank/Building Society

Desk, chair on either side. **Linda** *(now adult) in bank uniform.* **Callum** *comes in, carrying a can of special brew.*

Linda (*not sure about him*) Hello. (*No reply.*) Hello?

Callum *sits down.*

Callum I'm Callum.

Linda Hello, Callum. Would you like to open an account? (*Penny drops.*) Oh. Oh my God. Oh.

Callum Why did you leave me, Linda?

Linda How did you find me?

Callum Found your profile. Recognised your face. Bit different from Hackney round here. Is this where you went? When you went.

Linda (*talking about the can*) You shouldn't have that in here.

Callum Shouldn't have it at all. Eleven in the morning. I thought I'd try being one of those geezers in the park.

Linda Are you OK? . . . What do you need?

Callum Self-esteem, so they reckon.

Linda What?

Callum They say that's what I lack. Didn't you ever get no assessments? No lists of what's wrong with you?

Linda I mean, a place to live, or . . . Are you . . . I don't know what to say to you right now.

Callum Ah, sorry.

Linda It's not your fault.

Callum I'm sorry I'm still around. You must have thought I was dead. I mean . . . If you thought I was alive, you'd look for me, innit? I thought you would come. I thought that's what women did – normal women, women who weren't like Mum – looked after people.

Linda   Where are you living?

Callum   I got a place.

Linda   Is it OK? (**Callum** *shrugs*.) By yourself? . . . This is really difficult for me, I'm at work.

Callum   Have you seen Mum? (*She shakes her head*.) I found out where she is. You wanna come with me?

Linda   I'm working.

Callum   Later? (*Pause*.) She's still alive. At this address. (*He shows a scrap of paper with an address on it*.) Can't believe I found her.

Linda   What's your phone number? Here . . .

She gives him a pen.

Callum   Give us your hand.

He writes it on her hand. Releases her hand.

Callum   Funny . . . Don't change nothing.

Linda   What's that?

Callum   Seeing you. I thought it would make things different, I thought I'd feel something. But . . .

Linda   I'll call you.

Callum   I'm going.

Linda   OK. I'll call.

Callum   I was gonna say . . . I was planning this kind of . . . I really want to say Thank You. For . . . looking after me. Them years. That's what I wanted to say. You kept me safe. You tried. Before you left. (*Can't stop himself asking*.) Why didn't you take me with you? What did you think was happening to me? Why didn't you care? Why don't you care now? Look at me! How did you just turn me into nothing in your mind? Why was that so easy?

Linda   This isn't good for me.

Callum   No. (*Stands*.) Are you alright? You look alright.

Linda   I'm alright.

Callum   That's good.

Linda   I'll call you.

Callum   Don't bother. I ain't got a phone.

Linda   But . . . (*Looking at the number on her hand.*)

Callum   That used to be my number, when I had a phone. You should call it. See who answers. Might be my ghost.

The Park, the Tree

Josiah *is sitting under the tree.* **Callum** *arrives, running spikes round his neck.*

Callum   Been looking for you.

Josiah   What did you want?

Callum   Give you these.

Callum *puts the spikes down next to him.*

Josiah   I don't run.

Callum   You can find someone who does.

Josiah   So you quit running. Alright. Anything else you want me to know?

Callum   Nah. Just . . . Thanks for the coaching. Sorry for, you know . . .

Josiah   Yeah.

Josiah *takes the spikes.* **Callum** *turns away. End of conversation. Then* **Josiah** *stands up.*

Josiah   You might as well say it. Whatever you're holding in. What you got to lose? You'll never see me again.

Callum *produces the scrap of paper with his mum's address.*

Callum   Maybe you could help.

Passes the paper across.

How do I get there?

Josiah   It's on the Central Line. Zone 9 or something.

Callum   I don't know whether to go.

Josiah   What's there?

Pause.

Callum   My mum.

This has an effect on **Josiah**. *Not what he was expecting or wanting to hear.*

Josiah   You're asking the wrong man.

Callum   You told me you'd –

Josiah Yeah, yeah, I know about the question you're asking yourself. I can't answer it for you.

Callum You've been through all this shit, right?

Josiah All I got is my story. My story won't help you.

Callum (*pause*) D'you think there's a bus?

Josiah Out there?!

Callum You gotta help me, alright?

Josiah Why?

Callum You never got me spikes or a set of Nike gear.

Josiah If you'd made the times, I could've got the sponsors.

Callum You know what Multiple Sclerosis is?

Josiah Course. (**Callum** *waits . . .*) What? . . . No . . . No! Really?! For sure?!

Callum I'm dying inside.

Josiah You just been born inside. Your body carries you around. Like a car. Yours is gonna be in and out of the garage a lot, that's all.

Callum My life. I had all of it in front of me and now . . .

Josiah MS takes years.

Callum It's just straight downhill . . . Into the grave.

Josiah No.

Callum Josiah, can . . . (*Holds up the address.*) Do I go?

Josiah I reckon you got two choices. Five years of therapy, counselling, whatever . . . and build up to it. Or get over there right now and get it the fuck over with.

Callum You think I can handle it now?

Josiah I dunno.

Callum (*gripping the scrap of paper*) Can you get me there?

Josiah I ain't got a car.

Callum I don't mean that.

Josiah You mean give you the money for the bus?

Callum *shakes his head. Pause.*

Josiah You mean go with you? (**Callum** *nods.*) Come on.

Secure Mental Hospital

Two orange plastic stacking chairs. **Julie** *is there, in an overall, with a mop and bucket. She mops the floor.*

Callum   Why you doing that, Mum?

Josiah *realises that the woman is* **Callum**'s *mother. Gives* **Callum** *a look of moral support then disappears discreetly.* **Julie** *continues mopping the floor.*

Callum   Why you doing that?

Julie   I'm having the meds after. (*Pause.*) Do this once a day. I can't think after the meds, so I'm having them after this. It's better.

Callum *sits.*

Julie   Is Linda coming?

Callum *shakes his head.*

Julie   It's a good thing to have children. You should have children.

Callum   Why's it a good thing to have children, Mum?

Julie   Still living in the same place?

Callum   Which place? Which place you talking about?

Julie   I've been here a while. That explains it.

Callum   Excuse me? Hello?

Julie *looks at him.*

Callum   There's a chair. Can you sit down?

Reluctantly, she sits.

Callum   Why's it a good thing to have children? Tell me.

Julie   They bury you. (*Pause.*) It's very important to have someone who'll bury you. There's people who die, and no-one comes for them, you see? Imagine that. Being dead and no-one coming for you. Linda'll come. When the time comes.

Callum   You could live another forty, fifty years.

Julie   I've been here a while.

Callum   Do you remember . . . Saying that you didn't have a son?

Julie   When are you talking about?

Callum   When you said you didn't have a son. Do you remember?

Julie   Better to ask Linda, she's better.

Callum   You said I was a devil and you wanted to kill me. It wasn't your fault. You were just crazy. Just a crazy fucking loon. You didn't know what you were saying. So it didn't matter. None of it. All those years. None of them matter a shit . . . 'Cos you weren't there, you just looked like you were. So it's OK. It's OK, Mum.

Julie   I'm making progress.

Callum   This is supposed to help me, you know? It's, like, something I need to do. So I'm told.

Julie   D'you take something to help you sleep? I do. I've always needed to take something to help me to get to sleep . . .

Callum   I'd love to hear . . . one of your memories. Of me. Something I did. Something that happened.

Julie *is looking pained.*

Julie   They told you what to expect, right? From me. I'm making progress though.

Callum   What do you remember, Mum?

Julie   Remember the old flat. Are you still there?

Callum (*suddenly yelling*)   No! I left before you did, Mum.

Julie   I don't know what you want. I do everything I'm told. I'm good, I am.

Callum   OK, OK. Maybe you already let it go. Now I'm letting go. Of everything. That's a lot, Mum. Everything. Nothing left. Start from nothing.

Julie   Mm-hm.

Callum   That makes you free. I wish you could see that.

Julie   You just got to t-t-t-t-try your best. Every day.

Josiah *re-enters.*

Josiah   You need a break, man?

Callum (*standing, to* **Julie**)   You need the meds.

Julie   I'm having them after this.

Callum   This is over.

Julie   I'll have the meds now then.

Callum *stands, walks away.*

Josiah   You want him to come again?

Julie   I think it's Linda that likes me, really.

Josiah *hands* **Julie** *the mop. She smiles at him. He doesn't return it, turns and walks away.*

Sound of wind in the trees and birdsong.

The Park

Hannah *sits under the tree.* **Callum** *arrives.*

Hannah   There's a bird up there. See? Singing, singing.

Callum   Where's Paradise?

Hannah *looks up, then back down, shakes her head slowly.*

Callum   Where is she?

Hannah   Gone.

Callum   Where is she?

Hannah *shrugs.* **Callum** *paces nervously.*

Callum   You must know where she is. Where did you . . . Did you leave her somewhere? Where – where did you last see her?

Hannah   They took her away.

Callum   Who?

Hannah   I think it was doctors . . . Or police . . .

Callum *figures out what this means.*

Callum   How many came?

Hannah   Five or six I think.

Callum   Did you sign something? Did you sign –

Hannah *nods.* **Callum** *takes a deep breath.*

Hannah   Do you think I'll see her again?

Callum   I think they'll let you see her. But then she'll go and live somewhere else and you won't see her after that.

Hannah   Yeah I think so.

Callum   She won't be crying all the time. Making you worry.

Hannah   Having a baby is like having a bit of your insides outside you. Just hurting all the time. I kept wishing she could go back in me. That part was good. When I was heavy with her. She was warm and she was feeding all the time, even when I was asleep.

Pause.

Callum   Why couldn't you just look after her? (*No answer. Rising emotion in* **Callum**.) Why couldn't you look after her? Just stay with her? Just pick her up, for fuck's sake?! Why?! (*He kneels in front of her, holds her face roughly in his hands* . . .) Answer me. Give me an answer. Can't you just give me an answer . . .

He cracks and is overcome with sobs. His arms weaken. **Hannah**'s *hands hover over him for a second or two, hesitant. Then she draws his head in towards her belly and cradles it. Stay like that a while. Then* **Callum** *slides and sits with his back to her, his head still in her hands.*

Callum   Look. Sun coming up. Keeps on coming up, day after day, no fucking reason. Just does it. Like babies, keep on getting born, day after day . . . No reason. No reason to live . . . Or die. Just do it. (*Sits forward, no longer touching her.*) You gotta get her back. You gotta find Paradise and get her back. You can do it. You have to do all the things they say you can't do. You can do them. I'll help you. I've spent ten years with their questions and their answers and their rules. I know what you have to say, I know what you have to do. And you have to do it. Hannah? You listening? You HAVE TO. Paradise is your reason to live. And right now you don't want a reason to live. I see that. But I don't care. I'm gonna make you give yourself a reason to live. Sorry.

Hannah   It's OK.

Hannah *smiles.* **Callum** *smiles.*

Callum   Yeah . . . Yeah . . . (*As if he was seeing a joke.*) It is. It's OK.

Hannah *sings softly, 'twinkle twinkle little star'.* **Callum** *stands and pulls her to her feet. Then takes a step backward. Stops.*

Callum   I know you're there.

Spins round. The disease is there, we have seen him approach over a period of time.

The disease mirrors/echoes his every movement. **Callum**'s *expressions of confusion are reflected back to him, until he starts making movements just to see them reflected back – they are in a kind of dance . . . The dance shifts so that now the disease is making the movements and* **Callum** *is following – letting himself be caught up. They dance for a while, then* **Callum** *lunges towards him, arms outspread, like someone scaring off seagulls. The disease flits away.*

Callum *turns back to* **Hannah**. *She is laughing at him having watched his strange movements. The disease invisible to her.*

Hannah   You're crazy.

Callum   Yeah. You too?

Hannah   Me too.

They laugh, do the same dance. Watch each other laughing and mimicking each others madness.

The End.

In conversation with director Maggie Norris

BP *The play published here is an evolution of the first play that The Big House ever put on. Can you tell me a bit about the play in its first form?*

MN *Phoenix* was our very first project, just as I was setting up the company; it was an experiment to see if the programme that I was designing would work. And in fact, the emphasis wasn't on the production, it was on the programme of support given through the life skills, counselling and employment workshops. We only programmed that first show for a week because I was worried that exposing the young people for a longer public run and to reviews could be a little harsh and not the point. Anyway, I was wrong . . . People in the audience told me that more people should see it and, in fact, the young people didn't really care about the critics coming and most of them didn't read the reviews. But the discipline of sustaining a play over a four-week period, and all that that imparts in terms of their employability skills, was hugely important and became quite a big focus in our Open House Project moving forward.

BP *How was the process of creating the first* Phoenix*?*

MN It was such an adventure, and a transformative journey for the fifteen young people involved. The themes of the play emerged from the company and, at that point in our history, we were writing the play within the three month project. So pressure was on the writer to develop a first-class script in a very tight timeframe. One of the young people who was in the original cast had MS and he wanted to highlight to the public that this wasn't an old person's disease and that young people could have it too. I was very cautious about approaching the subject because I didn't want it to be his personal story. But actually, when we embraced that subject within a care story, he was able to input some brilliant, authentic detail, and he was able to use his experience in a creative way. It was a collaboration between the writer, the director and the cast.

BP *And so when it got to 2017, what was the reason you wanted to put it on again as* Phoenix Rising*?*

MN Very sadly, Kieran Dwayne Nero, who was the member involved in that first project, died. And we wanted to do something that would celebrate his life and his creativity. And so we discussed the possibility of putting on *Phoenix* for a new company with his family, as a tribute to Kieran. The family came to the production, which was staged in a car park underneath Smithfield Meat Market, which was a haunting and incredibly beautiful space.

BP *That car park . . . I've seen it with you – it's very beautiful, atmospheric, but I'm sure it posed quite a lot of challenges as a venue . . . Can you speak a bit about how* Phoenix Rising *evolved in that space?*

MN I really wanted to be able to find a space that could house the full hundred-metre athletics track so that (*laughs*) posed a challenge for me. I saw so many different spaces but, when I saw the underground car park, I knew that I had found the right place. It was so atmospheric and I knew that it would be such an adventure for the audience to come through the Meat Market and down the eerie steps and along the dimly lit tunnels that lead to the car park. The audience really loved the space. It was very difficult getting a sign off from the council however – it took months. I think that when we mentioned theatre they thought we were going to build a proscenium arch down there and have a conventional stage, not that we would use the whole car park and all its nooks and crannies . . . Seeing the actors emerge from the haze that we created, lit at such a distance away, was epic – particularly the disease coming towards us on crutches as he got more and more fragile. The sheer scale of the space is what made it epic..

BP *You mentioned to me recently that you used quite a lot of slow motion in the play. And I was wondering how you used that, what that was for you . . .?*

MN There are some surreal elements within the play. We decided to bring the disease to life and it was played by one of the actors who had an ability to move his body in a grotesquely skeletal and haunting way. We also go inside Callum's head, we experience his traumatic childhood through nightmare sequences. So, for example, the ever changing social workers in his life all morphed into one on the running track, with the same name, really to show how young people in care can be passed from parcel to post. Seeing all that in slow motion, and seeing his real motion reaction to that, was very powerful.

BP *In* Phoenix Rising, *were there any new characters that developed around the new cast?*

MN The part of the young mother Hannah. When Rebecca, the young lady who played it so beautifully, came to The Big House, she didn't speak for six weeks. She was totally silent. She huddled quite close to me at the drop-ins and, you know, I'd often have my arm around her. . . . so we developed a character that says very, very little but sings right at the end. . . . The character had a powerful impact on the audience and the silence was hugely moving. There was a moment in the play when that character broke into Callum's flat when he was in bed asleep and we had probably a minute of silence where Hannah just stands and stares at him in his bed. That made the audience cry. Because we felt her isolation, her loneliness, just standing there looking at another person sleeping was really powerful in a way that I didn't expect.

BP *Is there anything else you would want to say about* Phoenix Rising?

MN Well, I could tell the urine story.

BP *Oh, yeah. Always looking for a urine story.*

MN I decided to set the dank bedsit that Callum is allocated in a dark and dingy corner of the car park, and all we had in there was a manky bed and old sofa and a broken telly. What I didn't realise was that it was directly underneath some toilets, the car park toilets, and there was a crack in one of the pipes above and it was dripping urine into the scene. And one of the reviews commented on the stench of the scene being so authentic in his review. (*Laughs.*) But I found myself (because nobody else would volunteer for the job) having to create a sort of hammock to collect the drips so that it didn't actually land on the actors. As the production grew, so did the hammock of yellow urine above their heads!

BP *That is brilliant. Olfactory theatre.*

MN You couldn't write it.

Maggie Norris interviewed by Bel Parker
9 August 2022

Knife Edge

David Watson

Interview with writer David Watson

Who inspired the idea for Knife Edge?

Maggie's policy is that the writer generally doesn't sit down and write 'the story' of any particular member of the company. But you spend some time with the group in a room, get to know them as personalities and what their histories are, and then pieces of all that rub off on you and inform the play. With *Knife Edge* there was a particular individual, who didn't end up being in the show actually, but the thing was that her dad had died; he had been murdered in quite horrible circumstances, and the pain she was carrying around from that really stuck with me. Elsewhere in the mix there was a trainee chef who was very passionate about nutrition and about flavours, and Maggie had already got this notion of doing something around food, of the play taking place in a restaurant with a meal being served for the audience, so it was a kind of marriage between those two starting points that led to the play. The central thing of the girl finding she has all these step-siblings she didn't know about, with them all turning up at the restaurant at the same time; I think that was my idea – I liked the comedy of it and it was also a good way to give parts to lots of people!

What was the process of developing it? How did the members influence its development?

I think there is a sometimes an expectation with theatre like this that you're going to watch something very dark and gritty and raw, and The Big House has certainly done some really powerful stuff like that, and there can be a catharsis to that on the part of the actors . . . but one idea with *Knife Edge* was to do something much more comedic, which felt like a bit of a departure at the time, but I think the members really responded to it. Sometimes you'll turn up with a notion of a story which is very dark and bleak and you'll think 'this is the kind of stuff we should be doing'. . .but then you take it into a room full of young people who have such humour and wit and energy, and you find yourself wanting to tap into and celebrate that.

Can you tell us about the use of chorus? Was it performed as you imagined it?

Looking at it now, I think I was trying to play with some of the tropes around 'youth theatre', which can sometimes feel a bit patronising. . . . It was the idea of this Chorus being formed by a range of personalities, some of them are very jolly and hopeful, others more cynical, but they're all trying to keep the show on the road even as they lose control of it. I think the cast did a great job, although I remember some were initially a bit miffed because they didn't have 'proper' names and backstory; it took a while to persuade people they were still doing something really integral within the show! That was quite a good lesson actually, which I only half-learnt; there is often some kick-back against playing a more abstract kind of part. There is a sensitivity around 'Chorus Number 3'. . .but if you rename it 'Dave' and say he has two fish and lives in Dagenham – problem solved! But there was a genuine lesson there about trying to make sure every character in the company has their moment, and a sense of an off-stage life, however fleeting.

You've now written multiple shows for TBH, what for you is the best thing about writing in this context? And the most challenging?

I always love watching the show being brought to life by performers who might not have all the technical airs and graces but are really just using instinct and charisma and emotional truthfulness, which they often have in bucket-loads . . . Audiences respond to that, and it becomes something very special and unique. As for the challenges . . . there is often a lot of uncertainty, as inevitably people in the company have lots of stuff going on in their lives which can be difficult to juggle . . . sometimes you won't know who's going to turn up; is the lead actor going to make it through rehearsals? That keeps you on your toes and can lead to some frantic rewrites, but it's all part of the process.

What would be a piece of advice you'd give for a young company deciding to put on this show?

I just think it needs a lot of energy, and we have to care about the central girl. Even if it's framed in quite a comedic, heightened way, she has to feel her story going through it. Reading it again, I think there's loads of fun stuff in there, but it's also quite an eccentric piece, structurally. It rides on the energy of the performers and the set-pieces.

What's your process when writing characters that are very different from you?

I think you always have to relate on some level to the character you're writing even if you're worlds apart. I think we probably wouldn't be drawn to writing the characters we do if that wasn't the case. But, ultimately, for me it's an act of empathy and imagination, which is possibly quite an unfashionable notion at the moment; the emphasis is maybe now more on giving people the opportunity to dramatise lived experience, rather than the writer making a leap of imagination. . . . But I hope there's still room for both approaches. Plus it is always, to some extent, a collaboration. Big House members aren't slow to call bullshit on something that doesn't ring true, so that keeps you in check!

Knife Edge was first performed at The Pond, London, on 18 May 2016, with the following cast:

Ralph	Taurean Steele
The Girl/Yasmine	Tezlym Senior-Sakutu
Aaron	Adam Deacon
Delroy	Dymond X
Letitia	Jasmine Adolphus-Edie
Khalid	Moses Gomez Santos
Tania	Dilan Fox
Stef	Francesca Tokatlian
Kimya	Kismet Meyon
Trish	Tiffany Lambert
Girl's **Younger Self/Mia**	Naomi Banjoko
Chorus	James Atwell
	Ahmed Ahmed
	Haneefah Armstrong
	Kazeem Essoh
	Nadean Pillay

The play transferred to the Royal Court on 1 August 2016 and was staged in the basement restaurant and bar.

Creative Team

Writer	David Watson
Director/Designer	Maggie Norris
Lighting Designer	Amy Mae
Sound Designer	Ed Clarke
Musical Director	Louise Wellby
Assistant Director	Selena Lu
Assistant to the Director/ Musician	Kwame Dallas
Producer	Jo Hawkes
Production Manager	Nick Slater
Stage Manager	Samantha Gardiner
Sound Operator	Tom Wasley
Design Assistant	Kirsty Harris
Props Supervisor	Ellis Martin
Production Assistant	Kazeem Essoh

Characters

Chorus – (**One** *to* **Eight**)
Ralph
The Girl/Yasmine
Aaron
Delroy
Sylvia
Lester
Letitia
Khalid
Iram
Duane
Tania
Stef
Kimya
Trish
Girl's **Younger Self**
Mia

Note

A / slash indicates the point where the next speaker interrupts, and overlaps with the first.

Author's note – In the original production, at Pond Hawaiian Restaurant in Dalston, the show was followed each night by a meal shared between cast and audience, hence the build-up to the 'feast' at the end of the play.

As the audience enter, one of the **Chorus** *members is sat with a ukulele, cheesily and obviously miming along to maybe 'Hawaiian Ukulele love song.' Smiles and nods at people as they come in.*

Amongst the audience are members of the **Chorus** *– (***One***,* **Two***,* **Three** *etc). Our immediate impression of them is that they are maybe restaurant waiting staff, but there is something about the way they are dressed, the way they conduct themselves which isn't quite right . . .*

Once the whole audience has assembled, the music finishes.

A **Chorus** *member addresses stage management.*

One Head count?

Stage Manager Eighty. (*Or however many are in that night.*)

Two Perfect.

We're all here.

Some of the **Chorus** *members stare straight ahead, while others look at the audience, smiling benignly, almost creepily. A pause. Different Hawaiian folk music begins to play.*

A **Chorus** *member steps forward.*

One Of all the senses in the Human Physiology, the sense of Taste, the scientists say, is the most connected to the process of Memory.

Lights up on **Ralph** *in the kitchen, cooking, listening to earphones.*

Two So when Ralph Braithwaite fries chicken wings with rice and soy sauce – he is transported.

One To Hawaii.

Two To the beach.

One To the scent of his mother's home cooking, spilling out of an open window and across the palm trees and sky blue seas of Kawela Bay.

Three Funny thing about Ralph is that his name's 'Ralph' but he says it 'Rafe'?

Four He's a Pisces.

Five He's got two kids.

Six And another funny thing about 'Rafe' is that his mum's from Streatham.

Ralph What?

Five And the guy's never been to Hawaii.

Ralph (*removing earphones*) No what you saying about me? –

Two But we're not ready for Rafe just yet.

A **Chorus** *member fire-extinguishes* **Ralph**'s *cooking with one quick burst.*

Five   We'll stick him on the back burner.

Ralph   Oi! –

Lights down on **Ralph**.

Four   Chicken and chips.

One   Imagine.

Three   A homely favourite of all age groups.

Two   Take a well-known farmyard animal, which can taste dry and directionless on its own

One   But when combined with a herbaceous batter, and served –

Three   With chipped potatoes

Four   Chicken and chips.

Two   The most enriching experiences are born often of the simplest combinations.

Four   Chicken and / chips.

Six   Stop fucking saying chicken / and chips

One   Take eighty people in one room together and the only other ingredient we need is the ability to imagine.

Five   Yeah alright it's not a kids' show mate.

Three   Imagine:

One   Imagine we aren't here.

Two   Imagine we're transported. . . .

One   To Nando's.

Two   Nando's, in Westfield Stratford.

Five   It's a Saturday afternoon, at the start of the summer.

Three   It's raining.

The **Chorus** *begins to create the sound of rain.*

Two   In fact it's raining so hard that around eighty customers have chosen Nando's as their afternoon hang-out of choice, and are joined by seven waiting staff and eight kitchen staff, and between fifty and sixty dead chickens.

One   And in the middle of it all sits a girl

Three   A boy

Five   And a dog.

Four (*barks*)

Aaron (*to the dog, warning*) Dog!

Six (*to the others*) Are you allowed to bring a dog in Nando's / though?

Two It's a Staffordshire terrier, the dog, which is actually not as ferocious as you might have come / to believe

Five (*to audience*) Which is one of them ones you lot most probably cross the street to get out the way of, when you see some road man dragging it along, or the road man's getting dragged by the dog more / like

One *and* **Two** *are laughing nervously at the audience, feeling like* **Five** *is being a bit rough with them, and* **Five** *is then interrupted by –*

Four (*more barks*)

Aaron Sit!

Four (*more barks, even wilder*)

Aaron I said fucking sit!

Two (*to* **Four**) Yeah I think that's probably enough for / the time being

Five The boy's twenty-one and we'll call him Aaron.

One And as for the Girl.

Three She's sweet seventeen.

Two And we'll call her. . . .

Four Dorothy.

Girl What?

Two Yeah maybe that isn't quite / right

Girl I'm seventeen years old in 2016 and you're tryina call me Dorothy?

Five (*to* **Girl**) We'll call you what we fucking like.

One Erm –

Girl (*moving to confront* **Five**) Right –

Two And actually a big point about the girl is that she has quite significant anger issues, so for now maybe it's best just to call her –

Six (*putting plate of chicken and chips in front of* **Girl**) The Girl with no name sits in front of a plate of chicken and chips and says –

Girl (*to passing* **Six**) Excuse me?

Five And the boy called Aaron says –

Aaron Eat.

Girl (*to* **Aaron**)　Oi you see that though?

Aaron　See what man just Eat.

Girl　I'm looking at this bitch ten minutes like, my girl blanks me and serves next table.

Aaron　What you want?

Four (*barks*)

Aaron (*to Dog*)　I told you already!

Girl　They don't bring my sauce, man, true my chicken *cold* waiting on my hot sauce.

Aaron　Oh. Start eating.

Girl　Why?

Aaron　Looks fucking bad.

Girl　Looks bad?

Aaron　Looks bad that I'm eating, you ain't.

Girl　Bad to who?

Aaron　To people looking.

Girl　Someone looking at me I'll bang them over.

Aaron　Oi you know what it looks like though?

Looks like I don't care.

Girl　Do you care that I'm not eating or you care that people looking?

Aaron　What?

Girl　'Cos if I'm looking at us right now the only thing I'm thinking is 'She put on her one nice dress and he took her to Nando's.'

Aaron　It's Westfield man.

Girl　Nando's.

Four (*growls*)

Girl　And he bought his stinky fucking dog.

Aaron　Oi don't TALK –

Four (*barks*)

Aaron *yanks his dog's lead, then calms himself a bit.*

Aaron　Don't talk about my dog like that, my dog is a part of me, you know that?

Girl　Well maybe you should treat yourself a little better then.

Aaron Oi listen –

Girl You should think of a better name for yourself than 'Dog' anyway, How can a man just call their dog 'Dog'?

Aaron Shut your mouth and eat.

Girl Oh shut my mouth *and* eat?

Aaron Oi listen I take you out and I drive you here, and what do I get – just grief.

A moment. The **Girl** *assumes a posh accent.*

Girl Thank you so much for taking me out this afternoon. One has found it quite splendid. The only thing One wants is more sauce, to put on One's chicken.

Four (*barks*)

Girl And if the waitress doesn't bring some soon, One might have to push One's fork into her fucking eye.

Aaron Oi it's no wonder no one checks for you innit.

Girl (*kisses teeth*)

Aaron Some facety yat who thinks she too nice *and* too bad.

Girl Oh is that me?

Aaron You better fix up yourself from now you know, 'cos you see someone like you? – I'm the only one you got.

Six (*as the waitress*)   Is everything alright?

Aaron (*to* **Six**)   Yeah it's cool man, move.

Girl (*to* **Six**)   Can you be a bit more specific please?

Aaron (*to* **Girl**)   Did you hear what I fucking said?

Six Sorry?

Girl Is everything alright with what?

Six Erm, with the food?

Girl Oh the food.

Six Yeah.

Girl No everything is not alright with the food, I been waiting ten minutes for my peri-peri sauce.

Six Yeah the sauces are there?

Girl OK.

Six The sauce that you ordered is on your plate but if you want extra then basically it's self-service?

Girl If I want *extra*?

Aaron Leave it.

Six (*moving away*) Yeah basically it's self-service.

Girl These other tables getting real table-service, me I gotta self-serve myself? Story of my life.

The action freezes. Lights up on the **Girl***'s* **Younger Self***.*

Two The story of the unnamed Girl's life in a way actually could be summed up by this whole thing with the sauces, and different levels of access to sauces, characterised, as the Girl's life has been, by disadvantage, and by under-privilege, and by the feeling that whilst others have been waited on hand and foot – she has had to serve herself.

One This is the Girl when she was eight years old.

(*to* **Younger Self**) Hello.

The **Younger Self** *looks at her.*

One What's your name?

The **Younger Self** *spits in* **One***'s face.*

Six Oh shame.

Five Nasty.

Two (*to audience*) Her mother's just died.

One Which is obviously just a huge, huge thing for anyone at any age –

Two But for a child –

One Can you imagine?

Five And that's when it starts.

One Because after the death of a parent I mean it's really a massive amount of support the Girl needs, and as for her father –

Two Well we'll get to him.

Three *takes the* **Younger Self***'s hand and begins to lead her away.*

Three So for the Girl, from the age of eight, it's foster home, foster home –

Five (*taking the* **Younger Self***'s other hand*) Another foster home –

One And throughout all of this are these continuing issues of insecurity, and most destructively of anger –

Younger Self *suddenly slaps* **Five** *or gives her a massive shove, then runs away.*

Five (*to* **Chorus**) You see that?

Two (*to audience*)   But don't worry.

One   Because this is a story about finding a happy ending.

Girl   Can we get on with it now please 'cos my arm's kinda aching?

Two   And it's this sense of anger and frustration that's partly what's brought the Girl together with the Boy called Aaron and the Dog called Dog –

Three   Who aren't exactly strangers to anger and frustration either –

One   And which is partly what leads Aaron to face the Girl and say –

Aaron   Babes.

Girl   What now man I gotta get my sauce?

Aaron   What you like about me?

Girl   What?

Aaron   Like, why you choose me for your man?

A moment.

Girl   Because my self-esteem is so low right now I feel you're the best I deserve? And when the day comes when you blast your ting up inside me, and gimme one bun in the oven then leave –

Then at least what's gonna keep me warm at night, is the thought that I was right about you from the t-o-p.

One   She doesn't really say that.

Three   In her mind, she says that.

Six   What she really says is –

Girl   I dunno. What you like about me?

Aaron   What, you can't think a' nuttin?

Girl   I dunno man, fucking . . .

Aaron   What, how many months I been right here for you but you can't think a' shit

Four (*barks*)

Aaron   Dog!

Girl   What you want me to say? Like . . . I feel safe when I walk down the street with you, 'cos . . . I know no-one ain't gonna try nothing.

Aaron   Yeah. Yeah I'm good for you innit.

Take you out on a weekend.

Bring my dog.

Get you lunch, have a nice . . . conversation.

Girl OK.

Aaron I'm tryina' say that me and you . . . like we can take it to a different level, like.

Like we're built . . . to do stuff. Together. And . . . even maybe with other people . . .

Girl Yeah

Aaron (*angry*) Oi I'm tryna' fucking – . . .

(*He calms himself.*) Anyway.

He gets out a little box.

Happy Birthday.

The **Girl** *opens the box and takes out a necklace.*

Aaron What, you thought I forgot, innit.

You thought I forgot about that, are you mad?

Girl It's nice.

Aaron Yeah, you know it's nice.

Course it's nice, it's for my Queen.

Girl Yeah I swear I seen it before.

Aaron Yeah?

Yeah most probably . . . in your dreams, probably you dreamt that.

Dreaming 'I beg you let me get one a' these, up on / my –'

Girl Yeah I swear I seen it in your house.

Aaron Yeah?

Yeah well I dunno how you seen it round there like, 'cos . . . man only got the ting yesterday, still –

Girl Is this your mum's necklace?

Aaron What?

Jokes!

Girl Is it though?

Aaron Oi what you talking about, you think I'm the kinda man who gonna do some shit like that –

Girl My birthday was two weeks ago.

Had myself a cake.

Blew out my candles.

If I'm one of the girls you treat nice I'd hate to know the way you treat the nasty ones.

Aaron   Oi what you want outta life?

Girl   What?

Aaron   'Cos I can make it happen.

Girl   Yeah well first I want my peri-peri sauce up in / here –

Aaron   What you doing tonight?

Girl   Why?

Aaron   I can take you somewhere. I can take you –

Girl   Nando's?

Aaron   I can take you somewhere better than this.

Girl   I'm gonna see my dad.

Yeah?

So no, you ain't the only one I got out here.

Four (*barks*)

Aaron   Yeah the amount a' times I heard about your fucking dad, you know you're a grown up woman now, some Daddy's little girl ting is not a good look!

Four (*barks*)

Aaron (*to dog*)   Sit!

Girl (*standing*)   I'm gone, yeah?

Aaron (*to* **Girl**)   And you fucking sit!

A short pause. The **Girl** *sits.*

That's better.

Let's eat.

So I'm a couple weeks late.

But that's cool.

True there gonna be more birthdays.

More future.

Together.

Five   And when Aaron says the words 'Future' and 'Together'?

The Girl takes the necklace.

Dips it into her tiny portion of peri-peri sauce.

And then sticks it in her mouth and then swallows it.

And washes it down with a big gulp of a well-known multinational fizzy drink.

One   Not literally.

Two   She doesn't literally do that.

Three   Literally, she moves her eyes from the floor, to the ceiling, and then down –

One   To the chicken on her plate.

Two   And in her mind she's wondering about the chicken's short life, and what possible dreams the chicken might have had, and –

Two *realises the* **Girl** *is picking up the necklace, dipping it in sauce, and swallowing it, as described.*

And . . . And no, literally she does take the necklace, and . . . and dips it in the. . . .

And washes it down, with a big gulp of . . .

She swallows it.

Yeah.

She does that.

What's that all about do you think?

Aaron (*softly*)   You trippin' yeah?

Am I trippin'?

Five   And the Girl with no name looks at Aaron, and looks at the Dog, and kinda feels like they're both the same?

And inside she's kinda laughing?

And inside she's kinda saying –

Girl   I'm bigger than this anyway.

I got plans.

Five   And the Girl actually feels kinda sorry for them?

Two   Because when Aaron said –

Aaron   What you want outta life?

Four   In her mind, the Girl was saying –

Girl   Not you.

A musical transition – 'Dutch Pot Song'

> Steam fish and crackers inna di Dutch Pot
> Oxtail and rice inna di next

Steam fish and crackers inna di Dutch Pot
Oxtail and rice inna di next

Then everyone adds something to the Dutch Pot one by one

Say me want calalou
And me want ackee too
An mi want dumplin inna mi
Chicken back soup

Mi want bread fruit
Wid tropical juice
You know me love food
Ah nuh nuttin new

Steam fish and crackers inna di Dutch Pot
Oxtail and rice inna di next

Steam fish and crackers inna di Dutch Pot
Oxtail and rice inna di next

The audience move into Delroy's block of flats –

Two   Delroy Mitchell Smith is forty-two years and nine months old, and lives in a part of East London yet to be featured in the *Evening Standard* Property section.

Six   He lives in the flats.

Three   Which, like Del, were built just over forty-two years ago –

Five   And on the weekends, like Del, don't fully come to life until the sun goes down.

Three   At dinner time.

One   As ingredients hit pans and pots and plates up and down the block, and the air is alive with the smell of five different continents.

Delroy   Whatever you're saying about me I don't watch that – it's all love. And wherever I'm going right now – I'm free.

Two   That was Delroy to the Judge, back in 2013 after getting two years for possession with intent.

Delroy   I'm a force a' nature, and you can't tame that.

I'm living ten lifes at once!

Five   Which sounds like a load of old shit but actually <u>is</u> how Del's pretty much lived his life for forty-two years.

Two   Bit a' this

Three Bit a' that

Delroy Free-styling.

Two A trait that has definitely not rubbed off on his daughter –

The **Girl** *enters.*

One Who has taken the 69 bus out of Westfield Stratford and now enters Delroy's flat with her usual one-track, tunnel-vision sense of purpose.

Girl Dad.

Delroy (*to* **Girl**) Listen to my next proposal now –

Girl Dad when I move out my hostel yeah? – I wanna move in with you.

Delroy (*not hearing her*) The game of Monopoly –

A homely favourite of all age groups.

But what if you take the concept – and digitise it.

Hook it up to the world-wide markets in real time!

Suddenly your little family parlour game is a training ground for the next generation a' property developer and stockbroker in waiting –

Girl Dad

Delroy And suddenly your Daddy a rich man again –

He pops open some champagne.

– 'Ca that's some innovation concept right there, man 'a patent that quick-fast –

Girl Dad are you hearing me though?

Delroy What's to hear, Babes?

What's this urgency you got running through your veins, when your daddy by your side and he got the future locked?

He gives her a kiss on the forehead.

Girl You're the second one today chatting future to me you know.

Delroy Who the first?

Girl You don't wanna know.

Delroy Yeah you done know I don't, 'ca whatever future they're chatting 'bout – Ain't gonna be a patch on you, you and me's.

Girl (*half-smiling*) Is it?

Delroy (*kisses teeth playfully*) You mad?

Girl Monopoly, yeah?

Delroy　The remix. Amongst other concerns and projects I'm about to make happen – but in the meantime – let's see what's on the menu tonight.

Girl　Got stomach ache.

Delroy　What you been eating?

Girl　You live in some stinky-arse block you know.

Delroy　Yeah you wanna try living up in HMP, Princess.

Girl　Every time I come through bare different kinda cooking smells all coming out the place, all . . . Taliban cooking and Gypsy kinda cooking and all them stinky things there.

Delroy　What, you rather everybody cook the same way?

Girl　Yeah.

Delroy　Yeah?

Girl　Yeah. Furthermore I wish everybody <u>was</u> the same way.

Cloned. Factory style. Least then you know who you're dealing with.

Delroy　Well believe when I say you weren't made in no factory babes.

Luton Airport Travel Lodge, New Year's Eve 1998.

Girl　Dad.

Delroy　The taste of Cristal Champers! Every time it take me right back to where you started.

Girl　Have you heard of a ting called too much info?

Delroy　Can't all be no factory-bod, some of us gotta stand out from the crowd.

Girl　Yeah some of us standing out too much.

(*Half-smiles.*) With your cristal glass and your three piece suit and ting.

Delroy　What can I say, places to go and people to see.

Girl　What, apart from me?

Delroy　I'm a man a' means, you know a' mean by that?

Girl　No.

Delroy　Means Business – put me up in that *Dragon's Den* mek I *bun* the competition –

Girl　Yeah I beg you don't be going on *Dragon's Den* and chatting 'bout . . . remix-Monopoly or suttin like that, I think it's kinda off-beat?

Delroy　But my point is innovation. And speaking a' which –

He puts a flyer down in front of her.

Whoever said there ain't no such a thing as a free lunch – they're right. But a free dinner? Better come check me.

Girl (*reading flyer*)   The Belly Full Kitchen.

Delroy   Just the next big ting to hit the culinary-London-scene and who knows – maybe make another new star-chef-celebrity in the process.

Girl   That you yeah?

Delroy   Course. Me and my business partner. Opening night, fifteenth of the month, you bring that flyer down – you fill your belly up for free.

Girl   Who says I'm coming?

Delroy   Who said that?

Girl (*smiling*)   Later man, I might be busy.

Delroy   'Later man', my own daughter saying she ain't coming to my restaurant launch?

Girl   Oi for real though you ain't the only one who got plans out here.

I got plans.

Just dunno what they are yet.

Delroy   My princess course you got plans –

Girl   Basically I can't be living how I'm living right now like, I'm bigger than this.

Suttin gotta change.

Delroy   So what's happening in your life? You got that boyfriend, still?

Girl   Sometimes.

Delroy   He treat you good?

Girl   . . . ish.

Delroy   'Ish?' Ish ain't no fucking good, where's he live?

Girl   It don't matter, Dad.

Delroy   'bout 'Ish'. Some brudda getting ishy with my Princess?

Girl   Dad when I move out my place . . .

I was thinking . . .

Delroy   Yeah?

Girl   You could adopt me.

He stares at her.

Delroy   That what you thinking yeah?

Girl When I'm out a' my hostel place –

Delroy Babes I can't adopt you I'm your dad!

Girl Or what, let me move in here anyway, I can come and live with you!

I'm seventeen yeah, I ain't living in a hostel all my life –

Delroy And from you turn eighteen, babes, that mean you're an adult now, you don't wanna be living with me!

A moment.

Girl What, you don't want me here?

Delroy Babes –

Girl Yeah. Yeah I see clear now. Your own daughter too much trouble.

Maybe you should go prison again, won't have to deal with me there?

Maybe *I* should go.

Delroy Come on / now –

Girl No that sounds good! I don't wanna be close to no one in this fucking world, I just wanna move separate!

Delroy (*stopping her*) From your knocking, then my door's open.

Always.

A moment.

Girl Oi you're the only one I got out here you know.

One Moving, isn't it?

Two To see such vulnerability –

One And as for what Delroy does next –

Two (*smiling*) Well.

One I know you won't be disappointed by Delroy's next move because it really is a master-class in charisma, and . . .

Two In parenting –

One – and what he does is he takes his daughter's hands in his, and says –

Delroy The day you were born – it was a one-away kinda day, you know why?

'Ca that one day seventeen-summer-times back, there was a freaky ting that happened that we call the Total Solar eclipse, right?

Two (*to audience*) Stay with him.

Delroy And that mean only on that one day, for one hour only, everyone looking at the sky. 'Ca the moon get up in the Sun business!

And the moon block out the Sun and turn day half into night, and you had to wear some pair a' big stupid glasses to see the thing otherwise you gonna get blinded, except I weren't looking at the sky, Princess.

I was looking down at you in my arms. And inside I was thinking 'Yes. The world better put on his glasses from now, 'ca my little girl gonna shine so bright – she gonna bomb-blast the moon and the sun and the stars out the fucking ball park!'

One See what I mean?

Delroy Now you know what we're gonna do now?

Girl What?

Delroy We're gonna eat. Cupboards look a little bit bare but don't watch that.

I gi' you the full-nine-free dinner when you come to my Belly-Full launch, but for now – we haffi draw for the innovation.

Five And as if by actual magic –

In front of **Delroy**, *a shower of rice into a pot.*

Delroy We improvise!

Girl Alright.

Another ingredient or kitchen tool appears in **Delroy**'s *hand.*

One Every ingredient and apparatus that Delroy could possible need, to create the most heart-warming and soul-reviving dinner for two –

Four Appears.

Two And the Father and Daughter eat so well, in the spirit of togetherness, and hope for the future, it seems impossible at this moment for them to do anything other than live happily ever after.

Five Which makes it a double shame that in four hours time Del gets stabbed to death in a car park.

Girl What?

Delroy *freezes.*

Five (*to* **Girl**) Oh yeah. Sorry. Spoiler alert.

Delroy *remains frozen, as the* **Chorus** *slowly move towards the* **Girl**.

Girl No what you talking about, who's getting stabbed?!

Oi listen! What's going on?!

You're chatting shit!

Dad?

Dad?!

Chorus *members produce a syringe, and administer a sedative to the* **Girl**.

The **Girl** *sleeps.*

The melody to 'Kihawahine', a Hawaiian folk song, is played, almost as a lullaby, as **Chorus** *members gather round the* **Girl**.

One   That evening, the Girl without a name doesn't walk but flies, back to her hostel room in the grip of a natural sugar rush.

Two   And that night she sleeps like a baby.

One   With dreams as light as air.

Two   Dreams, that if they could speak, would be telling the Girl –

One   There's a place for you in this world.

There's a place for you in this world.

There's a place for you.

Three   But this is the bit where things get complicated.

Two   Because when Del said:

Delroy   Places to go and people to see! –

Five   He was talking about a drug deal.

Music stops. The sound of the streets at night. The **Girl** *grows restless in her sleep, meanwhile –*

Two   That night Del goes to meet a gentleman with the street name Red Cobra.

Chorus *member* **Four** *assumes the identity of Red Cobra.*

Who doesn't look like that but anyway –

One   Delroy goes about twice a month to the car park of B&Q in Leyton to buy cocaine.

Three   And Red Cobra goes about twice a month to sell it.

Five   It's a simple arrangement

Three   Made complex, by the fact that Red Cobra thinks Delroy's been ripping him off.

Two   And, by the fact that Delroy *has* been.

Three (*giving* **Four** *a knife*)   So tonight Red Cobra brings with him an eight by two inch Russell Hobbs kitchen knife

Six   Which he actually bought from B&Q.

Girl (*sleeping*)   Dad?

Two   Red Cobra doesn't really feature beyond this, in our story.

Maybe he can have his own spin-off. 'Red Cobra the re-match.'

'The curious incident of Red Cobra in the night time.'

But anyway.

Cobra does his job.

One   Which is to stick the kitchen knife deep into Delroy's left kidney.

Girl (*waking*)   No!

Four/*Cobra stabs* **Delroy**. *Then stabs him again, and then a third time. And with each stab, a* **Chorus** *member slams an egg into the* **Girl**'*s head.*

Street sounds rising in volume and mixing with the lullaby.

Two   And as Delroy sinks to his knees, the taste of Cristal champagne and blood takes him back to a mixture of Luton Airport Travel Lodge – and the first fight he had in primary school.

One   And as he dies, in his mind, Delroy's saying –

Delroy   Whatever you're saying about me I don't watch that.

It's all love.

And wherever I'm going right now –

I'm free.

The street sounds have engulfed the lullaby, and transformed into a sustained sound, the sound of numbness.

Chorus *member* **One** *addresses the* **Girl**, *who is still covered in egg, and is looking straight ahead in a state of numbness.*

One   Hello.

Girl (*dazed*)   What?

One   What's your name?

Girl   I dunno you know. . . .

A moment.

One   My name's Sarah.

Actually it's Sophie.

Call me Sophie.

Actually maybe it's . . . Mary, maybe you'd like to call me something more . . . maternal –

Girl   What are you talking about?

One (*coming closer*)   I am so very sorry about the way things have turned out.

Because you've been . . . such a victim, haven't you? Of everything.

Girl What are you saying?

One But don't worry.

Because I know it doesn't feel like it right now, but this – is a turning point.

Girl Who are you?

Five *has entered.*

Five (*to* **One**) Wasting your time.

One (*to* **Girl**) In the wake of your father's death –

Five She ain't gonna listen.

Girl Who ain't?

One In the absence of your father, we thought it best –

Five (*to* **Girl**) Oh the Father. Pinned all your little hopes onto him, didn't you?

Looks like you got egg on your face.

One – We thought it might be useful, at this point, for you to meet an Authority Figure.

I'm your Social Worker slash Key Worker slash Cognitive Behavioural Therapist.

Girl You're my what-slash-what?

Oi I'm cutting yeah, let me move from here –

One This is a story.

Stories need things.

People need things.

Girl Yeah I don't need this.

Five (*to* **One**) See?

One I've been looking through your records, from social services –

Girl Oh don't start on that I beg you.

Five Tell them about the carer.

Girl I don't wanna talk about care, I don't wanna talk about police, I don't wanna talk about no system-shit, all a' them just set me up to fall right back down.

One You've had a rough old time, on lots of different placements haven't you?

Girl I feel like I'm on suttin.

Five Yeah tell them what you done to your first foster carer.

Girl Have you given me suttin?

Five You want me to tell them?

One And there was an incident with your first foster carer, because according to your notes at the age of twelve you threw a kettle of boiling water in her face.

Five Oops!

Girl You don't know me.

Five We all know how it's gonna end.

Five *exits. A moment.*

One If you're not careful, your story ends badly.

Girl So?

One Because there's a pattern to a lot of these stories. A story that starts in care and ends in custody.

Girl You don't know about me.

One (*to audience*) And who wants to watch that?

Girl Who you talking to?

One But I can help you to find what you're looking for.

Girl I ain't looking for nothing.

One In the absence of your father –

Girl Yeah my dad is dead. The end.

One And what do you do now?

Girl I go out and I drink.

One And?

Girl I got out and I blaze.

One And would that make you feel much better?

Girl Yes.

One I see.

Girl I go out and fuck shit up.

One And how would you like to do that? Sugar?

A short pause. The **Girl** *stares straight ahead.*

Girl How to slit your wrists.

How to never wake up.

How to make absinthe.

How to be happy and not always mad.

*The **Girl** continues her list, as perhaps the audience are led to the next space. Over the top of the **Girl**'s list, a **Chorus** member speaks –*

Two   The Girl with no name spends the next two days mostly sleeping, and the next two nights mostly conducting internet searches.

One   Searches driven by paranoia, and loneliness, and mostly in fact by anger at this stupid, meaningless cunt of a world, and by the need to take this anger out on something, or someone.

Eight (*to audience*)   And how would you like her to do that?

Delroy   You haffi draw for the innovation.

Nine   And on the second night, at ten past two in the morning – she finds it.

Five   How to fuck shit up.

Girl   How to kidnap a dog.

Three   OK.

Six   How to kidnap a dog.

One   And how to make dog soup.

Four (*barking*)

*Members of the **Chorus** bring **Aaron** on, looking a bit pissed off and confused, and sit him down. Meanwhile the barking turns to yelping, and then stops.*

*The **Girl** faces **Aaron**.*

Girl   OK you want red or white?

Aaron   What?

Two   Three days after the incident with the necklace in Nando's, the boy called Aaron is sat in his mum's house, thinking possibilities.

One   He's thinking about the possibility of having a threesome.

Two   With the Girl with no name, and another girl, named Elodie.

One   Because when Aaron said to the Girl –

Aaron   Me and you . . . like we can take it to a different level like, We're built to do shit. Together. And . . . even maybe with other people –

Three   That's basically what he was thinking about.

Two   'Cos the Girl with no name owes him something.

Aaron (*in agreement*)   You get me though?

One   For taking her under his wing.

Three   Some hostel sket so beneath his level it's un-real.

Aaron   Blatantly.

Two   Aaron's pretty sure Elodie's up for anything once she's smoked enough, but the Girl with no name –

Aaron   Yeah it's tricky.

Two   He's thinking he might have fucked things up with the whole mum's necklace-birthday episode, but – is pleasantly surprised –

Aaron's *phone receives a message.*

– to receive a message from the Girl with no name saying –

Members of the **Chorus** *manhandle* **Aaron** *into sitting at a dinner table, maybe putting a napkin on him which he rejects, meanwhile –*

Girl   I'm sorry I was weird.

I'm sorry I got mad.

Come round tonight, I'll cook you dinner.

Kiss.

Kiss.

Kiss.

Aaron   What?

Girl   Red or white. Wine, man, I got wine. Gonna do this properly.

Aaron   Yeah?

Girl   Red wine you have with red meat, right? Or fish. Or is that the white? Anyway, whatever, red or white?

Aaron   Yeah you . . . You alright?

Girl   Yeah man, I'm good, What?

Aaron   Look a bit . . . stressed or suttin like that.

Girl   I ain't stressed. I'm feeling nice.

Aaron   Alright.

Girl   You look a bit stressed though.

A moment.

Aaron   No I'm cool.

Girl (*going back to kitchen*)   I should be the one who's stressed you know. Getting all these what's-it-called, fucking . . . ingredients together.

Aaron   Yeah?

Girl Spring onions like, what the fuck is a spring onion? What, they're the ones who think they're too nice, they only come out in the spring?

Aaron Yeah I leave that shit to my mum anyway.

My mum work in Asda these days you know that? What's that – staff discount. . . . Every day she bringing home all . . . leftover double chocolate / brownie cookies –

Girl (*coming back into the room, with cutlery, cutting him off, her anger bubbling over*) Stress enough getting clean plates and fucking forks like. Little trash utes living in here don't clean nothing.

Aaron Is it?

Girl Had to clean that shit my own self.

'Cos I wanna give you suttin nice.

Aaron Yeah?

Girl Give you suttin to remember.

Aaron *is staring at her, can't quite believe what he's hearing.*

Aaron To . . . to remember yeah?

Girl (*going back to kitchen*) Found one nice recipe you know.

Aaron Is it?

Girl From Korea or suttin like that.

Aaron Yeah? Yeah why you go through all this trouble just to get me round here / and

Girl 'Cos you deserve it.

A moment.

Aaron Yeah.

Yeah you know that.

Three Dog soup.

Four A homely favourite of all age groups.

Two Between two and three in the morning take the N38 night bus to your boyfriend's mother's maisonette –

One – And this is a little trick from your house-breaking days –

Seven Gain access via the Post Office sorting yard to said boyfriend's mother's maisonette's back garden and, very carefully –

Nine – And it's important to be wearing gloves when you do this –

Eight (*handing the* **Girl** *the sedative*) Administer a sedative to said boyfriend's Staffordshire bull terrier and remove him from his dog house.

One And what you get then is that really satisfying feeling, as you take a medium sized garden spade and –

Six Dash his fucking brains out on the concrete.

Five Yeah can I just say I don't think she does that?

Girl What?

One And as you're preparing to do this, what you really / do have to watch out for

Five No Hello, Excuse me, kidnapping his dog?

She ain't even got the brains.

Nine And it is a bit random.

One Because the Girl with no name is just in a state of complete . . . basically despair –

Five Yeah I get that –

One And basically just wants to fuck shit up

Girl Right

Five Yeah you said that bit, but I'm saying I thought we're telling this story together?

One Oh my God totally –

Five And I'm saying this bit don't feel real to me? –

One Oh my God I know but it's important to remember –

Girl (*to* **Five**) Who the fuck asked you anyway?

Five Oh you know what, why we telling your story anyway, fucking waste-gash, fuck's sake –

Five *exits, as a couple of* **Chorus** *members consider going after her. Meanwhile –*

Three Because it's important to remember this dog belongs to the boy who tried to give you his mother's necklace as a birthday present!

Two And who likes to think of himself as your only hope in the world.

One And remember your father is dead, and this pathetic excuse for a man is still breathing and so where – d'you know what I mean? – where is the justice in that, and so fuck it. Fuck it. Fuck it.

The other **Chorus** *members look at* **One**, *a bit surprised by her emotion.*

And then, erm – Put the dead dog in your bag and take it home!

Girl (*to* **Aaron**) I think you're gonna like this, you know.

Aaron Yeah?

Girl   Think it's gonna be the best thing you had in a long time.

Aaron   Yeah true say I have been stressed today you know.

Girl   Yeah?

Aaron   Yeah my Dog missing.

Girl (*coming back in, with pot of soup*)   WHAT?!

A moment. **Aaron** *a little surprised by her concern.*

Aaron   From last night.

Girl (*serving the food*)   Oh my God I love that Dog!

Aaron   Yeah?

Girl   Babes!

Aaron (*a little bit weirded out by her concern*)   Yeah.

Yeah and he missing from out the dog-house man, you know what that mean? That mean someone took him though.

Girl   Swear down?

Aaron   What, you think he gonna jump that fence?

My man can't jump.

My man . . . he just a baby anyway like . . .

Girl   Let's eat. Let's take your mind off things.

Aaron *starts to eat.*

Aaron   Yeah that dog is a part of me, you know that?

(*Eating.*) This is good.

Girl (*putting more on his plate*)   Have some more.

Aaron   What is it some . . . pork or beef or suttin / like that

Girl   I'm sorry I got mad on Saturday.

Aaron   Yeah?

Girl   Just kinda stressed, I guess.

Aaron   Yeah. Yeah you shouldn't have chatted to me like that.

Girl   I just get vexed at the world sometimes.

Aaron   Yeah I hear that.

Girl   Makes me wanna fuck shit up.

Aaron   So what, how was your dad then?

Girl I don't really care about my dad no more.

Just a wasteman.

Promising me things. . . .

Not like you.

Aaron Yeah believe.

Girl (*remembering*) Oh yeah. Red or white?

Aaron What, ain't you got any beers?

Girl (*standing*) Yeah I got beers. Took some beers off a girl yesterday.

She is getting a bottle of beer.

Aaron Alright. Oi you got a bottle opener though, man ain't got nothing / to open that –

Girl That's alright.

She looks at him as she proceeds to open the bottle with her teeth.

She gives him the bottle.

Drink.

Aaron Boy.

What, you feelin kinda freaky yeah?

Girl (*shrugs*) I dunno.

Aaron Yeah that . . . eating the necklace and shit, that was kinda freaky still.

Girl Did you like that?

Aaron Boy . . .

Girl Eat up.

A short pause.

Aaron Yeah me and you good together y'nuh.

Girl Yeah?

A short pause.

Aaron It's kinda comfy in here. Ain't too bad, for a hostel pad –

Girl No it ain't.

It's a shit-hole.

It's dirty.

Like me.

A short pause.

Aaron   Yeah me and you . . . like we can take it to a different level, like.

We're built to do shit. Together. Like . . . You see my friend Elodie yeah –

Girl   Slap me.

Aaron *stares at her.*

Aaron   What?

Girl   Slap me, come.

Aaron   You want me to / slap you

Girl   You can't say you ain't never done it before.

I'm nasty innit.

Aaron   Are you on suttin / right now?

Girl   You're gonna wanna slap me in a minute babes so you might as well do it now.
You're gonna wanna pull my eyes out.
You're gonna wanna splash that hot plate in my face.
I'm a fucking dog.
That dog was a part of you, right?
Yeah.
Yeah he is now.

Aaron   What you talking about?!

Girl   Just take it as a little thank you. For being you.

For being the only one who checks for me in this fucking world, now that everyone's gone, now that even my dad –

Aaron   Oi what you done?

Girl   Tastes like pork or beef or suttin yeah?

Wrong!

Aaron   Why you laughing for?

Girl   It tastes like a dog called fucking Dog!

Aaron   Come here!

Aaron *makes a lunge at the* **Girl**, *but one of the* **Chorus** *members sticks a napkin over his mouth and chloroforms him.*

The **Girl** *walks away as the scene melts away behind her and* **Aaron** *is taken off.*

She faces **Chorus** *members.*

One   How are you feeling now?

Girl   Good. Good man, It's done.
Dog soup, mate, he ain't never coming back.
World needs a slap like that certain times.

One   You fucked shit up.

Girl   Course.

Two   You gave the world a slap.

Girl   Like I said.

One   And I expect you're feeling incredibly happy now.
I expect you're feeling warm inside.

Girl   I wanna go raving, man.

Two   You're definitely not feeling empty.

One   You're definitely not feeling like there's a hole inside you.
And that you might be telling yourself you're happy but inside – you're only feeling pain.

*The **Girl** sinks to the floor. A short pause.*

Girl   So what then?

One   Please don't cry.

Girl   I'm not crying.

Two   We want to see you do well.

Girl   I don't care what you wanna see!
Tell me them!

One   As your Social Worker slash key worker / slash

Girl   Yeah whatever slash whatever!
Tell me the answer!

Two   Perhaps it's in your pocket.

*A moment. The **Girl** takes Delroy's 'Belly Full' flyer out of her pocket.*

One   The Belly Full Kitchen.

Two   Opening night?

Girl   (*staring at the flyer*)   Dad?

Delroy   You bring that flyer down, you fill your belly up for free.

Girl   What, you think a free meal gonna fix everything? And he ain't gonna be there! My dad ain't gonna be there, he's gone!

Two (*to* **Girl**)   Sometimes a story can take us by surprise.

Underscore begins.

Three   And the Girl with no name takes herself a bit by surprise –

Eight   Waking up the next afternoon, and wondering if the whole dog thing was all a dream?

Two   And then remembering her father's flyer in her pocket, and heading out the door, and taking the 56 bus –

Four   To Dalston.

In the transition, **Chorus** *members help the* **Girl** *get cleaned up.*

A Hawaiian restaurant in Dalston. Late afternoon.

Ralph – *a man in his thirties, intense and a bit wired, is sorting things out behind the bar, as the* **Girl** *enters, with her Belly Full Kitchen flyer.*

Girl   Yeah excuse me –

Ralph   We're closed.

Girl (*to* **Chorus**)   Oh well that's a good start.

One   Try again.

Girl   Yeah excuse me I come to get my free dinner / right now?

Ralph   Yeah which part a' Closed you don't get? Ah? Closed. Fermé – Yeah? That's French. Geschlossen – yeah? That's German. Atomu – that's the indigenous language of the Akan people of West Africa, but you ain't never heard a' that though, right? No – 'Cos you don't know your history.

Girl   Yeah I ain't talking history. I'm talking about the future.

Two   Nice.

Ralph   Oh the future, OK. Time traveller, OK, So what's happening for the future then, tell me.

Girl   Well the first thing that's happening is my free food right now, 'cos I got my flyer right here and my belly / empty –

Ralph   No no no, wait there wait there wait there wait there. 'Free food'? Are you saying to me 'free food?' Get out my place.

Girl (*with flyer*)   I ain't leaving 'til I get my free meal.

Ralph   Are you taking the piss?

Girl   Yeah I'm taking everything mate. I'm taking your peri-peri sauce right here –

Two (*to* **Girl**)   Easy.

Girl   You don't even know the frame of mind I'm in right now, I'm taking everything you got unless you gimme my Belly Full Kitchen, opening night, one-flyer-one-meal dinner for one.

Two   Perhaps we should start this again –

Ralph   Belly Full Kitchen.

Girl   Right.

One *indicates for* **Two** *to hold on and let them play it out, meanwhile* –

Ralph   Belly Full Kitchen opening night, what you talking about, what you know about this place?

Girl   This is my dad's place. Last thing he done he give me this invite.

Ralph   Your dad's place.

Girl   Yeah, dad. Papa. Abbah. Your business partner, yeah? Or maybe you don't know your history.

One   Perfect.

Girl   Your name Ralph?

Ralph   Rafe.

Girl   Says Ralph on the flyer.

Ralph   No, it says 'Rafe' on the flyer. Just 'cos you see it that way don't mean you say it that way. Like Eggs.

Girl   Eggs?

Ralph   Just 'cos I'm cracking eggs then putting them in a pan, don't mean I'm making omelettes.

Girl   OK.

Ralph   But I do make omelettes, you don't know about my omelettes. My omelettes so good – eggs cracking themselves just to get in my pan.

Girl   Yeah I never really come for no omelette like, I'm more kinda thinking maybe jerk chicken and / then

Ralph   Oh! She said that, She really said that.

Girl   What?

Ralph   Because I'm a proud Black man just running my own place you think it's Jerk Chicken I'm serving here?

Girl   Because your restaurant named Belly Full?

Ralph   Yeah Delroy named the place Belly Full, that was not my scenario no way mate.

But we had a disagreement. Multiple. Yeah?

Then two in the morning he come down here – fix that fucking sign above the door and now we're stuck with it.

Girl Yeah that sounds like him.

Ralph That sounds like him yeah? Let me tell you suttin –

Girl Oi if it's not jerk chicken then I beg you let me just get couple fried dumplings and / maybe

Ralph We don't do jerk chicken! We don't do dumplings, and you know why?

Girl No.

Ralph 'Cos the place is Hawaiian. Hawaii – yeah? Go Mexico Bay and then south-by-south-west, 'cos you don't know your geography –

Girl What you know about Hawaii?

Ralph What do *I* know about – (*Laughs.*) What do I know about Hawaii, Yeah. Yeah, you're Delroy's kid alright, I can smell the same smell a' just attitude and bullshit.

Girl Oi you better *watch* what you're saying about my dad you know, 'cos I swear to you right now I'm in a mood to do suttin I might come / to regret –

Ralph Listen.

I heard about your dad.

Girl What you heard about my dad?

Ralph I heard he's dead.

I'm sorry to hear that.

But – what can I say? Del . . . that's a man who had fingers in all kinda pies. Sometimes the pie bites back.

Girl Yeah that don't even make sense, and furthermore –

Ralph Furthermore I ain't seen Del for six months, right?

We met in prison.

Shared a pad together.

Shared a few plans together. And between us . . . we led some lives, that's true.

Both got a bit a' money stashed, both decided, on the out – Restaurant. Gonna put that cash together, make a dream real.

Girl I hear that.

Ralph But Delroy had a lot of dreams.

And when it come to actual really putting in the work?

Let's just say he kinda slept on the job.

Girl (*idly picking up a packet off a surface*)   Well it don't exactly look like it's jumping off in here / right now

Ralph   Oi don't touch that!

Girl   What?

Ralph   That's my quinoa, don't be touching my quinoa, someone like you don't know about quinoa.

Girl   Oh someone like me yeah?

Ralph   Yeah.

Girl   Tell me then.

Ralph (*indicating quinoa*)   Calcium, fibre, protein, that's all up in this bitch. You don't know about food, What did Delroy know about food?

All printing out flyers for opening night, this look like opening night to you? Fucking Belly Full. . . . Brain empty.

Girl   Why you think you so special, Ralph?

Ralph   What?

Girl   You ain't special.

And I know I ain't.

(*With flyer.*) But the world owes me just one thing right now, and I come to get what's mine.

Meanwhile, members of the **Chorus** *have been squabbling over a Belly Full flyer – and thus who should next enter the scene.* **Chorus** *number* **Six** *grabs a flyer and enters, assuming the identity of* **Letitia**.

Letitia   Yeah excuse me?

Ralph   We're closed.

Letitia   Yeah excuse me I come to get my free dinner right now –

Girl (*to* **Ralph**)   You see what I'm saying?

Ralph (*to* **Letitia**)   What?

Letitia   Is this the Belly Full Kitchen yeah?

Girl   Except he don't like calling it the Belly Full Kitchen but yeah.

Letitia   My dad called it the Belly Full Kitchen.

Ralph   Ah?

Girl (*to* **Letitia**)   Your dad?

Letitia   Yeah this my dad's place?

Girl   What?

Letitia   Basically my dad died yeah?

Ralph   Hold up –

Letitia   I was kinda sad after it happened but then I stopped 'cos like – feeling sad is kinda long?

Girl   Oi what you talking about *your* dad?

Ralph   Oi listen –

Letitia   Are you Ralph?

Ralph   No

Girl   Yes

Ralph   Rafe.

Letitia   Rafe?

Girl   He says it 'Rafe'

Letitia   But on the flyer it / says

Ralph   Yeah 'cos you see it one way don't mean . . . Like the eggs! Fucking . . . never mind –

Girl (*to* **Letitia**)   Oi what you talking about this *your* dad's place?

Letitia (*getting flyer out*)   The last thing he gave before he died you know, was this.

Ralph (*in despair*)   Oh . . .

Letitia   And if I come to the opening night then he said I get a free meal?

Ralph   No. No this ain't happening

Meanwhile **Letitia** *has grabbed a bag of rice, and is stuffing it under her top to represent a baby bump.*

Letitia   By the way I'm pregnant yeah? So I guess that means I should get two meals.

Girl   You need to stop waving that around and talk to me.

Letitia   No, babes, I don't think I need to do that. Unless you're gonna bring me my food.

Ralph   No there's no food for neither of you!

Letitia   To be fair I had quite a big lunch though, but even so if you got some jerk chicken maybe –

Ralph   Oh! She said that, she really said that.

Girl (*to* **Letitia**)   Oi listen yeah –

Ralph   We don't do jerk chicken!

Letitia   Why man?

Ralph   'Cos I'm a proud Black man just running my own place you think it's Jerk Chicken I'm serving, it's Hawaiian, yeah? Hawaii – get your little phone out and look up Hawaii –

Girl   Where you get that thing?

Letitia   My babyfather goes to me 'From your pregnant then don't smoke, don't drink and eat so much sweets', I'm like 'This baby pissing me off already.'

Girl   My dad don't know you.

Letitia   What you talking about your dad for? (*To* **Ralph**.) My dad didn't say it was Hawaiian though.

Ralph   Your dad was a wasteman who didn't know shit.

Letitia   Excuse me?

Ralph (*to* **Girl**)   And so was yours!

Girl (*to* **Ralph**)   You better watch / yourself –

Ralph   'Cos you both got the same dad! Oh no, but you didn't even know it!

Girl   What?

Ralph   But he give you the flyer the same way! Oh – Del you gimme trouble even after you're dead and gone.

Letitia   Yeah what you talking about though?

Ralph   Bad seed – that's you, and that's you: Attitude and bullshit, passed right down from your big daddy.

Girl (*to* **Ralph**)   Oi you might think you're special yeah, but me and you the same!

Ralph   No you and her the same.

Letitia   Er, no –

Girl   I see you, fucking Rafey-Ralphy.

Letitia   Excuse me?

Girl   Mr 'I'm a Businessman', but you met my daddy in prison, right?

Ralph   Yeah?

Girl   Yeah. Yeah you might be wearing them hipster creps, but you're from the road. Just like my dad. Just like me.

Letitia   What's hipster creps?

Girl   So you ain't so special after all.

Ralph   Oi you know what, maybe I was like you. Once upon a long time ago.

Letitia   What, is it story time now?

Ralph   But the difference is that I switched my life *up* – upwards – *up* being the operative word, 'cos you can't keep a man like me down, you know why?

'Cos I'm skilled.

Turned my life around in the kitchen, mate. What you know about Vitamin A through D? What you know about balance? All munching on your box of fried chicken or glugging down your energy drink, yous are living in the ghetto, mate, I'm living in Kawela Bay!

Letitia   What's Kawel Bay?

Girl   Teach me then.

Ralph   What?

Girl   I wanna turn my life around, so come.

Ralph   Get out of here man –

Girl   Nah man, I'm all about the 'Yes Chef, No Chef. Three bag full a' quinoa, Chef.'

Ralph   Nah –

Girl   You saying you turned your life around. Well you done know mine needs turning too.

Letitia   What's quinoa?

Ralph   No you lot don't know –

Girl   So teach me.

Letitia   Oi teach me too!

Girl (*to* **Letitia**)   Move.

Letitia   Yeah I wanna turn around, I wanna live in Koala Bay!

Chorus *number* **Seven** *enters, and assumes the identity of* **Khalid**.

Khalid   Er, excuse me?

Ralph/

Girl/

Letitia   We're closed!

Khalid   Is this the Belly Full Kitchen?

Girl (*to* **Ralph**)   Oh I beg you don't start –

Ralph No it's not called the Belly Full Kitchen, ignore the sign, don't look at the sign.

Khalid OK –

Girl (*to* **Ralph**) You so special then pass the specialness on.

Ralph No this chat is done –

Khalid (*producing flyer*) It's just that – erm –

Letitia (*to* **Khalid**) Where d'you get that?

Khalid I think this is my dad's place?

Girl/Letitia What?

Khalid My dad had a place called the Belly Full Kitchen.
I don't even know if I should be here right now –

Ralph No you shouldn't.

Khalid But part of me felt I should come . . .
Because my dad invited me . . .
My dad passed away –

Girl Shut the fuck up.

Khalid Sorry?

Ralph (*to* **Khalid**) Bruv –

Letitia (*to* **Khalid**) Are you taking the piss?

Ralph Bruv you're stepping into something more than what you bargain for.

Khalid One of the last things he said was for me to come here and . . . and if I came on the opening night he said I'd get a free dinner.

Girl Why you lying for, who's your dad?

Ralph Fuck's sake.

Letitia Why you beggin' my dad for, I ain't never met you before, or you.

Girl (*to* **Letitia**) Why you beggin' mine?

Khalid I don't understand.

Ralph It seem like your dad had more than one kid mate – two more than you, two more than you, and two more than you.

Girl You're lying.

Letitia (*to* **Ralph**) Can we go Koala Bay now please?

Khalid Are you Ralph?

Ralph / Rafe!

Letitia Rafe, he says it Rafe!

Khalid I don't know what's happening here but I feel my dad wanted me to come.

Girl Yeah I think he wanted *me* to come.

Khalid He said . . . 'Come fill your belly on jerk chicken –'

Ralph Oh – / He said that, He really said that –

Letitia (*to* **Khalid**) It's not a jerk chicken joint, it's Hawaii, bitch!

Girl (*to* **Letitia**) Why you beggin' this guy for?

Letitia Who you talking to?

Girl When's you birthday?

Letitia When's yours?

Girl (*to* **Letitia** *and* **Khalid**) And both of you right, what's your dad's full name?

Khalid What d'you mean?

Girl I mean what's his first second and third names right, you should know your own dad.

Letitia/Khalid Delroy Mitchell Smith.

Ralph That's the one.

Khalid From Leyton.

Letitia No he weren't *from* Leyton.

Khalid He lived there.
He died there.

Letitia Don't.

Khalid My friend text me.
She said turn on the news.

Letitia Oh I don't wanna think about all that again.

Khalid They said he lost eight pints of blood . . .

Girl Shit.

Khalid Sorry.

Girl Shit.

Ralph I ain't got time for this –

Girl You're telling me you're my sister and brother?

Khalid   So you're telling me you're mine?

Letitia   And mine?

Ralph (*to* **Girl**)   So you ain't so special after all then, right?

Chorus *number* **Three** *has entered, and assumed the identity of* **Stef**.

Stef   Do you do pizzas here?

Ralph   We're closed.

Stef (*producing a flyer*)   I think this is my dad's place?

Girl/Letitia   What?!

Ralph (*calming himself*)   OK –

Stef (*looking at them*)   What?

Khalid   What is your dad's full name and when did he die?

Stef   How do *you* know he's dead?

Girl   / I swear to God you know . . .

Letitia   Is it actually for real though?

Ralph (*to* **Stef**)   No! No – Don't ask for me no free meal, or opening night bullshit-bullshit, just – Sit down here, with your brand new sister and sister and brother – yeah? And the whole lot of you Delroy-half-sibling can just – have your half-sibling convention and sort shit out.

Chorus *member* **Eight** *emerges from an unlikely place and assumes the identity of* **Tania**.

Tania   Is this the Belly Full Kitchen?

Girl   / Oh my days

Ralph (*to* **Tania**)   No how you get there?!

Tania   I think this is my dad's place.

My dad got murdered.

I've been feeling kinda low since then. But the last thing he did before / he died was to give me this.

Said if I came on opening night then I'd get a free meal.

I'm quite an impulsive person.

I kinda just had a feeling I should come?

Like almost like my dad was calling me?

I didn't know my dad too well but anyway.

Saw him on Easter weekend.

He gave me two Easter eggs he'd made – Guinness and chocolate and rum punch mix.

And he gave me the flyer and he told me come down.

Didn't tell me he was gonna get killed.

Didn't tell me I was gonna meet this lot.

Have I got brothers and sisters?

Chorus *member* **Nine** *emerges from another unlikely place and assumes the identity of* **Kimya**.

Kimya   Yeah excuse me is this the Belly Full Kitchen?

I know its kinda weird but I think this is my dad's place?

The last thing he did before he died was give me this?

And he told me to come here / and on like . . . the opening night, he said I could get a free meal?

Haven't eaten since Sunday.

That's when I heard, that he'd been killed.

I just went out the house and I didn't come back.

I say 'House'.

Hostel.

That's where I'm at.

I think.

I can hardly remember.

Everything's been just a blur.

Is this lot my brothers and sisters?

I feel like they're my brothers and sisters?

My mum said if I ever went to live with my dad then my life would just be fucked.

I guess now I'll never know.

Confused and excited chatter among the **Siblings***, as* **Tania** *and* **Kimya** *continue their speeches, which lasts approximately thirty seconds while the* **Chorus** *continue over the top of it –*

One   A human being.

Four   A homely favourite of all age groups.

Delroy   Take your one Sperm, and bomb-blast the ting up inside your one Egg – Stick it in the oven for nine months and then –

One   A human being.

Two   Delroy, it turns out, had spent the last twenty years making human beings all over London.

Four   With mothers from all over the world.

One   And here they surround the Girl with no name, in the restaurant that isn't named the Belly Full Kitchen, and this – is wonderful.

Two Because when Aaron asked the Girl –

Aaron What you want outta life?

Two What she didn't say –

One Because maybe she doesn't even know it herself –

Two Is that she wants to be a part of a Family.

The action freezes.

One Brothers and sisters.

Aunties and Cousins.

Bottoms to smack and cheeks to kiss and shoulders to cry on.

I think – finally – the Girl is feeling happy.

Girl I do not fucking believe this shit!

Ralph Can you hold your noise down please –

Letitia (*in agreement*) You get me though.

Girl I come to get what's mine! I come to get what's promised to me by my own dad, now you're telling me he promised it to half the fucking world!

Kimya But are we all brothers and sisters?

Girl I don't need no brothers and sisters –

Khalid But it's almost like our dad – like he planned for this to happen?

One Actually he didn't but isn't it wonderful to think that he did?

Ralph Yeah sorry to buss 'tru your bubble and that, but your daddy could not plan shit.

Girl And here we go again.

Ralph And all a' you wortless' ute just take after him innit, you think I need that in my place? A man like me, who's on a upward-ting, just turned my life around?

Girl So teach me then!

Fran What?

Girl My man's all about the 'turn his life around in the kitchen', and now he's looking down from Kawela Bay, but I'm saying you come from the same as me – so teach me!

The **Siblings** *all chime in with her 'Yeah and me, teach us then, haven't got anything to lose' etc.*

Ralph *is moving to turn away from them, but* **Chorus** *members* **One** *and* **Two** *face him. They seem to compel him to slowly turn around, and then –*

Ralph Alright, alright, alright, alright, alright, alright, alright, alright.

Alright.

You don't get no – (*tearing up a flyer*) – no free meals – yeah?

You don't get no jerk chicken.

But if you wanna learn about kitchen?

You wanna learn about skills?

You wanna just . . . break out from the pattern and don't be no wasteman like your dead-daddy-Del?

Then Saturday.

Saturday morning, you reach and you get the full download, anyone who's here then we'll do suttin, now move from out of my place, come we go.

*As **Ralph** dismisses the **Siblings**, they face each other for the first time. There is some chatter amongst them, and some of them perhaps beginning some kind of choral piece. It is a moment of tentative discovery.*
*The **Girl** keeps her distance, looking back at **Ralph**, trying to work out what his game is – **Ralph** looks at her too.*

Meanwhile –

Two   But why does he do it? –

One   – an observer might ask, at this point in our story, why Ralph

Ralph   Yeah Rafe.

One   Why Rafe performs this charitable u-turn, and turns father-figure to a field of Orphans.

Girl   Yeah why you do that?

Ralph   Yeah you lot don't know about that. 'Cos you don't know my history.

Two   History going back just eighteen months, to Pentonville Prison – D-Wing.

One   To a cell, and to Del, and to Ralph.

Ralph   Rafe.

Delroy   Rafe?

(*referring to cell paperwork*) R-A-L-P –

Ralph (*interrupting*)   Yeah just 'cos you see it that way don't mean you say it that way.

Delroy   Alright, cool nuh bad man.
Rafe.
Two months I been naming you wrong, you never tell me.

Ralph   My dad called me 'Ralph.'
My dad was a wasteman.

Delroy   So you switch up the format?

Ralph   Right.

Ralph *begins putting a Hawaiian poster up on the wall.*

Delroy   You see from you stick by me young man . . .

Ralph   From I stick by you . . .

Delroy   We're gonna switch up the format on the outside, king.

Ralph   God willing.

Delroy   Yeah you know God willing.

(*Indicating poster.*) Your little dream there about. . . . Escape to Hawaii and that, you gotta hold on to that.

Ralph   Believe.

Delroy   A restaurant. I'm telling you that's the clean-hearted business ting, you know a' mean by that?

Ralph   Clean-hearted.

Delroy   'Ca food is life!

Ralph   Right.

Delroy   An essential ting that!

From you're running a place, and you serving the people what they need –

Then when the time come, you look God inna the eye and say 'Yes. I used my time and I used it good.'

Ralph   I hear that.

Delroy   You leave suttin real to pass on.

Ralph *nods. A pause.* **Ralph** *decides to tell* **Delroy** *something.*

Ralph   You got kids, Del?

Delroy   Yeah I got a couple here and there.

A short pause.

Ralph   I got kids.

Delroy   Yeah?

Ralph   Yeah two. Boy and a girl.

Delroy   And that's the best combo.

Ralph   Right.

A short pause.

Yeah I don't know them too good you know.

Last time I see 'em. . . . Nearly two years.

Delroy   Bwoy.

Ralph   Me and their mum split a long time ago.

Meantime, she flips out.

Last I hear . . . she getting sent to a nut-house or suttin like that.

Then the last I hear. . . .

Kids getting fostered.

And that's the last I hear.

Delroy Someone name you 'Father' then they take the name away.

You're the man without a name.

Ralph But it's still in me. You see what I'm saying?

I wanna know them, I wanna be there for them, but . . .

A short pause.

Delroy You'll be there for them, king.

When you least expect, that's when they're gonna come to you.

Most probably up inna we restaurant!

Ralph (*half-smiling*) Probably.

Delroy You're gonna sit down one day and cook food for your kids.

Believe that.

Lights down on **Ralph** *and* **Delroy**.

The **Girl***, and the* **Siblings** *begin to assemble again.*

During the transition, they sing maybe the Hawaiian folk song 'Shake the Papaya Down'. The **Girl** *doesn't join in, and is generally irritated by the presence of the* **Siblings***.*

> Mama says No play,
> This is a work day,
> Up with the bright sun,
> Get all the work done,
> If you will help me,
> Climb up a tall tree,
> Shake the papaya down.
>
> Shake them down,
> Shake them down,
> Climb the tall tree,
> Shake them down.
>
> Shake them down,
> Shake them down,
> Shake the papaya down.

The Hawaiian restaurant. The following Saturday.

*The **Siblings**, including the **Girl**, are all assembled, with ingredients and cooking utensils in front of them. They are all preparing a basic Hawaiian starter-dish, maybe a salmon poke. The **Girl** has placed herself a little separate to the rest.*

Ralph *stands at the front, working and addressing the group.*

Ralph Right. Now as you're doing this it's eyes to the front, and looking at me. Always.

Khalid / Yes Chef, eyes front. (*Speaks in Somali – something like 'You're the boss.'*)

Kimya / I feel like I'm in the army?

Stef / What, forever?

Tania / (*Sings to herself, reprising a line of a previous song.*)

Girl Shhh!

Letitia (*to* **Girl**) Who you shushing?

Ralph Apart from if you're cutting suttin. If you're cutting suttin and using a knife then always . . . then you're looking at the knife, but apart from that – Anyway –

You see food? That's an essential.

Kimya / Yeah that's right you know.

Tania Erm, obviously?

Girl Oi can you lot just shut the fuck up for one minute?!

Letitia (*to* **Girl**) Oi what's wrong with you man?

Ralph (*working with the food*) You running your place and serving the people not just what they want but what they *need*.

*Affirmative comments from some of the **Siblings** – 'that's true'. . .*

And then when the time come –

You look God straight in the eye and say 'Yeah. I used my time and I used / it good –'

Kimya Ah this tomato just spunked right in my face.

Tania / Maybe you're cutting it up too sexy babe.

Letitia Oh my days you lot are too funny you / know

Stef Can we not just get a pizza in here?

Girl I swear to God –

*The **Girl** starts moving to confront the **Siblings**, but the **Chorus** gently move her back. Meanwhile –*

Ralph Yeah you better start treat that tomato with a bit more respect. 'Cos that's a alkaline food, and you don't know your science –

Khalid Alkaline's the opposite to acid

Ralph Yeah Alkaline's the one mate, 'cos of what it does for the *brain*.

Now you're mixing the salmon and the rice up good like I told you.

Girl   The brain?

Letitia (*to* **Girl**)   Yeah shame you ain't got one innit.

The **Girl** *moves to confront* **Letitia**, *but one* **Chorus** *member blocks her, as another* **Chorus** *member moves* **Letitia** *away.*

Ralph   Alkaline food, they come in like the mechanic. Repairing the brain cells, after the brain seen trauma.

(*For the* **Girl**'s *benefit.*) You got trauma in your life, don't be thinking about no big-dutty box a' no chicken and chips, you draw for the cherry tomato, the broccoli –

Stef   The pizza?

A burst of agreement and disagreement from the **Siblings**.

Girl   Excuse me, can I make my ting separately please?

Letitia   Yeah can she though?

Ralph   From your life too greasy, you draw for the salad. And that's the first step.

Kimya (*to* **Ralph**)   Why did you go prison for?

Ralph   I went prison for ABH.

(*For the* **Girl**'s *benefit.*) I got a temper. Matter of fact I got what we call anger issues. But Food –

He strikes a match.

It turned on a light.

With the match, he lights a hob and begins frying something.

Khalid   My dad told me one time. About the Nine Night.

Letitia   What you know about Nine Night?

Khalid   That's in the Caribbean . . . it's like a tradition. Nine Nights after a dead man's dead the family gathers in celebration –

Kimya   Oh my God we should do that –

Tania   Hawaiian nine nights?

Kimya (*to* **Ralph**)   That's how you should open your restaurant up

Ralph   Yeah and who's gonna cook it?

Letitia   Oi we are if you're teaching us.

Ralph   What, are you really on this yeah?

Khalid   Maybe it's what Daddy-Del would have wanted.

Ralph   Yeah food is family.

(*For the* **Girl**'s *benefit*.) One ingredient out on its own, it don't count for nothing.

Might not even like how that taste its on own, but you put them all together in a one pot?

Then you getting somewhere.

Tania I'm not being funny you know, but this salmon smells like pussy.

Letitia / Oh my God did she really say that?!

Kimya / I know, right?

Stef / That's disgusting

Girl Oi you know what I'm cutting –

Letitia Yeah do that

Ralph No wait there

Girl Move

Ralph Why you wanna move separate for?

Girl 'Cos I'm the only one who never let me down!

Ralph (*to* **Girl**) So you gonna let down your kitchen staff?

Kimya Are we staff now?

Ralph Who knows what you gonna be if you stick to suttin and you stand by it?

(*To* **Girl**.) Your siblings.

Your co-ds, yeah, you gonna walk out the door?

Girl Oi this lot ain't nothing to me.

Letitia Are we gonna let her talk to us like that?

Kimya Yeah but I can understand how she's feeling though 'cos we're all in a bereavement –

Khalid But this is a chance to make a family

Tania No thanks.

Girl Family ain't a word to me. Family was my dad.

Ralph (*to* **Girl**) Yeah you ain't never heard 'bout you can't choose your family?

Girl (*indicating the* **Siblings**) Yeah and I never chose them!

Ralph Yeah that's the point!

Girl Oi for real though, me and them don't relate!

*A **Chorus** member has taken the box of matches and now strikes one, and holds it out in front of **Khalid**. He begins his speech. Meanwhile, another **Chorus** member strikes a match in front of **Kimya**, and she begins hers.*

*The following speeches have a slight musical underscore, and overlap with each other, as the **Chorus** members strike a match in front of each sibling, and they begin their speech.*

Maybe we find a way of hearing the whole of each speech, or maybe each just lasts for the time it takes for the match to burn out or has to be blown out.

Maybe when one speech is cut off, the next sibling continues the same speech from the same point . . .

Maybe it doesn't involve matches at all. Either way, the atmosphere is that of the Siblings sharing parts of their stories together – of the differences and similarities within the new family, and of the unpredictability of life.

Khalid   I was born in 1994, and my dad came to see me every birthday. Except he never remembered my exact birthday but anyway.

Every year he brought me a meal, and told me I was gonna do good at everything.

One year, when I was thirteen, my mum told me she didn't want me coming home any more because I was bringing her shame. She said (*He speaks in Somali.*) – 'Go and find your dad.'

I spent a whole day walking. There was this guy, this tramp, who was trying to steal my shoes? So I stopped walking and I ran.

I found a hostel, and then they found me a children's home. And two years later – two days after my fifteenth birthday – my dad turned up. He'd found me.

Kimya   I'm not a trouble-maker.

I never have been.

I even did alright at school.

I was better at the creative stuff.

I think I got that from my dad.

I think that's why I've spent so much time wondering.

Wondering how I got like this.

A head-full of dreams, but no dinner table.

Up against the wall down alleyways, doing favours for favours.

Mum's still Mum, but she don't pick up the phone that much.

And as for Dad.

I liked him, when I saw him.

He made me laugh.

He made me lunch.

Sometimes that's all I wanted.

Stef If I was a pizza I'd say I was a Pepperoni double. The Domino's one, not Papa John's.

Just straight-forward, I guess. Dependable.

My dad was kinda Ham and Pineapple. Some people just aren't into it. But if you are, then you love it.

My mum's more like Cheese and Tomato deep-pan you make in primary school.

Not in a bad way.

You feel proud when you look at it. I feel proud of what she's done for me. Held it together like cheese and tomato, when my dad was too busy hamming it up with the pineapples.

Why am I talking about pizza for anyway? Is there gonna be pizza soon?

Tania Like most kids I used to think the world of my parents, and according to my mum I liked to do some crazy things like throwing flour around the kitchen to make it look like it was snowing?

Like most kids, I would sit in front of the TV and daydream about how one day my life would be like the life of the teenage kid played by an actress much older than I was.

Some people wanna travel back in time to their childhoods, but I pray to God that never happens to me because standing here right now I can't barely think of one good memory.

Got to know my dad a bit better now I'm older.

Did grown-up things together.

Like throwing flour round the kitchen to pretend that it was snowing.

Sometime parents fuck it up.

My friends are my family now, and that suits me.

Letitia I was just born, and then I was just a kid, and then I just grew up.

Like everyone does.

Life was hard.

Got kicked out of school, went unit.

And my mum was my Mum, and my dad was my Dad.

Didn't see that much of one – saw too much of the other.

And this baby's just gonna be a baby.

Ain't gonna see much of its dad – thank God.

And then it ain't gonna be just a baby 'cos it's gonna be a mum or a dad, and then it's the same thing.

I dunno what else to say.

When the other siblings have finished, a **Chorus** *member strikes a match and holds it out in front of the* **Girl**.

She blows it out.

Another **Chorus** *member offers another match.*

She blows it out.

Another **Chorus** *member begins to offer another match, when* **Ralph** *takes it.*

Ralph (*quickly, looking at* **Girl**)   Felt so angry at the world sometimes, felt like burning out. But I didn't. World gonna burn out before I do.

He blows the match out and discards it. He offers the **Girl** *her apron. A moment.*

Girl   I'm doing this for my dad you know.

Ralph   Maybe it's better if you're doing it for you.

An underscore begins, softly. **Ralph** *moves back to the cooking.*

(*To group.*) Now you're chopping up the lettuce in parallel lines, that's gonna make the texture come correct.

And when you're done –

Hawaiian culture all about the *Luau*, you know what that mean?

That mean sharing.

Some of the **Siblings** *begin to share the food they have made amongst the audience.*

Girl (*to* **Ralph**)   Oi my one looks shit you know.

Letitia   True that.

Letitia *knocks the* **Girl** *as she passes – the* **Girl** *moves to confront her but* **Ralph** *stops her.*

Ralph   Oi why you giving her power like that?

Girl   What?

Ralph   Some people in life just got a bad taste – so don't bite.
Write your own recipe.
Don't let no-one be dropping chilli powder where it ain't meant to be.

Kimya   I swear to God you know . . .

Stef   What?

Kimya   If I could go back and tell myself . . . I got brothers and sisters.

Tania   I've got five already.

Stef   Six.

Khalid   But Delroy-kids are kinda different.

Kimya (*in agreement*)   Do you know what I mean?

Khalid   Yeah it would have been better to have known.

Middle of the night.

Hostel room.

Kimya   Or in the mornings.

The **Girl** *is listening.*

Tania   When you're feeling like 'Am I even gonna bother getting up today?'

Letitia (*to her bump*)   You gonna have a lot of half-Aunts and half-Uncles

Ralph (*to* **Girl**, *and* **Letitia**)   Right. You, and you – you can help with the demonstration – Next course we're gonna fry chicken wings with rice and soy sauce, So spark up a pan and drop the cooking oil –

Letitia (*to* **Ralph**, *indicating* **Girl**)   Do I have to do it with her though?

Ralph (*moving towards kitchen*)   Need my paprika in here, where my paprika at? (*Referencing the* **Girl**'s *food as he passes.*) What you talking about that look shit? You learn the ting up good.

Letitia *kisses her teeth.* **Ralph** *exits into the kitchen. Underscore increases in volume.*

One   And the Girl <u>is</u> learning the ting up good.

Two   And, in Ralph –

Two   – She has found what wouldn't be too optimistic to call –

One   Someone to look after her.

Two   A mentor figure.

One   Someone to look after her.

Two   And the Girl with no name –

One   This nameless victim of so many years of neglect and misfortune –

Girl   Yasmine.

They all look at her. Underscore stops.

My name is Yasmine.

The **Girl/Yasmine** *lights a match.*

Yasmine   In the mornings. When you feel like 'Am I even gonna bother getting up today?'

When you feel to just blow out the light.

She lights a pan with match, and puts in some oil.

Feeling like it's gonna be meals just for one, just for you, just forever.

'Cos no-one don't give a shit.

And God knew you ain't Godly.

That's why he took away your mum.

And as for Daddy-Delroy.

He might swing by for breakfast, but he won't be round for dinner.

So what's the point in cooking?

Only ones who care, it's 'cos they're paid to.

That's why you splashed that foster-mum, hot-boiling-water in her fucking face.

That's why it felt so good to get arrested, finger-prints taken, you're thinking 'At least now I exist.'

And after dark you're thinking is it always gonna be like that.

Middle of the night. Hostel room.

But I guess you ain't the only one.

She has slowly turned to look at the others.

I guess you ain't alone.

Ralph *re-enters from the kitchen.*

Ralph Right, Now you're turning up the heat and give it a good splash around. Now you get to understand about real fried chicken that you don't get in Nando's –

One And the one son and five daughters of Delroy Mitchell Smith do turn up the heat and give it a good splash around.

Two Unified.

One A found family.

Two And in memory of the past –

One And celebration, of the future –

Two Together, they begin to plan a feast

One And with every dish their mentor teaches, they are brought even closer together, in the / spirit of –

Letitia (*to* **Yasmine**) I feel fucking sorry for you know.

Foster ute.

Can't take the pressure.

Gets all violent and shit like she can't control it.

And no wonder innit.

Her mummy died you know.

Eight years old.

Out of all of us, ain't she the one our dad shoulda taken in first?

Guess not.

Guess Daddy-Del didn't love you enough to do that.

One   And the Girl with no name –

Two   Who remember has eaten jewellery and killed a beloved family pet –

One   Who would, at an earlier point in our story have reacted to this provocation with extreme violence –

Two   Does not.

One   And instead, she calmly turns to face her half-sibling.

Two   She looks her in the eye, and she says –

Suddenly the doors crash open, and **Aaron** *bursts in.*

Aaron   Alright, stop that, shit is stopping right now!

Sound of consternation from the **Siblings** *– 'Who's that?', 'What's going on?' –* **Aaron** *grabs a big kitchen knife.*

Nobody fucking move! Nobody fucking move, and you better listen how the fuck it's gonna go down –

Two   And . . . and the Girl with no name looks in her / in the eye –

Aaron   No she does not! No she does not, mate – Who the fuck are you anyway, Jackanory-story-time –

Kimya   They're the Chorus!

Aaron   Oh the Chorus yeah? The Chorus, well here come the fucking Verse!

Ralph (*to* **Aaron**)   My brudda *my* restaurant you gate-crashing yeah, better put the ting down and we can talk shit through –

Aaron   Shut up

One (*to* **Aaron**)   The siblings are reaching towards a bright future –

Aaron   Yeah I ain't come to talk about future yeah, I come to talk History –

(*To* **Girl**.) You.

That dog was a part of me, you know that?

Tania   What's he talking / about?

Kimya   I don't understand

Ralph   What dog?

Aaron   Yeah. Yeah, this bitch killed my dog. (*To* **Chorus**.) You forgot about that though, right? Killed up the ting and then –

He tries not to become emotional.

And then fed him to me.

Sounds of disbelief and horror from the **Siblings**.

Killed up my baby then fed me that!

Letitia   Oh my days, this girl's cracked.

Aaron   You get me?

Letitia   This hostel sket –

Another burst of argy-bargy from the **Siblings**, *which the* **Chorus** *tries to subdue –*

Two   And the Girl looks her Sibling in the eye and says –

Aaron   No shut the fuck up I come to get what's mine. (*Shouting off.*) Mum?! Mum come through, I got this.

Another burst from the **Siblings** *– 'What?' – then* **Aaron**'*s mother* **Trish** *bursts in.*

Trish   Right. Which little twat had my jewellery then?

Aaron   It's this bitch right here!

Khalid (*to* **Chorus**)   What is she talking about?

Trish   What am I talking about – she only jacked my best necklace!

More argy-bargy from **Siblings** *as* **Aaron** *continues –*

Aaron   Yeah not even jacked it, she ate that shit! Straight up and down, stuck it in her mouth and swallowed it! Real!

One   And the Girl with no name –

Trish (*to* **Kimya**)   Right. See you, you thieving little fucking freak –

Trish *gives* **Kimya** *a massive slap round the face. A burst of consternation from the* **Siblings** *as* **Aaron** *says –*

Aaron   No that's the wrong one, Mum, it's her!

One (*to* **Aaron** *and* **Trish**)   The Girl with no name has found a family –

Ralph   Yeah these my apprentices right here, I vouch for them

Trish   Apprentices?

Ralph   Turn their life around through the cooking!

Trish   What is this, the Great British Wank-off?

Aaron   Innit though. (*To* **Chorus**.) Oi what's this fucking fairy tale business anyway, 'The sons and daughters of Delroy-bullshit'?! What, and they all get together and they're learning cooking skills, what you take this ting for, man?

Khalid It's a story based on hope, and based on / possibilities –

Aaron (*indicating* **Khalid**) Furthermore you tryina tell me that's a Jamaican father's son? My man's pure Somali mate, that ain't no mixed-race ute no way, and she's as white as the Queen, so why you trying it for –

Trish (*picking up a flyer*) The Belly Full Kitchen?

Aaron Yeah alright, Mum, I'm dealing with it –

Trish I could murder a bit a' jerk chicken

Shouts of consternation from the **Siblings***, and* **Ralph** –

Ralph Oh – She said that, she really said that!

Aaron (*to* **Ralph**) Oi who you calling She, that's my mum you're talking about y'nuh – (*To* **Girl**.) So what, you ain't got nothing to say?

Ralph Eh fall back my bredda yeah?

Trish / Oh don't get out your pram, sunshine.

Aaron (*to* **Ralph**) Don't touch me yeah, you touch me again I'm gonna pass this through you –

Two And the Girl with no name looks her / sibling in –

Trish / Shut it!

Aaron (*to* **Chorus**) Shut up!

(*to* **Yasmine**) What, you ain't got nothing to say?

Yasmine *says nothing.*

(*Half-laughs,* i*ndicating the* **Chorus**.) How you let these neeks just dictate your story for you anyway like, that's weak. I shoulda binned you off early.

Two The Girl with no name has found a family –

Aaron No fuck that! Fuck a fairy tale bruv, a yat like this don't live in no fairy tale.

One She looks her half-sibling in / the eye

Aaron No that ain't what she does!

Play it again!

Play it again and show them what she does!

A short pause. **Letitia** *stares at* **Yasmine***.*

Letitia I feel sorry for you, you know.

Foster ute.

Growing up, no mum or dad.

Growing up with so much anger, at yourself, and at the system,

When maybe it ain't the system.

Maybe it's just you.

And as for Daddy-Delroy.

Who you loved so much.

Guess he didn't love *you* enough to take you out of it.

Guess he didn't love you much at all.

Two And the Girl with no name . . .

One Who has lived her life so many times on a knife edge –

Two So many times on the edge of doing something that would make her lose everything –

One (*not wanting to say it*) Like doing something like . . .

Like doing something like –

Aaron Like dashing the hot fucking pan in her face!

Yasmine *splashes her pan of hot cooking oil into* **Letitia**'s *face.* **Letitia** *screams.*

A transition –

During the transition, the **Girl** *faces her* **Younger Self**.

Then lights up on –

Yasmine, *in a prison cell.* **Chorus** *members are with her.*

One This is the last part of the story.

Two It's the part where the Girl –

It's the part where Yasmine finds what she's been looking for all this time.

One And even though she's sat in Holloway Prison.

Even though she's gone down for GBH, and is looking at three years in these four walls –

Yasmine's story, as stories do – may yet have a glimmer of hope in its tail.

Two And even as she faces what she faces at this point, inside, her mind is saying –

One (*clears throat*)

The **Chorus** *member realises that* **Yasmine** *has moved over to the toilet at the side of the cell, pulled down her trousers and is now sat there, hunched over.*

Two Erm.

Sorry about this.

One Yasmine?

Yasmine Fuck off.

A short pause.

Two   Yasmine we've reached the last part of your story.

One   The best part.

Yasmine   The story's done.

My dad's dead.

I killed a dog.

I splashed that stupid bitch and now I went prison.

And now I got a stomach ache like I don't even know like – like I got appendicitis or suttin like that –

Two   Yasmine

Yasmine   Like you given me suttin. Have you given me suttin?

One   People are hungry, Yasmine.
People want to eat, and then go home.

Yasmine   Tell 'em go then. Go fucking Nando's.

Two   Stories need things

Yasmine   I told you already the story done! (*Winces in pain.*)

One   We're here to help you to get to the end –

Yasmine   There is no end!

One   Can't you see we're trying to help you redeem yourself!

Yasmine   What?!

One   And people have paid a lot of money to see you do it, Yasmine, or whatever your fucking name is, and this constant . . . making of stupid, destructive choices is really – selfish!

Two (*to* **One**)   I think Yasmine maybe needs some time alone –

One (*to* **Yasmine**)   I told you you'd end up like this!

Stories need things!

Yasmine   This ain't a story it's my life!

Yasmine *suddenly shouts in pain, clutching her stomach and hunching over. The* **Chorus** *watch.*

She shouts in pain again.

A short pause.

She gets some toilet roll. Her hand goes down into the toilet bowl, and the **Chorus** *narrate, un-sure, a bit disgusted –*

Two   And the Girl with no name –

And Yasmine reaches down –

One   And pulls out . . .

Yasmine *slowly pulls out the necklace given to her by* **Aaron**, *and holds it in the toilet paper.*

Two   Aaron's mother's necklace.

The . . . the necklace from Nando's.

One   She expels it from herself, and holds it out.

Two   As a metaphor, for . . .

One   As a metaphor, for . . .

A moment.

Two   As a metaphor, / for –

Yasmine (*dazed*)   It better be a metaphor for something mate, I spent five minutes pulling it out my arse.

Stef/Chorus *number* **Three** *has entered.*

Three   As a realisation.

That she is the queen of her own destiny.

Yasmine *slowly stands and moves from the toilet.*

One

One (*gaining confidence again*)   That . . . that whatever the world throws at her, deep down inside, all along –

The **Chorus** *is interrupted by a triumphant scream of defiance coming from the toilet bowl – and* **Delroy** *emerges from out of the toilet.*

Delroy   Princess!

Yasmine   Dad?!

Delroy   My fifth favourite daughter!

Yasmine   What?

Delroy   No I'm joking, babes!

Two   At her lowest low, a voice inside her head –

Delroy (*to* **Chorus**)   Do I look like a fucking voice inside her head?

(*To* **Yasmine**) Babes. Look like you seen a ghost!

Yasmine   Have I?

Delroy (*getting out of the toilet*)   Me? You mad?!

You think a lickle internal bleeding and fatal cardiac arrest and ting gonna hold *me* back?!

You gotta draw for the innovation, babes!

At your lowest low!

Yasmine   I fucked everyting y'nuh.

Delroy (*getting out of the toilet*)   What?

Yasmine   Now even *you're* gone.

And I can't even come to your nine night.

Delroy   My nine night?

Suddenly, **Ralph** *emerges from the toilet bowl, blowing a big load of water out of his mouth as he does so. For a bit, he seems a bit traumatised by the experience.*

Ralph (*traumatised*)   Oh.
Oh.

He pulls himself out of the toilet.

Yasmine (*half-smiling*)   What took you so long?

Ralph   Nah. Nah, nah, that's – Oh. That's some *Shawshank Redemption* in reverse right there.

They don't get the reference.

Shawshank Redemption. Where the brudda getting out the prison and he climb out through the – (*Gives up.*) You don't know your culture. Anyway –

Delroy   Rafey-bwoy.

Ralph   Delroy.

Delroy   Didn't I say you'd be cooking one day with your kids up in your restaurant?

Ralph   Yeah didn't say the kids'd be *yours*.

Delroy   You teaching 'em good?

Ralph   Yeah you owe me for this.

Delroy   Alright.

Ralph (*to* **Yasmine**)   Listen –

Yasmine   What you want? I can't tell you nothing, mate, everyting fucked.

Ralph   You gotta stop thinking on the past, and start think about the future.

Yasmine   What future? Future's in here.

One   The future of when you're no longer in here, and / are

Ralph (*to* **Chorus**)   Yeah can you fall back please yeah, I'm dealing with it. (*Turns to* **Yasmine**, *then back to the* **Chorus**.) What you doing after this by the way, me and you should exchange business numbers and chat / business and pleasure –

Delroy (*to* **Ralph**)   Nah get on with it, fam, come.

Ralph (*to* **Yasmine**)   You smell that? I can smell that. That's the smell of that nine nights, opening night, Hawaiian-celebration-feast getting prepared.

Yasmine   Yeah that's the smell a' the feast I ain't going to

Ralph   But what about the next feast? What about the future feasts?

Yasmine (*not convinced*)   What about them.

A short pause.

Ralph   You done some bad things.

Delroy   True.

Ralph   You had some bad things done to you.

Yasmine   True.

Ralph   But if you keep your head held high in here –

And remember you're my chef-apprentice-in-waiting –

Delroy (*to* **Yasmine**)   You hear that?

Ralph   Then one day soon you're coming back to the table.

A moment.

Yasmine   Swear down?

Ralph (*to* **Yasmine**)   You smell that, yeah? You keep hold a' that smell.

That's the smell that make me remember, mate – Hawaii, the smell a' Kawela Bay!

Yasmine   How can you remember somewhere you ain't been?

Ralph   You gotta remember in reverse.

It's not where you been.

It's where you're going.

A final transition. **Yasmine** *steps forward, and faces her* **Younger Self**, *who now assumes the identity of a girl called* **Mia**.

Yasmine *and* **Mia** *face each other across a big table in a kitchen in a hostel, three years later. Both are carrying shopping bags of food.*

Mia *is quiet and withdrawn.* **Yasmine** *is watchful, and not immediately friendly.*

Yasmine   What's your name?

Mia *says nothing.*

Alright, don't tell me then.

Yasmine *starts to unpack her grocery shopping. A short pause.*

You new though, right?

Mia *nods.*

First time in a hostel?

Mia *nods. A short pause.*

Where you come from before?

Mia   Watch your own business.

Yasmine *looks at her. She smiles. A short pause, then –*

Yasmine   You fucking talking to me?

Mia (*scared*)   What?

A short pause.

Yasmine   No I'm only joking.

You wanna know where I come from before?

I come from prison, bruv.

You wanna know what I done?

A pause. **Mia** *looks at her.*

Mia   Holloway?

Yasmine *nods. A short pause.*

Mia   I was in Holloway too.

Yasmine   Yes!

Mia *looks at her.*

Yasmine   I knew it.

I knew you was in prison like, I got the sense for that.

A short pause.

Alright, you don't have to tell me. Like, what you done, or reh-reh-reh.

So you're the girl with no name.

Mia (*getting a box of fried chicken out from her shopping bag*)   My name is Mia.

Yasmine   Mia?

Are you really gonna eat that shit?

Mia   What?

Yasmine   That greasy chicken and chips and grease, are you really on that?

Mia   Yes.

A short pause.

Yasmine   Gimme some then.

Mia   No.

Yasmine   Oi you want me to bang you over?

Mia *quickly passes the box over to her.* **Yasmine** *smiles. She takes some chicken, then goes back to her own groceries.*

You need to get educated y'nuh. If you gonna be in here with me.

Mia   Educated about what?

Yasmine   Everything mate.

So what, how old are you then, nineteen, twenty?

Mia   Eighteen.

Yasmine   Ain't you got no mum and dad?

Mia *says nothing. A short pause.*

Yasmine   Prison is one thing, yeah?

You got through that.

Congratulations.

Now on the out – that's a next thing to get through now.

Yasmine *begins chopping up some vegetables.*

Gotta learn up the next set a' tings.

To get through it.

Mia   Prison was alright you know.

I didn't mind it.

It was kind of like a family.

Yasmine *watches* **Mia**.

Mia   But then you get out to this.

A short pause. **Yasmine** *brings out some cherry tomatoes.*

Yasmine   Cherry tomatoes. That's a alkaline food, you know what I mean by that?

Mia (*shakes her head*)

Yasmine   That's like your fruit and veg, your broccoli, your apples . . .

Alkaline means not no acidy food, it balances out with the acidy food, like chicken or what-not. You need the balance.

She offers **Mia** *a knife.*

Come. Chop some veg up with your chicken, man, come.

Mia *takes the knife and starts to chop with her.*

Musical underscore begins.

Meanwhile, one of the **Siblings** *enters and puts one of the completed dishes for the feast down on the table.*

Alkaline food work for the brain.

If the brain been through trauma –

They help fix that.

Another **Sibling** *enters with another dish.* **Ralph** *enters, ordering the* **Siblings** *around.*

Ralph   Alright come we go people, opening up in two minutes, two minutes doors are opening!

Yasmine (*to* **Mia**)   Food is essential, right?

Mean you gotta give it respect.

You see when you chopping up this lettuce and shit you gotta chop it in parallel lines.

That make the best texture.

Some of the **Siblings** *begin to offer some of the food to the audience.*

A Pizza Delivery Guy *arrives with a pizza.*

Pizza Guy   Someone call for a pepperoni double?

Stef   Mine!

Muttering and consternation from the other **Siblings**, *as* **Stef** *collects her pizza.*

Ralph   Two minutes!

Yasmin (*to* **Mia**)   Nah; *parallel,* man, what you doing?

Mia *gives her a bad look, as she continues.* **Yasmine** *smiles.*

Yasmine   That's better.

Yeah, you're getting better.

The music rises in volume. **Yasmine** *and* **Mia** *continue preparing their salad, whilst around them, the final preparations to the feast are made.*

The End – The Feast. The audience and cast sit down together to eat.

In conversation with director Maggie Norris

BP *Where was* Knife Edge *first performed?*

MN The play was performed in a Hawaiian restaurant in Dalston. It was not supposed to be a Hawaiian restaurant, we were planning on using a Caribbean restaurant but they pulled out at the last minute. However, it was a stroke of genius that it was Hawaiian and it lent a sort of quirkiness to the whole piece that was really beautiful. So originally it happened at a restaurant called Pond and had a very successful run there. And then it was performed at the Royal Court.

BP *And the audience ate with the cast at the end of each show . . . Can you talk more about the decision to do that?*

MN Well, I realised that the young people that we work with loved our annual Galas, when we invite lots of people, have a lovely meal, and talk about the work and there's a lot of intermingling between guests and members. They are not formal and are great fun. People dress up and party. And they became a favourite with the young people. So I thought, wouldn't it be lovely if we could have that favourite night every night? I'm always looking to get rid of barriers between audience and cast at any opportunity, and that's an ultimate removal of a barrier, if they actually sit down at the end of a show and share food. Also, it's a lovely thing to do because lots of our young people have not been brought up with that tradition and love it, perhaps even more because of that. The candlelight, the food, the meeting of people that perhaps wouldn't ordinarily meet. It was very celebratory. And so the ticket price included a meal, a Hawaiian meal.

BP *It's very distinctive; the chorus in* Knife Edge, *that narrates the action and transforms into different characters . . . and I was just wondering about how you developed and directed that chorus.*

MN Well it's such a brilliant way to comment on what you're seeing – deconstructing the play as you're watching it. It's very funny, seeing the characters question their authors' decisions about their character. We played around with that a lot in rehearsal and decided that we wanted many people playing the Chorus, as opposed to just two. And so the Chorus ended up being about seven or eight people! Also it gave the cast the ability to multi-role which they loved. Really it was a very playful rehearsal period. We didn't get set in – we kind of threw ideas around constantly and there are some really surreal elements in the play that challenged our imaginations. Dad returns from the dead, emerging up through the toilet, for example, and the dog of the aggressive boyfriend is eaten by his owner in a stew served up by his vengeful girlfriend. Very dark but hugely funny!

BP *How else did the company affect the writing of* Knife Edge?

MN The play was very much influenced by the young actress who played the lead, who came to The Big House with anger issues – not surprisingly, given the incredibly hard time that she had emerged from. And so she was able to channel that anger into the creation of the leading character. And that in itself was hugely therapeutic for her.

Although she wasn't playing herself, and we wouldn't want her to play out any of her story, she was able to release a lot of pent up frustration and have control of it.

BP *What was the biggest challenge about directing* Knife Edge?

MN It was . . . What's the right word? (*Laughs.*) There was *turbulence* within the company. And a lot of the young people were dealing with quite complex issues that were impacting the rehearsal room. It felt, the company felt, that we were precariously placed on the edge of a precipice. But that's very exciting artistically, I've found, and something I've learnt from working in this way is that feeling unsafe doesn't mean you can't be creative and produce work of brilliance. Sometimes being on the precipice makes you make choices that you wouldn't necessarily make, which can be breathtaking. Is that a bit obtuse? (*Laughs.*) It's about how a rose blossoms in hostile territory, and how exciting the work then becomes as a result of the challenges that you're facing.

BP *Can you speak about how you have used* Knife Edge *to provoke discussion or challenge your audience when they watch it?*

MN Well, actually, that's a really interesting question and one that I've been thinking quite a lot about recently because *Knife Edge* is a great play to provoke debate. Why is that? One of the things that we see in the play is a young lady who's massively angry at the world. And what we see at The Big House is the criminalisation of care leavers for what is considered to be 'bad behaviour' when actually I know and you know that this behaviour is totally natural and totally understandable when contextualised. But context is not always considered in this country. So people are put in a secure placement or they're sent to a youth offending institute or they're put in prison. I went to court for *Knife Edge* in order for one young lady to continue her part and go to the Royal Court because she was looking at a potential long sentence for effectively being exploited by a gang and forced to be a drug mule. And so I appealed to the judge and put together an application to allow her to continue the work. And the judge listened. So sometimes judges do listen, but I've met a lot of people in prison who shouldn't be there and sending a care leaver aged eighteen, nineteen, twenty to prison for what are often minor offences or offences where they have clearly been exploited by elders who know they are vulnerable, is ridiculous. The whole system needs to be overhauled.

BP *And* Knife Edge? *Why do you think it's so successful in raising those ideas?*

MN Because we see an angry adolescent. And we follow her journey and we see the transformation when she's surrounded by the family that she gets to know and how that healing process impacts her character. So it's a great starting place for discussion as to how we treat traumatised young people generally, and particularly people who've been in care and who are likely to have suffered abuse or neglect.

BP *Anything else you'd like to add?*

MN I really enjoyed watching the Girl watch the Boy eat his dog in a stew every night. An absolute stroke of genius from David. Gruesomely funny! (*Laughs.*)

Maggie Norris interviewed by Bel Parker
9 August 2022

Bullet Tongue (Reloaded)

Andrew Day

Inspired by Sonya Hale

How it was written

Sonya Hale was commissioned to write a play for The Big House in 2018. With the Artistic Director, Maggie Norris, Sonya developed the theme of a teenage girl, mixed up in a trap house, with a need to find her own voice and her own path.

When the various elements of the story weren't settling into a theatrical structure, Maggie asked me to get involved. At first, Sonya and I worked on it together, organising the plot and drawing out the characters. But unfortunately, Sonya fell ill and so we agreed that I would finish the play.

The show was really successful. When it was revived in 2019 (under the title *Bullet Tongue Reloaded*), I took it on and further refined the plot and characters. The theme of an alternative economy outside the legitimate one emerged from conversations with members and was weaved through.

Sonya's influence is very present in many aspects of this script. Bumper's final monologue is a tour de force, a composite edited together from a number of Sonya's drafts. The 'mouse's heartbeat' and the 'bullet tongue' were phrases that she came up with and then discarded, but were rescued – gems of poetic brilliance that encapsulate Sonya's unique vision and her idea of an emerging female voice.

Interview with writer Andrew Day

As you've mentioned in your Author's Note, Bullet Tongue Reloaded *evolved from the show* Bullet Tongue. *What were the new things you wanted to address in the rewrite?*

First, I wanted to bring in the County Lines/Going Country angle properly. Previously, we had a trap house and a bunch of kids who were becoming a gang but it didn't show how county lines worked. We wanted to make the process more clear.

I also wanted to get across the idea that some young people are in a gang almost by default. They're in danger as soon as they step onto the street – the very same streets that are not dangerous for me.

Second, Bumper's final speech became much more defiant. She rejects mainstream society and her supposed place within it: docile, low-paid, law-abiding. Her stance goes against certain assumptions made by liberal media, social services, and many who might want to sympathise with her.

How did you research for this show?

Over ten years of working with Maggie Norris at The Big House. Regarding the particular gang/dealing stuff in this show, many of our young people (though not all) have been near that kind of activity if not actively involved. They know what goes on and can tell you about it. And one or two have 'been there and done that'.

How does this show engage with the narratives around the drug dealing underworld shown in the media?

The media/politicians etc. need simplified, ultra-communicable narratives. So a person is either a victim – an object of pity – or a perpetrator – an object of revulsion. That makes for crap drama and crap politics – and crap policy too. Nearly everyone in this story is hurting someone and being hurt. Even the outright villain, One Ton, tells Bumper he's driven by pain. That is a technique to manipulate her but it's still the truth.

Did your understanding of county lines drug-dealing change in the writing?

I didn't know anything about it to begin with. What surprised me was how all the different accounts I heard of it tallied. And I was fascinated by the way it was a replicable business model, like a franchise.

The other shocking thing was the sheer number of missing teenagers. Nobody is looking for them. Because of what kind of children they are assumed to be, they are seen as having chosen to run away, disappear or get involved in crime. But a teenager can't be a long-term missing person without someone systematically committing some sort of crime against them. It's legally impossible. It's similar to all the taxi-paedophile victims in Rochdale, Rotherham and all those other towns, where the girls were seen as consenting/complicit or guilty by background. Looks like those paedo rings are a kind of replicable model too . . .

What's your process when writing characters different from you?

I hope I only write characters different from me. For me, it's essential as a dramatist to hear and transcribe the voices of other people. If those voices don't pop up in your head, you should choose another medium.

I suppose part of the process is to pay very close attention to the distinctive language people use. Not so much the slang as the vocabulary they use to articulate ideas and arguments important to them. That's how you represent their mental process. The way a character reasons is key.

I suppose it comes down to learning where your own experience and the experience of the character touch. If you can do that across the divides of gender, race, age etc . . . you've struck gold.

Who do you want to see this show, and why?

If the question is about the moral, political or social point that the play makes . . . that's totally secondary for me. Obviously, a play has to be about something. Now, if it's about something urgent and topical, like this, of course that helps. But as a writer you're striving to tap into universal human experience – nothing more and nothing less. So, while it's easy to know whether you've made a 'point' in your play, it's much harder to know whether you've ever got hold of that more elusive thread that runs through everyone ever – but that's the only thing I'm interested in. To answer the question, I hope everyone comes to see it and comes out thinking 'Shit, it's complicated, and I get why'.

You've written a lot for TBH, what for you is the best thing about writing in this context? The most challenging?

There are a lot of 'best' things: large casts mean you can fill the stage with people, the openness of the members to share experiences, the raw emotion. It also means I can write about subjects that I wouldn't otherwise be qualified to deal with – and to a depth that means I'm having to alter my own worldview to assimilate the perspectives that young people with very different experiences are opening up to me.

To be honest, all of those things I just listed are challenging to deal with. But the concern that hangs over it all is whether I can do justice to the people who inspire the shows and are then delivering them to audiences: what if I create something that looks authentic to another person who is just like me, but not to the people who really know? You have an obligation. I know I fell short once (in one of the plays that didn't make it into this anthology).

You can never be sure but it's gratifying when someone comes up to you and says 'Wow, that was my life, right there.' That's happened a couple of times, which gives me hope that we've hit the mark more often than we've missed it.

Bullet Tongue (Reloaded) was first performed at The Big House, London, on 22 May 2019, with the following cast:

Bumper	Shonagh Marie
Hawk	Jesse Lihau
Mad Mick	Dymond X
Yasmin	Auzelina 'Cookie' Pinto
Nadia	Charde Pinnock
One Ton	Andrew Brown
Lil Psyche	Rhys Lanahan
Tirella	Phoebe Rain
Nico	Teslim Oyegbade
Gizzy	Tyler Barnett
Shaznay	Elizabeth Rochester
Skanka	Rapheal Addai
Marlon	Tyrone McLeod
Celine	Amber Bryan
Imani	Ramzia Swaray-Kella
Julian	Taurean Steele

Creative Team

Writer	Andrew Day
Director	Maggie Norris
Dramaturgy	Maggie Norris
Set Designer	Zia Bergin-Holly
Video Designer	Mic Pool
Lighting Designer	Michael Harpur
Sound Designer	Ed Clarke
Graffiti Artist	Tizer
Costume Designer	Paulina Domaszewska
Executive Producer	Peter Huntley for Smart Entertainment
Stage Manager	Bex Snell
Production Manager	Jack Greenyer
Assistant Director	Freddy Wilson
Assistant Director	Steffi Igbinovia
Assistant Set Designer	Alessia Mallardo
Associate Sound Designer	Joe Dines

Characters

Bumper
Hawk
Mad Mick
Yasmin
Nadia
One Ton
Lil Psyche
Tirella
Nico
Gizzy
Shaznay
Skanka
Marlon
Celine
Imani
Julian

Director's Note

In order to stay authentic to the time and place, actors and directors are encouraged to customise the characters' words.

The play is designed for promenade performance with projected images.

Intro: As the audience assemble.

On screen, coming up one at a time. Text messages.

    3g for 25 shout me Thurs 9 May 12.46

    About. Thurs, 9 May 13.25

    Best buds shout me Fri, 10 May 16.14

    Big bags best buds shout me Sat, 11 May 21.05

    Quick service about shout me Sun, 12 May 14.34

    Best bags shout me asap Tues, 14 May 13.19

    New high breed fuckin amazin shout me asap Wed, 1 May 11.09

    Big sexy tasty smelly ones shout me Thurs, 16 May 12.02

    10 10 flavours shout me Fri, 17 May 16.28

    The foods so loud the bitch is screaming at me Fri 17 May 17.31

    10 10 bits shout me. Sat 18 May 14.45

    Best bags around shout me Sat, 18 May 15.28

    3.5 for 25 shout me Sun 19 May 12.46

    Girl Scout cookies of gelato 33 best bags shout me Mon 20 May 12.46

    3.4 for 25 shout me Tues 21 May 12.46

    Lemonade Peng Peng Peng shout me Thurs 23 May 15.55

    Lemonade Peng Peng Peng shout me Thurs 23 May 16.44

    Lemonade Peng Peng Peng shout me Thurs 23 May 17.49

    3 grams of the best for 25 Fri 24 May 16.29

    3 grams of the best for 25 Sat 25 May 12.28

Scene One: Prison, visiting time.

Prison Visit. **Bumper** *waits.* **Hawk** *is brought in. Two orange plastic chairs. Also seen on CCTV.*

Hawk   Are you good? (**Bumper** *shrugs.*) You going school? (*No answer.*) Where you living?

Bumper   I got something.

She takes out a packet of Rolos. Puts it on the table. Opens it, takes out a Rolo.

Hawk What's that?

Bumper What you need. In here.

Hawk I told you I don't need nothing.

Bumper You don't wanna smoke it? Then sell it. Next time I can get you a phone.

Hawk What for? Mum dead, so she ain't suddenly gonna answer the phone. No point you calling. We can't think of things to say to fill the time when you visit.

Bumper 'Cos you won't let me do nothing for you.

Hawk You want both of us in jail?

Bumper I don't get you these days.

Hawk There's one thing you can do for me.

Bumper Name it, fam.

Hawk Don't call me 'fam'.

Bumper Hawk . . .

Hawk Don't call me 'Hawk'?

Bumper What's the matter with you?!

Hawk That's a road name. I ain't on road no more.

Bumper You in here innit? Then you out. You back.

Hawk Nah.

Bumper What?!

Hawk (*smiles, shakes his head*) I can't explain it all to you.

Bumper I ain't a kid no more.

Hawk How old are you, huh?

Bumper It ain't a number make you full grown. It's where man been, what man seen. I ain't no child – don't speak to me like one.

Hawk You listening now? . . . The caravan . . . in Eastbourne.

Bumper What the fuck you talking about?

Hawk The caravan . . . in Eastbourne! (*No response.*) Mum's caravan. Yeah?

Bumper . . . Yeah?

Hawk Go check it out. It's empty. We don't want some waste-man squatting in it. Get down there and take a look, yeah?

Bumper That's long.

Hawk That's family business, so . . .

Bumper Why you care about that bucket of shit?

Hawk (*points*) That door you come through. . . . Same door I came through one year ago. I put all my clothes, phone, chain, ring . . . in a box . . . (*Shows with his hands.*) . . . this big. That caravan's the only thing I got that ain't in that box. If I find some stinky tramp sleeping in it, I'm gonna murder him. So get down there, will you?

Bumper Fuck that.

Hawk I'm counting on you.

Bumper You can't tell me what to do. You don't put no roof over my head. You don't give me protection.

Hawk I'm in here!

Bumper True dat. So you don't get to tell me nothing. Gyal doing fine, if you wanna know.

Hawk I do. I wanna know where you live, how you get money, and how social services ain't crawling over your case.

Bumper People been asking me about you. When you coming out . . .

Hawk Tell them I died.

Bumper Come . . .

Hawk One thing . . . you seen Mad Mick?

Bumper Mad Mick? No. Fucking piece of shit.

Hawk You think they gave that piece of shit Mum's ring – the one that used to be Granny's wedding ring?

Bumper Scumbag probably cut it off her hand before he called the ambulance.

Hawk Huh. Sort the caravan out.

Bumper Fuck the caravan.

Hawk Just do it.

Bumper (*gets up*) Uh-uh.

Hawk Bumper . . . (*Points to Rolos.*) Take that. (*She picks them up.*) Don't forget, Bumper.

Bumper Fucking Eastbourne? No. Fuck off.

A string of texts comes up in real time with audio notifications.

Where are you? 12:08

Where u at Bumper? 12:17

Who r u? 12:17

Psyche. New phone. 12:27

Later 12:17

Your ment to be working. 12:17

Missed call: 12:24

Missed call: 12:25

Missed call: 12:27

Missed call: 12:27

Missed call: 12:27

Missed call: 12:28

Missed call: 12:28

Missed call: 12:28

Missed call: 12:31

Missed call: 12:34

Missed call: 12:36

Missed call: 12:37

Missed call: 12:41

Scene Two: Eastbourne, Caravans

татрTRANSITION: First, voice of **Mad Mick**, *one almighty roar, then yelling a tune . . .*

Second, banging . . . (drumming on the BBQ with the spatula)

Third, music (something old school)

SCENE: Audience arrive at caravan site. There are two little gardens/plots divided by a fence/hedge about a foot high. caravans behind. On one side is **Yasmin**, *in a folding chair, tapping on a laptop (which has stickers on), wearing shades, earphones in. Her bag next to her. On the other side is . . .*

Mad Mick, *in Speedos, a cowboy hat and an apron, behind a BBQ, acting as if he was a DJ behind decks: sausages on the BBQ, sizzling. He is drinking, smoking the biggest, phattest reef. His suitcase lies open behind him.*

Mad Mick Let's av ya beast! Come on, let's 'ave eeeeeet. . . . Come fam! Awwww sweet sausages. . . .

He sings – dementedly – for a bit and dances, gyrating . . . getting sexy with the spatula.

All this is for **Yasmin**'s *benefit, obviously, but he's pretending he's just doing his thing.*

The track comes to an end (N.B. needs to be a track that ends not fades). **Mad Mick** *finishes with a flourish. For the first time, he turns to look at her, as if expecting marks out of ten for his performance. Tucks the spatula into his trunks, like it's the best place to keep it.*

Yasmin *finally looks up. Takes out her earphones, and takes off her glasses.*

Yasmin OK. You've got my attention.

Mad Mick Finally, after four hours, she's ready to introduce herself.

Yasmin I didn't introduce myself. I said you got my attention. Now you got it, what are you gonna do with it?

Mad Mick Woah, OK . . . I'm gonna welcome you to the party.

Yasmin Oh, nice. What party?

Mad Mick *Our* party. We can like start a lickle off over dis side . . . den move it on over your side of da fence, ya get me? As dah night draw in we can get a lickle hot and sexy.

Yasmin You think it's gonna be that easy?

Mad Mick Oh, no. It's gonna be a long ting for ya to win me over, but . . . you're a real woman, I'm a real man. We all know what happen.

Yasmin Man, who are you? What are you?

Mad Mick Whatever you want. Bad man, Good man, Hot man, Sweet man, Heavy man – every man you ever meet.

Mad Mick *holds out his hand ceremoniously.* **Yasmin** *is amused, but not showing it too readily.*

Yasmin I met a lot of men. I don't want to meet them all again.

Mad Mick (*changes tack, pretends to 'drop the act'*) You see right through me, innit? You see into man's soul. See this? (*Holds out his hands, as if cupping a delicate creature and offering it to her.*) Mad Mick's life. In your hands.

Yasmin I'm only here for a couple days.

Mad Mick (*switches again, conversational, neighbourly*) Here for pleasure?

Yasmin Business.

Mad Mick Is it?

Yasmin D'you live here? D'you own the caravan?

Mad Mick What's mine is yours. For one night only.

Yasmin But is it actually *yours*?

Mad Mick *goes to fetch her a drink.*

Mad Mick   This caravan was owned by this one up jewel of a lady but then she pass and now it's like a family ting. I come here in a spirit of remembrance and love and peace.

Bumper *is there listening. They didn't see her approach.*

Bumper   What the fuck? You?!

Mad Mick *and* **Yasmin** *both look at her, shocked.*

Mad Mick   Do I know you? Wait . . . Bumper?

Bumper   Get ya stinky dutty motherfucking ass away from that caravan!

Mad Mick *introduces* **Bumper**.

Mad Mick   This wonderful young lady co-owns the caravan with –

Bumper *marches up and headbutts him. He goes down.*

Yasmin   Oh my God!

Bumper   You teafing cunt! You teafing fucking pagan gypsy cunt! .

She kicks him in the groin. **Mad Mick** *is curled up on the floor, in agony. But he still extends his arm in a gesture introducing* **Bumper**.

Mad Mick   This . . . my . . . Step-daughter

Bumper   I ain't related to you.

Mad Mick   We ain't seen each other for year or so and –

Bumper   Fuck you talking that shit.

Yasmin   Shit. . . . Wait a minute . . .

Bumper *hurls* **Mad Mick**'s *hat away. Boots his suitcase.*

Mad Mick (*to* **Yasmin**, *hands over his bleeding nose*)   Lot of passion in this family.

Bumper   You ain't my family, boy! (**Bumper** *grabs* **Mad Mick**'s *other stuff and starts flinging it off the plot.*)

Mad Mick   Easy gyal,

Bumper   Ya move yaself right in with my Mama, slithery feet all under the table – you ain't teafin this gaff too.

Mad Mick   There was real love between me and your –

Bumper   Don't talk shit. Ya fill ya mouth, ya fill ya pockets, then run.

Mad Mick   Run? When she got sick, I gave up work!

Bumper   You never had no work!

Mad Mick   I rushed to her bedside every time she called!

Bumper   You rush to any woman bedside, any fucking time . . .

Mad Mick   So man got too much love for just one woman . . .

Bumper *picks up a fork from the grill.*

Bumper   Hawk was on road, trying to provide, 'cos you dint bring home nuttin'. That's on you that Hawk got locked up, on you that we lost the flat, and on you that our mother died.

He backs away, still performing for **Yasmin**'s *benefit. Points spatula at* **Bumper**.

Mad Mick   My religion – and my honour – forbid me to give you the whuppin' ya deserve. I will retire . . . (*Picks up his hat*) with . . . my dignity.

He thrusts the spatula into his Speedos. Plonks his hat back on.

Mad Mick (*to* **Yasmin**)   Nice to meet yah.

Mad Mick *exits.* **Yasmin** *is Standing there,* **Bumper** *makes a brief bad-tempered inspection of the caravan and plot.*

Yasmin   God . . . (*Trying to pull herself together.*) I don't know what to say.

Bumper   What makes you think you gotta speak?

Yasmin   I'm sorry about your mum.

Bumper   Did you know her? . . . Well then. People you don't know die every minute, every day.

Yasmin   I just know how that feels. I lost my mum same age as you.

Bumper   Shit!

Yasmin   What?

Bumper *picks up her phone from the floor. Presses buttons, it's not working.*

Bumper   Ah, for fuck's sake. (*Preparing to go.*) If that stupid motherfucker shows his ugly face tell him my brother come for him soon.

Yasmin   Wait!

Bumper   What?!

Yasmin (*shaking her head*)   Forget it. Sorry.

Bumper *exits.* **Yasmin** *still reacting.* **Mad Mick**'s *head appears, peering round the side of the caravan.*

Mad Mick   Is that crazy bitch gone yet?

Yasmin *smiles when she turns to see him.*

Mad Mick   Whoo! She put on a bit of muscle since I last seen her.

Yasmin   How old is she?

Mad Mick (*thinks*)   Sixteen. No, fifteen. maybe . . .

Yasmin   The same age as this missing girl. Victoria Carson? On the news? (**Mad Mick** *looks blank.*) She got a train here, to Eastbourne. Then disappeared.

Mad Mick Ah, yeah.

Yasmin That's why this whole place is crawling with journalists. Did you notice? Trucks, cameras . . . microphones . . . that's why there's no hotels left. That's why I had to hire a caravan.

Mad Mick (*admiringly*) So, you a journalist type gyal?

Yasmin Freelance journalist slash documentary maker. Which is another way of saying skint . . . and hustling . . . and desperate for a story I can sell.

Reaches into her bag, presents him with a card. **Mad Mick** *gets his glasses out and studies the card.*

Mad Mick (*reading the name slowly out loud*) Yas-min . . .

Yasmin What's her name?

Mad Mick Who? Her? Bumper. She hate me like a religion. She got like a jihad on me.

Yasmin Must be a reason.

Mad Mick Her mum was with me, kind of . . .

Yasmin 'Kind of . . .'

Mad Mick Mad Mick a party animal. And I mean *animal*. Bumper and her brother blame me when her mother out partying hard. RIP and that. First her brother tek agains' me, then she do the same. And they both . . . you know . . . making their own way, you might say.

Yasmin Trapping. She's 'on road', right?

Mad Mick Trapping? I wouldn't call it that. She shots a bit of weed and that. Normal teenager. Brother's gone for a lie down in the big house. (**Yasmin** *looks blank.*) Prison. Out soon.

Yasmin Bumper's on the edge of that world, back in London? This whole other London that runs under the official London. It's people like her I need to talk to. On camera.

Mad Mick Why you wanna talk to that bag of fireworks?

Yasmin To give people a dose of reality.

Mad Mick I could take you to her . . .

Yasmin So . . .

Mad Mick Ting is . . . I got these tingling doubts. Ya need to win me round. Work on me. Gain me trust.

Yasmin Uh-huh. How do I do that?

Mad Mick Ya got to mix da business with pleasure. Mix it right up till ya can't tell which is which.

Yasmin *thinks.*

Yasmin   What pleasure you offering?

Mad Mick   You like a barbecue?

Yasmin   Depends.

Mad Mick   On what?

Yasmin   The sauce.

Mad Mick *springs to life. Offers his hand for a high-five.*

Mad Mick   The sauce!! Got to be sweet, and tickle-prickle and smooth and sexy hot.

Yasmin *high-fives him. Slides her hand away slowly. He fetches a beer and hands it to her. She takes a big swig.*

Yasmin   Alright, barbecue man. Tell me your story.

Mad Mick   Whole story?

Yasmin   About the jewel of a lady who passed away, and the girl who's left, and the man who's come up to her caravan.

Scene Three

Nadia *is waiting on the corner. Singing some really grimy tune to herself. Messaging on her phone.*

Bumper *arrives, a little hyped, all ready to pitch . . .*

Nadia *sounds pleased to see her, maybe a bit fake, not 100 per cent paying attention. She is a bit stony, a bit shot away, as if there was always a tune she was nodding along to that we can't hear.*

Nadia   Bumper . . . fam . . .

Bumper   Whassup.

Nadia   What you doin'? No-one told you to be here, so . . .

Bumper   I wanna speak with the man.

Nadia   What man?

Bumper   One Ton.

Nadia   You don't speak to One Ton.

Bumper   It's business.

Nadia *just snorts. Then looks patronising, like she's making a concession.*

Nadia OK, baba. What you want me tell him?

Bumper I got a nice line for him. Seaside town, I scoped it all.

Nadia You better not waste his time.

Bumper Dis proper tings.

She considers . . . Only half-sure . . . Shrugs and reaches for her phone.

Nadia I tell him.

Whoosh. Lighting change. Lights down on last scene. **One Ton** *is up high, looking down. Motionless. Bathed in blasted blinding light – as if he's the source of it.* **Bumper** *climbs up to meet him. He doesn't turn to look at her.*

One Ton You don't talk to me, you talk to my boys.

Bumper I got this town for ya. I know it, from young. I got caravan there, I know where all the junkies sit – the benches, the bridges . . . I scoped it all. It's fresh and ready.

One Ton What town?

Bumper Eastbourne. Seaside.

One Ton So what?

Bumper I just thought . . . You could send your boys down there, check it out.

One Ton Why would I do that?

Bumper I was . . . just trying to bring you something . . .

One Ton Why would I send one of my boys when I could send you? . . . Yeah, you.

Bumper Wait, no, yeah . . .

One Ton (*interrupting*) You wanna stay small? Shotting out in the rain and the cold?

Bumper Nah, I'm cool, we're cool.

One Ton You know how it go. Get off the train. Find some nitty sleeping on the street. Give him a free sample. Tell him to spread the word. Give out your number. Write it on bits of paper 'cos those junkies got fuck all memory for anything. Sell their phone every time they start clucking. Sit and wait. They come.

Bumper What about back up? Who do we call if . . .

One Ton You call each other. It's time, Bumper. (*She doesn't know what he's getting at. He changes tone.*) Your mum passed, innit?

Bumper (*shrugs*) Last year.

One Ton And Hawk inside.

Bumper He's out soon.

One Ton Yeah but he's on his own mission now.

Bumper How d'you know?

One Ton I got eyes everywhere. That's all you need. (*He turns his gaze full on her, as if he's assessing her.*) People say I'm cold, innit? (**Bumper** *shrugs*.) Secret is, man ain't cold. Man is burning pain. Made of pain. No skin, no bone, no brain, just pain. Pain make man sharp like a knife. I see you. You got nuff pain. You could burn down a city with it.

Bumper (*not sure how to take that*) Me and the mandem on point, every second, every day.

One Ton Man want to see good stuff come to you. Rise up through the ranks. Till you right next to One Ton. One day. Yeah?

One Ton *puts his arm round her shoulder, man-to-man.*

Bumper Yeah.

One Ton We gotta make sure nothing hurt you. Never again. You took a blade last year too, innit?

He pulls out his phone. Messages. Pauses to explain.

Always someone out there hating, some stupid greedy cunt gonna fuck you up just for a bag. Ain't no time to call for back up. Time to back yourself up.

Bumper Alright.

One Ton (*takes a bullet out of his pocket. Holds it up to the light, admiringly*) You will never see anything in the world more beautiful than this. Hold this in the chamber and every man will do your will. Here. (*He touches it to his lips and hands it to her.*) Your virgin fucking bullet. When you pull the trigger, and you let it fly, you remember me. You never forget that I believed in you.

On screen. Messages coming in from different senders.

Shout me 14:22

Active 14:22

Happy Hour. 8 for 7. 14:22

                      Skank this is Rez. Is it calm to come over 14:23

No. It's bait. 14:23

                                                                             When? 14:23

I shout you. Asap. 14:23

                                      Fuck u at? Im waiting. 14:23

I been there. You weren't there. 14:23

                                                    I'm here now. 14:23

Wait there 14:24

                                Fuck waiting. When u comin? 14:24

Chill. You best be there this time. 14:24

I'm fucking here. 14:24

Yo, Skank. I'm here N12TR. You around. 14:24

We be there quick. 14:24

Scene Four: The Trap House

TRANSITION: On screen, gang video – drill music. Message going out to opposition gangs . . . staking their claim. Faces covered. Putting up the sign . . . One girl in the mix too . . .

SCENE: The youths we just saw in the video, watching the video, which they've just made: The Mandem: **Little Psyche, Skanka, Gizzy, Nico, Marlon** *plus* **Tirella, Little Psyche***'s girl.* **Tirella** *is glamorous, thinks a lot of herself.* **Shaznay** *is lying full length on the sofa – out of it.*

Bumper *enters, carrying a backpack, watches the end of the video.*

Tirella   Where you been?

Bumper   You gonna put that up? That video. Serious?

Gizzy   Send out a message, innit? Who we be.

Bumper   That's boydem pussy-o. Bare videos on internet all talk, talk. . . . You think crews in these endz gonna get all shook when they see that? They gonna laugh at you.

Nico   Fuck you.

Skanka   Where you been anyway?

Bumper   Family business.

Marlon   Don't take two days to visit your brother in Belmarsh.

Bumper   I had some shit to take care of and – what the fuck is that?

She is pointing at a bike. It's a new but old-fashioned lady's bike with a basket on the front and a child seat on the back.

Little Psyche   Tell her, Nico.

Nico (*affronted*)   It's a bike!

Skanka   She can see it's a bike.

Gizzy   Some nitty brings it to him to pay for point-3.

Nico   That's worth two hundred. Point 3 is only twenty. That's good business.

Little Psyche   You're forgetting the opportunity cost, nah? That'll take you half a day to sell for two hundred. In that time you could be all over the endz, shotting bare food. Make more than two hundred.

Gizzy He don't know what you're talking about.

Nico Neither do you!

Gizzy Who d'you know is gonna buy a bike like that?

Little Psyche Gizzy! Nico! Talking about Time Is Money.

Marlon Yeah. That's why I wanna know why Bumper's gone two days and don't say nuttin' to nobody.

Little Psyche (*to* **Bumper**) You didn't get none of my texts?

Bumper Why you all bitching and moaning 'cos I ain't there? So I could do what? Stand in a video trying to look gangsta. I'm more gangsta than you. My baby cousin more gangsta than you.

Marlon What if we need you?

Bumper For what? You can't bag up without me?

Skanka Gizzy found out we got opps moving onto our turf.

Gizzy I dealt with it, though.

Little Psyche What if we say come now the opps is busting the door in – you gonna text me back 'Later'?!

Bumper I say bring on all the opps right now. I say come right in and meet Ugly Betty.

She pulls out a gun. Holds it up. Next few lines overlap.

Little Psyche What?!

Skanka Wait. . . . Shit!

Gizzy No fucking way.

Marlon Shit, Bumper fam . . .

Nico Where the fuck did you get that, Bumper?

Bumper One Ton.

Skanka When?

Little Psyche We don't deal with One Ton. We deal with One Ton's soldiers.

Bumper One Ton, deal with me, innit?

Marlon What the fuck?

Gizzy Fam, tell the fucking story.

Bumper I scoped this new town, all juicy fresh. Told him about it. He tells me WE go set it up. And Betty gonna play on our team. Settle any beef.

Skanka   He just gave you that?

Bumper   Next time some yout pull a blade on me . . . I pull Ugly Betty. Betty a nasty gyal. Betty got bad temper. Betty got bullet tongue. One word from Betty and you no speak no more never.

Skanka   He just gave you that? Business ting?

Bumper   He don't want us running to him for back-up.

Nico   He moved us up a level, innit?

Bumper   I moved us up.

Little Psyche *moves over, takes the gun, gets a feel of it. Starting to like it.*

Little Psyche   Army issue. Ain't no souped up starting pistol. Kiss of death, right here.

Gizzy (*looking round to everyone*)   Come on. This is cool.

Little Psyche   We go from making business to taking business.

Skanka   It's protection, Psyche. We don't wanna . . .

Little Psyche   Don't wanna what? Step up a level?

Silence.

Marlon   Fucking hell . . .

Tirella   True say, that's a sexy look, Psyche.

Little Psyche   Innit?

Marlon   We gotta get smart if we keep dis ting.

Gizzy   We're smart. I'm smart. Who's not smart?

Nico   Marlon, we could go rob a fucking jewellers! Fucking rob any cunt. Drive over to the opps put the Bucky in their face, they'll shit their self.

Skanka   That's fucking bait, Nico . . . You go waving a gun round on the street, you'll be dead or in the bin, one week maximum. Grow a brain.

Gizzy   Yeah but FUCK. This is fucking . . . (*Can't think how to say it.*) Look at it!

He starts to laugh. Others join in. It gets almost hysterical then dies down.

Little Psyche   It's not loaded.

Bumper *pulls out the one bullet she was given. Shows it.*

Bumper   All I got right now.

Psyche *doesn't take it. Turns the gun at* **Shaznay**.

Little Psyche   Wake up, junkie. Wake up you sloppy bitch.

He nudges her forehead with the gun. She wakes up. As if from a trip to another universe. She's slow to find her bearings, looking around. Focuses on the gun, finally.

Shaznay What?

Tirella Wakey, wake.

Shaznay Obeah. Obeah. What you fi-do?

Tirella What?!

Shaznay Nah, nah. Na innah mi yard.

Little Psyche You think this is your yard? You really think that?

Shaznay Di yard inna mi name.

Little Psyche Ha! I kick your dirty arse out on the street what you gonna do about it?

Marlon Leave her, man.

Little Psyche I ain't gonna DO it. Am I? Eh? I love this girl. (*Hugs her roughly.*) I known this girl since time. We seen things. Innit, girl?

Shaznay Yuh haffi find somewhere to kip dat.

Skanka For real.

Gizzy Like where? You got some bando we don't know about?

Bumper Keep it calm, innit? (*She takes the gun back.*) Betty no chat, chat, chat, chat, like some people. Betty a bark, Betty a bite. (*Quieter, down to a whisper.* **Bumper** *hides the gun carefully under one arm.*) Most of the time, Betty quiet, Betty hide away. Betty a secret gyal.

Shaznay *stares towards where the gun is hidden.*

Shaznay It haf history.

Gizzy What??

Shaznay Di ting there. Can feel a killer finga pon di trigger. Me na wa it innah me yard.

Bumper Shut up, Shaznay.

Shaznay Weh ya ah get dis?

Bumper One Ton.

Shaznay (*turning her head slowly, and ominously to look at* **Bumper**) One Ton?? My God.

Gizzy Shut the fuck up.

Nico Someone give this bitch a hit.

Skanka *takes a wrap out of his pocket and throws it. It bounces off her. Feebly she picks it up and pockets it.*

Tirella (*starting to snigger*) Can't believe you lot got a fucking gun!

They all laugh. **Bumper** *holds the gun high. They all whoop, celebrate as if they've scored a goal. Start to chant: Oo-weh, Oo-weh. . . . Except for* **Skanka**. *He smiles, he nods, he doesn't want to show his doubts, but he doesn't join in.* **Shaznay** *looks haunted.*

Scene Five: Outside the Trap House

Bumper *marches across the space.* **Mad Mick** *is there, stops whistling abruptly.*

Mad Mick Bumper . . .

Bumper *stops and looks at him.*

Bumper I don't know you.

Mad Mick Bumper . . .

Bumper I'll kill you. I wouldn't blink.

Mad Mick One second . . . imagine your Mama standing right here now, what would she want?

Bumper She probably want to go out to some bar then get wasted in your car, leave me to do what the fuck I want, like always.

Mad Mick Gyal . . . all that anger and hate, it's weighing you down . . .

Bumper You wise man, now? Reverend Mad Mick?

Mad Mick I'm here 'cos of your mother, her memory.

Bumper You come to give back everything you stole from her?

Mad Mick I never stole. We shared.

Bumper Shared . . . that's a nice watch. I wanna share it. Come on. Those trainers, let's share them, and all your money. Where's the key to your car, it's time you fucking shared it with me.

Mad Mick Someone I want you to meet.

Bumper What they looking for? Crack or smack? One of each?

Mad Mick I want you to hear this person out.

Bumper Gotta get my phone fixed.

Mad Mick (*grabbing her arm*) Come . . .

Bumper Get your fucking hands off me . . . I'll fucking . . . Oy! . . .

She wriggles free. Pushes his chest.

Mad Mick Alright, I pay you. Come for one little chat. Fifty.

Bumper A hundred. Five minutes.

Mad Mick You know, I'm gonna pay you to do yourself a favour, out of the tender love I still hold for –

Bumper Don't mention my mum. Don't talk about her.

Scene Six: The Trap House

Little Psyche Quit that, fam. (**Gizzy** *turns and pretends to fire at him.* **Psyche** *snatches the gun.*) Fuck's the matter with you? I got bare texts on my phone. We gotta get out there. (*Points at* **Gizzy**.) You're going Ashford.

Gizzy Fuck Ashford, fam. That's long. Why me?

Little Psyche You the man, innit?

Gizzy I ain't fucking staying there.

Little Psyche That little Dwayne, he's there, you just drop the food and back same day.

Gizzy Why me, though?

Nico 'Cos you're fourteen.

Skanka 'Cos you look like a nice little civilian kid.

Little Psyche If the feds bust Marlon, he can't plead intimidation. Look at him! If they bust you, you put on a sad face and say we threatened you. They ain't gonna sling you in the can.

Gizzy Time we got a younger in to do this shit.

Skanka We have. You.

Gizzy Give me the piece. Now. I'll go over this corner I know in Clacton. I'll rob the food, I'll rob the cash. I'll do it now. Come on.

Marlon Chill, Gizzy.

Gizzy Fuck you, pussy-o. You all pussies. That's what it is. You make out I'm some wet boy.

Little Psyche Gizzy . . .

Gizzy I'm the one that ran that girl off our turf yesterday. No blade, no piece. She fucking ran.

Marlon She's a fucking GIRL, fam!

Nico Course she fucking ran.

Skanka Any chicks give us trouble, we send you in, fight for mandem, innit?

Gizzy Fuck off . . . fuck you. . . .

Tirella Tell you what, Gizzy, you got me shook right now!

They're all laughing at **Gizzy**. *Then FIVE DIFFERENT TEXT ALERTS GO OFF on each of their phones at the same time. Confused looks.* **Marlon** *is the first to read.*

Marlon   Shit . . . shit, shit, shit. Did you get this?

The message comes up on the screen/wall for the audience, as the other four check their phones:

'Yo. Now U R tooled up for big league. OT wants 5 by Friday.'

Little Psyche   Where's Bumper?

Marlon   What the fuck has she done?

Tirella   What? What?

Nico   One Ton wants 5 Gs for the piece.

Tirella   Five Gs . . .

Nico   By Friday.

Gizzy   Fucking Bumper . . . making out he just gave us the ting.

Skanka   Five Gs!!

Little Psyche   We do it. We get on it. We get out there. (*To* **Tirella**.) T, you bag up, starting now.

Tirella   All of it?

Little Psyche   Course fucking all of it. We gotta move all of it.

Tirella   What about Shaznay? (*Yelling.*) Shaznay!

Shaznay *wanders out, calm, smoking.*

Little Psyche   Nah. She'll fuck it up. Look at her.

Tirella   About time she paid her way.

Shaznay   Ah yuh know mi ah pay mi way . . . unu walk in an out mi yard any time yuh like. Yuh need mi. Yuh pay yuh way, likkle gyal? Tell mi how?

Tirella   I ain't talking to you, sket.

Shaznay (*sucks teeth*)   Fighting words . . .

Little Psyche   Shut up with that shit.

Shaznay   You all best fix up and pay di man. Mi no want One Ton in mi yard.

Marlon   Or you'll do what? If we didn't give you no food, you'd be out on the street.

Gizzy   Selling your pussy, selling your mouth, selling your arse.

Shaznay   Ickle boy, learn some respect, or mi lick yah.

Gizzy   Can't fucking respect that.

Little Psyche   Hey! If that money ain't in One Ton's hand by Friday, he's gonna be round here and I ain't gonna look the same after he's done with me. So stop standing around chatting shit. We are on road 24/7 till this is done.

Nico   This shit is on Bumper, man.

Little Psyche   This shit is on me, on you, whoever One Ton say it's on, you get me? I ain't gonna fucking argue with him. Now fucking move! Move!!

Scene Seven: Yasmin's flat

TRANSITION: Smooth, sophisticated music. Coffee maker bubbling. **Bumper**, *abusive and mocking stands looking around the place as she talks to* **Mad Mick**.

Bumper   Fuck is this place? It's peng. Man come back and rob it up, I think. Yeah . . .

SCENE: **Yasmin** *enters*

Bumper (*to* **Mad Mick**)   Remember I got shit to do, yeah, just a few minutes, right?

Yasmin   How did he get you to come?

Mad Mick *hands* **Bumper** *the cash. Makes his way over to* **Yasmin**.

Bumper   Who are you?

Yasmin   I met you in Eastbourne.

Bumper   Yeah, who the fuck *are* you?

Mick *puts his arm round* **Yasmin**.

Bumper   Ah. You in love again, Mick? (*To* **Yasmin**.) Least you know how long he'll be around. Till the exact day your money run out.

Yasmin   You don't have to stay. (**Bumper** *takes that in, nods, turns to leave*.) I've got an offer.

Bumper   You? What you got to offer a gyally?

Yasmin   I want to make a film. Documentary thing. Maybe a report for the news, I don't know. About the people that get talked about . . . but don't get to talk. Like you.

Bumper   I talk bare shit. Fuck you know about me, anyway?

Mad Mick   She thinks you're all 'county lines', and 'feral youth', and 'gangs' and I told her you know about that shit, but that shit ain't you.

Yasmin   Mick, can I talk to her? Woman to woman.

Mad Mick   You know da girl can get a little . . . violent. Like, murderous.

Yasmin   I'll take my chance.

Mad Mick *inclines his head, accepts.*

Mad Mick   Man thrown out on the pavement, rejected by his lover. Always *one* friend ready with open arms. The bookie.

Mad Mick *exits cheerfully.*

Yasmin   I get it that me hanging with Mick isn't a great way for you to meet me.

Bumper (*she shrugs, then frowns*)   Offer?

Yasmin   OK. Have you heard of this Victoria Carson girl ? On the news. (**Bumper** *shakes her head.*) She disappeared. And, people think . . .

Bumper   Make me an offer right now, or I walk out that door.

Yasmin   Do an interview with me. Talking like you talk. I've got a producer interested.

Bumper   I still don't hear no offer.

Yasmin   The interview is the offer.

Bumper   This . . . this . . . filming thing you do – you're a professional, right? Right?

Yasmin   Yeah.

Bumper   Me too. So . . . What. Are. You. Offering to pay. Me?

Yasmin   I can't pay you.

Bumper   Shit . . .

Yasmin   People won't believe you told the truth.

Bumper   You pay someone, that's a offer. You asking me for a *favour*.

Yasmin   What? OK, maybe I am.

Bumper   Why this neek waste my time . . .

Bumper *sighs and gets up to go.*

Yasmin   Wait . . . I want you to watch something. What you got to lose, you come this far?

Bumper *shakes her head, but stops to think.*

Bumper   Go on then.

Yasmin   Here . . .

Yasmin *goes to her laptop and finds a news update of the Victoria Carson situation. The audience see this projected on the wall.*

Yasmin   I'll get my camera.

Bumper *checks* **Yasmin** *has gone then starts to search the place, as the news update plays, pockets a couple of things.*

News   The search continues for Victoria Carson. Victoria disappeared on Wednesday after taking a train to Eastbourne.

Bumper   This? I seen this. . Eeediot . . . Fucking Muppet

Then her attention is attracted by the clip. She starts to settle. She laughs, watches, heckles. **Bumper** *talks over the* **News** *not between it.*

News   Extra police have been drafted in to help with the search for the fifteen-year-old, who was described as a bright, bubbly girl who recently had become increasingly withdrawn.

Bumper   Cha. Fuck you fam. I been on road since way back, nine years old. I know how to handle it.

News   Teachers and friends were interviewed today. Both said that concerns had been growing over Victoria as she had been missing a lot of school. Fears are mounting that she may have been exploited by so-called 'County Lines' drug-dealers . . .

Bumper   Check me. Check dis. We drive fast car we look damn good, man want this, they can't handle what comes with it . . .

News   Victoria's parents, Martin and Lisa Carson, issued this plea . . .

We see the parents at a press conference. Long awkward silences in the mother's speech. Photographers cameras click in the silences.

Lisa Carson   Victoria . . . please, please contact us. . . . Wherever you are . . . whatever might have happened, we don't mind . . . You're not in trouble. We just want you back . . . We just want to give you a hug. . .

Bumper *stops the news report on the computer.* **Yasmin** *re-enters, carrying her camera.*

Bumper   Cha. Not man's problem innit? Man is dying out there on the street. Every day. Getting shot and killed and we grow up around this shit, it's what we know, it's what we do. Cha.

Yasmin   You see? *That!* That is what the world needs to hear. Your voice. We need to get a bit of truth into this. What it's really like in this country, right now, for some people. These reports just make people scared of you, stop them seeing you as other people, just like them.

Bumper   We *AIN'T* like them.

Yasmin   This is your chance to tell the world what you got to say.

Bumper   We ain't got nuttin' to say to the fucking world.

Yasmin   Tell them the truth. Spit in their faces. Like you did just then. You wanna do this, I know.

Bumper   Told ya. Ya gotta pay to play.

Yasmin   If we can get a documentary, then . . . *then*, you could make money. There'd be media opportunities. You could blog, get sponsors . . . that sort of shit.

Bumper *fishes out a rolled spliff.*

Bumper   Why you wanna mek a video so fucking much? You mek money from it?

Yasmin   If I sell it, yes, if I don't, no.

Bumper   Can I smoke this here?

Yasmin   Only if you share it . . .

Yasmin *sets up the camera focusing it on* **Bumper**. **Bumper** *lights up. They share it.*

Bumper   OK I'll school you up. You people . . . looking down . . . you see gang dis, gang dat, stabbin', shottin', everything wrong. You news people always telling everyone to get all shocked and shit. You miss one thing out. Always.

Bumper *sits back, like she's not gonna tell.*

Yasmin   What thing?

Bumper   LOVE. Mandem got the love, you know? No other motherfucker gives a shit.

Yasmin   About what?

Bumper   About us.

Yasmin   You know people would say . . . what about . . . I don't know . . . social workers, teachers, outreach all that?

Bumper   That's jobs. You can't pay people to give a shit. How about the government pay someone to be your boyfriend, huh? Some stranger gonna come round and say 'Hi, I'm your new boyfriend, I'm taking over from Dan.' That's a joke. That's not real. I tell you what's real. After my brother went jail, I got beat up outside this chicken shop. When mandem see my cheek all swelled up, I see pain in their face. My pain in their face. They ride out, beat that boy till he blow bubbles of blood out his mouth. That's LOVE. Who loves you enough to do that?

Yasmin   No one.

Bumper   I got more than you, better than you. I don't shake when I walk the street. Our streets belong to us.

Yasmin   Shit. . . . Wait till I tell people about you.

Scene Eight: Imani's flat

SCENE: Dark. Bed in the middle of the room, someone in it. Gasps and grunts as **Skanka** *climbs through an open window. Inside, he uses his phone as a torch, searching the room for a light. When he switches the light on, he has his back to the bed.* **Celine** *leaps out from the duvet, and grabs him from behind in a choke hold, pulls him back onto the bed, sits on his chest and strangles him with both hands. He struggles, but this is serious. She's trying to kill him. Suddenly, she realises, and loosens her hold*

Celine Shit . . . wait . . . I know you.

She climbs off him. He doesn't move, gasps for breath.

Celine Get up. Get off my bed.

She pushes him off with a foot. He slides to the floor.

Celine How did you get in?

Unable to talk, **Skanka** *points at the window.*

Celine That window? You'd think a police officer would be into security. She's out by the way. Next time if we don't answer the door, the fucking window ain't a catflap for dickheads. (*Calming a bit.*) I know who you are. I seen your photo all over your mum's living room. (*Imitating the mum.*) 'Please God, help my son, he's a GOOD boy . . . Please Imani, help your brother, he's a GOOD boy'. Good boy . . . boy, boy, boy. I told her. You've got a daughter too, you know? Sitting right here, and you know what – she actually IS a good person. Only problem is she's a girl. So all she does is get your prescription and your shopping, check your blood sugar and come round on your birthday and listen to your boring stories with no booze to drink and that stupid clock on the wall going tick-tick-tick . . .

Skanka *smiles, recognising the description of an evening with his mum.*

Skanka (*curious*) Imani took you to meet our mum?

Celine What's funny? Am I funny to you?

Skanka Fuck, no!

Celine Why you here? Don't tell me. It'll piss me off.

Silence

Skanka I forgot your name. (*No answer.*) Said I forgot your –

Celine Fuck my name.

Silence again. Then **Imani** *comes in wearing her police uniform, carrying a bag, looking tired.*

Imani Woah! OK. You two met then. Door was locked.

Celine He came through the window.

Imani Fuck's sake, Kelvin. (*To* **Celine**.) You alright?

Imani *gives* **Celine** *a quick kiss.*

Skanka I need to talk to you, Imani.

Imani *looks to* **Celine**.

Celine Alright. But don't ask her for money.

Celine *exits.*

Imani   Does Mum know where you are?

Skanka   Right now?

Imani   At all. Ever. Does she know you're alive? She's doing mad prayers to save your soul.

Skanka   That woman pray if I cross the road. If I got one lace untied she pray I don't break my neck. If I bite a sandwich she pray I don't choke to death on it.

Imani   You boys, you're never gonna know. Never gonna know what it's like to care about anything else but your sweet little self.

Skanka *is crushed. Can't deal with this subject.*

Skanka   Alright. Forget it.

Imani   Wait. (*Pulls a pack of sandwiches out of her bag, offers them. He doesn't take one, she puts them back in.*) You came for something. I might as well know what it is. (**Skanka** *shrugs.*) It's OK. I want you to come, Kelvin, if you need something.

Skanka   Why you always bawl me out when I come?

Imani (*matter of fact*)   'Cos you do such stupid things. What? You want pats on the back for the shit you get up to?

Silence. He looks away. He tries to say it, but can't. She can read him.

Imani   How much?

Skanka (*mutters*)   An amount. (*Like it's not much.*) Two grand.

Imani   Two grand?

Skanka   We gotta pay it.

Imani *wasn't expecting this. It's a whole new level.*

Imani   Who to?

Skanka   One Ton.

Imani   SHIT!! NO!! Listen. You are all babies, I know that. They don't. So now you got a debt with some proper Badman?

Skanka   I shouldna come here.

Imani   How do you think this is gonna end? My colleagues pull in One Ton's boys all the time. One of these days they'll be kicking Mum's door in, looking for you!

Skanka   That's why I don't go back there.

Imani   They'll still go there first. . . .

Skanka   I'll pay it back.

Imani   I ain't got that kind of money.

Skanka Can't you get a loan?

Imani You think I joined the police force so I could get money to pay drug dealers debts?!

Skanka Why *did* you join?

Imani So it would be me... who makes the arrests, who speaks to the families... to use what I know to get you baby shotters and runners off the road and put the heat on those people that put you out there.

Skanka (*sarcastic*) How's that going for yah?

Imani They come to you like they are your family, your parents, your brothers. Then they burn you – easy as they burn a ten-pound pay-as-you-go phone.

Skanka What other life you want for me? Just hide in the house? You know the second I put one foot on the pavement the game is on – like it or not. The opps could be up in my face, with a blade, with a bullet. We is all in the game ... in the game, from young.

Celine *re-enters with two cups of tea.*

Celine So? What's he after?

Imani A way to get out of all the madness.

Celine Just get out the hood. Get on a train. Do what Imani did.

Skanka Ain't so easy.

Celine I'll give you the money for the train ticket myself.

Imani I've seen boys like you standing in the dock. Trying not to show the fear. Judge sentences them and they go down. They don't ever come back up. Not like they were. Every prison sentence is a life sentence.

Skanka We do what we gotta do, innit?

Celine Nah. Human beings always have a choice. Even with a gun to your head, you still got a choice.

Imani (*without much hope but trying to persuade him to stay*) Sleep on the sofa. (*Beat.*) *I'll* sleep on the sofa, you take the bed ...

Celine (*objecting*) Er ...?

Imani – (*across her*) ... remind yourself what a home feels like.

Skanka (*laughs*) Tell Mum I.... No.... Don't tell her nothing. Don't tell her I came.

Imani Call her. You don't have to tell her where you are, what you're doing... Use my phone ... (*He shakes his head. She holds out the sandwich again. He doesn't take it. Just leaves. She calls after him.*) You *know* I don't have that kind of money, right?

Scene Nine: The Trap House

Bumper *and* **Yasmin** *waiting.* **Yasmin**'s *camera is set up on a tripod facing the sofa. She checks her phone, avidly.*

Bumper   You love the news, innit?

Yasmin   As long as this girl's missing, the gangs and the county lines story is hot.

Bumper   What's that got to do with us? We ain't got the gyal.

Yasmin   But you're a gang. And they think a gang has got this girl. So if I get a report from right inside a gang, right now. . . . Boom. Perfect.

Bumper   I ain't gonna talk about that, though. I don't give a fuck about that stupid gyal.

Yasmin *picks up a notepad.*

Yasmin   If she's in with a gang then what? Why would she be in Eastbourne?

Bumper   In some trap house?

Yasmin   Trap house. . . .

Bumper   Ya go up country, get off train, find some nitties on the street. Find one who's got their own crib, ya take it over, keep the food there. That's the trap house. She's probably sitting on a stinky carpet all day waiting for her phone to ring. Junkies come round, pay up, cook up.

Yasmin   She could be working for a gang?

Bumper   Maybe. Or maybe she's a junkie, lying face down in her own sick on the carpet. Maybe she got some boyfriend. Maybe . . . Whatever . . . There's bare gyals gone missing from every endz. What's special about this one?

Yasmin   This producer I know, he's into the story. He wants this report. He's a total prick but he's important. (*Looking around.*) Where is everyone?

Yasmin *takes out a bunch of animal masks.*

So we can have the guys all sit on this sofa. These are lame . . . are these lame? (*Looking at the masks.*) To keep them anonymous.

Bumper   Whatever. Do me. Real talk, Right now.

Yasmin   OK . . . while we wait.

Bumper   I wanna say all the shit that never gets said, you know?

Yasmin   You wanna choose a mask?

Bumper *takes a half pig mask.*

Bumper   Fuck You Tube. Fuck Instagram. We gonna cross over now. Any little pussy-o boydem, mek a lickle video, all stand round, tryna look gangsta. Fuck that shit. This straight on Sky News, BBC – big, big proper telly . . . That Donald Trump on his plane gonna go – 'who's dis gyal'?

Bumper *puts the mask on. Hood up.*

Bumper   Weird.

Yasmin   OK . . . (*Starts recording.*) So . . . when did you first start hanging round here? What drew you in?

Bumper   Right, so . . . OK, Since long I been beefin' with my mum's man . . . dis wasteman . . .

Yasmin   So bad home life. Cool.

Bumper   My mum's man – man's a fucking cunt.

Yasmin   Woah, that's heavy.

Bumper   Ya want this real, or what?

Yasmin   You're right. Real is good. Heavy is good. Fucking cunt is good.

Bumper   OK, so . . . This fucking cunt called – ah, never mind his name, he's my mum's boyfriend.

Yasmin   Just one . . . problem. With the mask on . . . we can't see if you're a boy or a girl. Maybe hood down?

Bumper   This is how I roll.

Yasmin (*has an idea*)   We'll put a name at the bottom of the screen. A made-up one. . . Lisa or something.

Bumper (*lifting the mask up*)   Fucking *what*?

Yasmin   Doesn't have to be that but something so the audience knows they're looking at a girl.

Bumper   Why they need to know that?

Yasmin   Because this is about Victoria. Well, it's not about her. It's about where she is, or might be.

Bumper   It's about *me*.

Yasmin   Precisely.

Marlon *enters. Tired and stressed. Sees* **Bumper** *and* **Yasmin** *and the camera.*

Marlon   What the fuck?

Bumper   Fam, listen. This is cool. This my gyal Yasmin, she gonna get us –

Marlon (*interrupting on 'cool'*)   We been texting you all day – again!

Bumper   My phone's fucked.

Marlon   You went to fix your phone. (*To* **Yasmin**.) Who da fuck are you? (*To* **Bumper**.) Are you mad, fam?

Nico, **Skanka**, **Tirella** *and* **Shaznay** *enter. Chaotic reaction. They talk over each other to begin with.*

Gizzy   Hey, what the fuck is going on here?

Tirella   Oh look who it is.

Shaznay   This gyallie head gone . . .

Nico   Bumper, you fucked up bad, fam.

Bumper   What you talking about?

Skanka   You still don't know?!

Tirella   Girl, you bring it on top bad. And you don't even know? That piece you walked in here with? You're all like, look at me, I'm in with One Ton, look what he gave me. . . . He wants 5 Gs for it. Psyche's gonna fucking kill you.

Bumper   What? Wait my phone's all fucked, when you hear about –

Skanka (*interrupting*)   How could you not know? You took the piece off One Ton, you didn't think to tell us he wants five Gs for it?

Bumper   He didn't say nuttin' about that.

Nico   Fam, you fucked up big.

Bumper   The Big Man tell me to go Eastbourne, give me the tool to take care of whatever. What am I gonna say no to him?

Skanka   You didn't ask him about payment?

Bumper   I don't ASK One Ton, I fucking do what he say.

Marlon   You go seek him out, don't speak to his soldiers, go straight to the plug, and now you bring it on top for all of us. Fuck you, stupid bitch.

Skanka   We been out there trying to fix this shit, and what was you doing? What? Who da fuck is dis? (*Points to* **Yasmin**.)

Bumper   Look, how was I meant to know?

Nico   What the fuck is she doing here with this shit?

Yasmin   Making a film.

Simultaneous lines/reactions from Mandem. Less anger, more disbelief, different vibe:

Nico   Huh?!

Skanka   What?

Marlon   You serious. Bumper??

Tirella (*contempt*)   A film?

Yasmin I wanted to meet you. Bad time, right?

Shaznay (*looking down the lens of the camera*) Nah, it's good. Nico, how much you a get for dis?

The others look at the camera.

Bumper Wait, ain't her fucking fault, is it?

Shaznay What she even come yah for?

Yasmin (*nervously*) You won't get more than a couple hundred –

Shaznay Couple hundred . . . sweet.

Bumper *tries to stop them taking it. A struggle.* **Little Psyche** *enters with* **Gizzy**. *They're not stressed at all, in fact they're glowing.* **Gizzy**'s *pockets are stuffed.*

Little Psyche Woooah.

Gizzy What the fuck?

Little Psyche What a happen while we gone?

Tirella Bumper been making a film, 'cos she thinks our video's bait, and she gonna do one better, while we all out grafting to pay up her debt with OneTon.

Nico So we tek this nice-nice camera, mek a bit of gwop.

Bumper Lef the gyal, innit?

Yasmin You can get more money if you don't sell my camera.

This gets their attention.

Shaznay Say, what?

Yasmin I . . . I . . . I could get you . . . I mean you want cash fast, right? I could pay you. But you gotta give me what I need.

Little Psyche And what's that?

Yasmin A fucking good interview. Really lift the lid. No-one's got a good interview with – with a . . . well, you're a gang right. All this talk about gangs – you're a real gang.

The boys snigger.

Shaznay Interview fi wha'? You want these boys snitch on themsel'?

Yasmin No, anonymous.

Nico No face, no case . . .

Little Psyche What we got that's worth that kind of money to you?

Yasmin The truth. About gang life. About what happens to young people.

Little Psyche Truth? You in the market for truth, is it? Mandem got bare truth to tell.

Bumper I say we do it. That's fast gwop. We fucking smash this.

Skanka   I dunno.

Little Psyche   Bumper . . . you know where this chick live, innit? She know what happen if she bring it on top for us?

Bumper   She wants the story. She ain't a fed or nuttin.

Skanka   You know that?

Gizzy   Come on, she ain't no fucking fed, fam. She's shook. Look at her.

Little Psyche *starts to chuckle.*

Little Psyche   How mad is this? Alright, we do it.

Yasmin   You do it? Yeah? . . . Yeah! OK. Oh my God, right, take one of these.

She shows them the masks. Some take them, some have their own balaclavas, some just put up hoods and sink behind collars. Maybe one has a bandana. They've hidden their faces before. **Shaznay** *doesn't want to be involved.*

Shaznay   Ya nah point di ting at me.

The Mandem arrange themselves on the sofa, some sitting on the back of it. **Bumper** *goes to join.*

Yasmin   Hmm – Bumper. If you stay out of shot. actually . . . (*To* **Tirella**.) Can you like perch next to one of them.

Little Psyche   Fuck you, she my gyal, innit?

Tirella (*sitting with* **Little Psyche**)   I go with Psyche.

Yasmin   Yeah, yeah, that works. OK, I'll level with you. To get this broadcast, I need you guys to look like the real thing. You know, gritty, grimy, whatever. The people in their nice safe homes have gotta think 'Shit these kids are scary'. That's what my man the producer is looking for. Cool. Action . . . (*Switches on the camera.*) Great. So, who are you, and what're you about?

Little Psyche   We is like . . . a gang.

They all snigger.

Yasmin   We hear a lot about gangs. What is a gang?

Marlon   Family.

Skanka   Mandem close, mandem touch blood.

Yasmin   And you sell drugs.

Little Psyche   Cha.

Gizzy   We serve up country, an' all.

Nico   No man is badder than we. Believe!

Yasmin   Can you explain 'up country'?

Ltttle Psyche   Means our kingdom is fair range, fam.

Bumper   Innit!

Yasmin *puts her finger to her lips to* **Bumper**.

Yasmin   Can you tell people what going up country is?

Marlon   You take the business out of town. Go countryside, seaside. Find new markets. The local nitties, yeah? They call us up in London, and we call our kid in their town.

Yasmin   Kid?

Little Psyche   We don't need no big man in the trap house. Just some kid sit there give the food, tek the money, come back up, give the money, tek the food. Easy. Proper business.

Skanka   Innit?

Little Psyche   Supply chain. Wholesale to retail. Personal service. Protect the margin 'cos no middle mans.

Yasmin   OK. What would you say to people who accuse you of preying on young people in those towns? Turning them into drug-users.

Gizzy   Fuck them.

Marlon   Ain't converting no-one. We jut tap up da junkies what's already there. Find dem in the streets. They better off getting the real ting from us 'cos we get it straight from the plug.

Little Psyche   No middle man, like I say.

Marlon   And we don't cut the food with no shit. No poison in dem veins, jus' pure produc'.

Skanka   We serve a need for dem.

Marlon   It's win-win.

Gizzy   Whatever you gonna buy – brown, white, pills, skunk – you best get it from a pro. Not some forty-year-old guy with no teeth and dirty fingernails and scabs on him. Can't trust no junkie.

Nico   . . . is what I'm saying – we the pros, you get me?

Skanka   That's why we make bare Ps.

Yasmin   Right, right, so you're making good money?

Little Psyche   Let me tell yuh. My cousin works Burger King, alright? He's a Manager. And he wears a clip-on tie, and a cardboard hat. And he works a fourteen-hour shift and he eat his lunch in a cupboard. And the girls on the tills disrespect him. And what he earns in a week, I make in a day, if I feel like it. If I don't, I go spend some of it. Cha!

The others cheer or laugh, high-five.

Marlon You da man, Psyche.

Little Psyche See people think we on road 'cos we too thick to get a job. Nuh. People get jobs 'cos they too thick to survive on road.

Gizzy Maybe they ain't thick. Maybe they don't wanna take the risk.

Skanka Right!

Nico Any day of the week, we could get shot, shanked, kidnapped, shut up in the bin . . . I know bare youts who ain't on road no more. It's sad, I tell yuh.

Little Psyche That's why you get the high margin, yeah? Any business, it's the high risk that make the profit. You selling a tin of beans, there ain't no risk in that, yuh gonna sell it sooner or later and everybody know what price. So you gotta sell a million cans to make proper dough. Every time the feds crack down on us, they drive up the risk, so they drive up the margin, so the smart money want in.

Yasmin What d'you spend it on?

Nico Mandem sick in dem garms.

Gizzy We look good, smell good, eat good, drink good.

Nico And we fuck good too, innit?

More laughter.

Marlon Chicks like us 'cos we look cris and fly.

Gizzy (*fishing cash out of his pocket and waving it*) I'm a walking, talking, good time for any girl.

Yasmin What about girls like Victoria? Victoria Carson? The missing girl. People would say she's a victim of your greed and selfishness.

Tension rises. They roll heads, suck teeth.

Nico So what?

Gizzy People can say what they want.

Little Psyche Man don't come from where we come from, innit? We all born with you people treading on our face. Then some stupid bitch come lie down in the gutter with us, and that's on the news – why? 'Cos she one of you. We down here all the time, cuz, ain't nobody bothered about that.

Yasmin I hear you. I have to ask this next question. Do you use violence to do business?

There's a moment of silence before the first answer. . . .

Marlon We told you, this is family, right? What would you do if someone threaten your family?

Yasmin I dunno.

Marlon (*harder*) What would you DO?

Yasmin Call the police, I guess.

Marlon Right. 'Cos the police got the cuffs, and the tasers, and the cars, and the law behind them. We ain't gonna do that. If I go out there, I gotta know that I can pick up my phone and say to my brethren – 'Come rise' –

Nico Man would buss up any fucking ops for you cunts.

Gizzy One word, we ride out and deal with it.

Yasmin It?

Skanka Any beef. We dere for each other.

Marlon Ain't nobody else – nobody! Nobody care what happen to us. Like dat from day one.

Yasmin What about family? I mean not everyone's got much family, but some of you do, right?

Skanka Yeah, there's people. But listen. They all powerless. They don't wanna see us busting up other youts, and getting locked up, but all they do is beg and cry – no solution.

Gizzy Like Psyche says. You people think when I see someone go work on the bus, go mosque on Friday, buy their clothes down the market – that's a role model for me? Nah, that's telling me what NOT to fucking do!

Skanka Truth is. . . . Man's trapped. Man's lost and dis is all man knows.

Little Psyche Yeah . . . truth is money, girls, cars . . . dat come with danger and destruction . . . like chicken come with hot sauce.

Nico Innit, fam!

Gizzy Innit!

They laugh so much they fall over, start pushing each other – the interview is over.

Yasmin OK, cool. I think we really got something there. Jeez. Thanks. I'm gonna call Seb and tell him we got something pretty explosive.

Little Psyche So now the gwop.

Yasmin Sure. Give me, I dunno, half an hour.

They gradually start to surround **Yasmin**. **Psyche** *switches – menacing.*

Little Psyche Where's our fucking money?

Bumper Psyche, fam, chill. All of yous.

Yasmin Look I just don't carry a thousand pounds in cash around on me, yeah?

Bumper Innit? Gyal is cool. We go walk, get the gwop.

Little Psyche Two Gs.

Yasmin What?

Little Psyche Two thousand. I reckon we gave you double, so we get double.

Bumper Come on, Psyche.

Yasmin Listen, I can max my credit card at one thousand. That's it –

Little Psyche Better idea. She pay all five.

Yasmin Listen, please. . . .

Little Psyche (*grinning*) She can work to pay off the debt. . . .

Bumper Shut the fuck up.

Shaznay Lef di gyal, Psyche.

Little Psyche What?! (*Glares at her, then transitions from threatening to charming.*) You think I'm serious? You think I'm going back on my word? Nah, we mek a deal, innit? I'm jokes. (*Pats* **Yasmin** *on the shoulder.*) I'm jokes. They know me.

Bumper (*to* **Yasmin**) Come.

Nico We all go, innit?

Skanka That's bait.

Marlon Gyal's shook. Look! (*To* **Yasmin**.) Come. Don't worry.

Bumper (*to* **Yasmin**) He's cool.

Marlon *leaves with* **Yasmin**

Shaznay Yuh fi de out pon di road, Bumper.

Bumper I just brought in a G for us.

Gizzy SHE did, more like.

Little Psyche Don't sweat it, Bumper. (*Looks at the camera, gestures to* **Nico**.) Switch it on. Shoot me with it.

Nico *points the live camera. Films* **Psyche**. *We see the image projected on the wall.*

Little Psyche Wanna know why you all good, Bumper? 'Cos Gizzy and me took a ride over Clacton. Walked up to the trap. Knock on the door. (*Whips out the gun, points it into the camera.*) Don't fuckin' move, boy, jus walk back, walk back, where's the cash? Wallah di money pussy-o. We clean out the place. We stepped up. Betty pay for herself. 'Cos Betty a good gyal. Betty a-love Little Psyche. (*Brings the gun to his lips, murmurs as if in its ear.*) Ain't that right, Betty. (*Turns to* **Tirella**.) Feel that babe.

Tirella *steps forward and touches the gun.*

Little Psyche   That sexy?

Tirella   Uh-huh.

Nico *leaves the camera, but it's still pointed and running.*

Shaznay   Yuh done what?

Nico   What d'yuh get?

Gizzy (*patting his stuffed pockets*)   Six, seven, maybe.

Skanka   Wait, so . . . where in Clacton? You know dat crew? Dey know us?

Gizzy   They don't know who fucking hit 'em, fam.

Nico   You fucking sure about that?

Bumper   So we good? We got 5 now? I best take it over to One Ton, innit?

Little Psyche   I make it, I take it.

As **Psyche** *puts the gun back in his trousers,* **Tirella** *steps in front of the camera. Talks into it.*

Tirella   Don't look at my man. You! I said don't look at my man. You look my man in the eye, he'll bury your arse deep in soil, fam. You look down, boy, you look at your shoes when you see us come.

She tilts she camera down. Laughs.

One Ton *enters. The room goes silent.* **Nadia** *is in tow.*

Nadia   Look. This is like a little nursery . . . little playground . . .

One Ton   My boys tol' me it's all good down here . . . But it's not good, not no more. 'Cos I'm hurting for five grand. I give this one (*indicates* **Bumper**) a piece, trying' to help the mandem up. Nobody come with my money.

Bumper   You never said . . .

One Ton   My man text you all, innit? So why ain't you out there?

Gizzy   We got it.

Little Psyche   We got five. We on it, we done it. (*Nods to* **Gizzy** *to show* **One Ton**.)

Gizzy *unloads his pockets.*

Gizzy   I think that's five.

Nadia   Think? Don't fucking think, boy!

Gizzy   It's five, it's five.

One Ton   Alright . . . Huh. (*To* **Nadia**.) Look, dey all looking at me like I'm gonna go now. Like I'm jus' gonna pick up the Ps and walk out the door.

Nadia (*laughing*)   Dese pickneys don't know One Ton then. (*To the gang.*) One Ton, the king, innit? So you . . . roll out the red carpet for man, innit?

One Ton *strolls to the sofa.*

Little Psyche   Cool . . .

One Ton (*sharply*)   I'm sitting – you got a problem with dat?

Little Psyche   No.

One Ton *turns his attention to* **Tirella** *who is sitting on the sofa.*

Nadia (*to* **Tyrella**)   Hey gal. We know each other from time, innit? (**Tirella** *nods, shrugs.*) Wait, you're Shannon. . . . No, Kahdija? . . . Shireen? . . . Samantha.

One Ton   Dat gyallie name, Tirella. Innit, Tirella? Yeah . . . And you . . . (*Turns his attention to* **Shaznay**.) You is a different ickle kitten. Come, sit.

Shaznay *stares wide-eyed, still as a statue.*

Nadia   De man say come sit. . . .

Almost robotic, **Shaznay** *gets up, walks over, sits and kneels at* **One Ton**'*s feet.* **Tirella** *is moving away very slowly and secretly from the sofa.*

One Ton (*to* **Tirella** *without looking*)   Gyal! . . . Hey.

She turns back to look at him. He produces a pre-rolled joint for **Tirella***. She takes it but makes no effort to light it.*

One Ton   Where's the piece?

Little Psyche *pulls it out, hands it over.* **One Ton** *cuts a line along the barrel. Holds it for* **Shaznay** *to snort. With only a slight hesitation, she does. Then he does the same for* **Tirella***. He turns the gun in his hand.*

One Ton   I hope you all are gonna look this sad at my funeral. You boys need a ickle lesson here. You!

He beckons **Nico** *over.* **Nico** *comes round in front of him, dutifully.* **One Ton** *shows* **Nico** *his watch. Really upbeat, snappy.*

One Ton   What's this?

Nico (*unsure*)   Your watch . . .

One Ton   Fucking bumbaclot. . . . Get down, look proper.

Nico *gets down on his knees. Peers at the watch.*

One Ton   What does it say? . . .

Nico   Rolex.

One Ton   Kiss the Rolex.

Nico *hesitates. Then does what he's told.*

One Ton   Now go out and kiss the car. Go on, then come back.

Nico *stands. There is a tiny pause where we think he might rebel, but then he walks out.* **One Ton** *is getting into his stride.*

One Ton (*laughing*)   You all should be gassed. You're fucking proper in with One Ton. You just paid your debt and we all good. We peachy. Time now to lock dis shit down. Mekk-a ting a bit more solid. You get me? (*To* **Shaznay**.) Now, Mandem come find you innit? Find this house. Since time, they look after you goo-o-o-o-od. You get the pengest food . . . Yeah?!

Shaznay   Yeah.

One Ton   Where dat food all come from? My boys, innit. My boys, they get it from me. So who's feeding you? Who?

Shaznay   You.

One Ton   And ya take as ya like. And now the time has come. Man take as Man like. Now . . . (*He turns to look at* **Tirella**.) Sometime I like it when the gyallie heart beat faster for One Ton (*Lays the gun down.*) Yuh ickle heart beat faster for One Ton, lemme feel. (*Feels her heart.*) Mmmmm. (*Takes her hand and lifts her to her feet.*)

Tirella   Um . . . . Little Psyche is my man.

One Ton   That's cool. 'Cos . . . Little Psyche – he's my *boy*. My boys' boy. Da boy (*points to* **Little Psyche**, *then down*) down here. . . . Da man (*points to himself, then up*) up here. (*To* **Tirella**.) Come. Baby girl. Come sugar wings. Come fly with man a lickle.

Nadia (*to* **Shaznay**)   I say one ting, you got a clean crib for a junkie – mm-hm.

Nadia *beckons* **Tirella** *into the bedroom.* **Nico** *re-enters as they are leaving.*

One Ton   Ya kiss the car? (**Nico** *nods.* **One Ton** *chuckles.*) Ras . . .

One Ton *follows* **Tirella** *into the bedroom.* **Little Psyche** *looks distraught. The gang members are shocked by what's just happened.* **Nadia** *stands in the doorway, takes her phone out, takes a photo, takes more photos and then hovers in the doorway distracted by her phone. Then takes the camera into the bedroom.*

Bumper *sits on the sofa, picks up* **Tyrella**'*s joint from the ashtray. She looks at it, thoughtful.*

Shaznay (*hard, to* **Bumper**)   You just gonna look at that, or you gonna smoke it?

Bumper   Shut up, I'm thinking.

Shaznay   Thinking what? How you bring it on top for Mandem, then go AWOL?

Bumper *grabs* **Shaznay**'*s hair and forces her head down onto the sofa next to her.*

Bumper   I'll put this in your eye, you fucking bitch.

Shaznay *gets a foot to* **Bumper** *and shoves her right across the room. The others turn and come over.*

Skanka Bumper, fam.

Gizzy Chill . . .

Marlon Get that fucking gun out there.

Shaznay Me tell yuh, dat ting a bring trouble.

Skanka Fuck me, Bumper, why did you have to go to him? Everything was down. All calm. All good.

Bumper When I went to him, I didn't ask him for nuttin'.

Nico You went to him. You cut his men out, went direct. That's a risk.

Gizzy I say it's all good.

Bumper It's like One Ton say. We change up now.

Nico That's it.

Little Psyche You out there kissing a car? That's changing up? Bullshit.

Gizzy Ain't no time to pussy out. We take the shit. 'Cos that's how *we* get the car, get off the fucking wet road, and the junkies and sitting on trains with condoms up our arses. And sleeping in stinky crack houses and all that filthy shit. Get some youngers to do that, we be the elders now.

Skanka Yeah but we can still roll the way we roll – not like him.

Gizzy (*disagreeing*) One rule. Eat or get ate. The moment you stop eating, that's the moment you get a bite taken out of you. 'Cos there's always some boy out there who's meaner and madder and he ain't gonna let you roll nice and easy, the way you wanna roll.

Nico That's the truth.

Gizzy Top man, that's the last man standing. Yeah, we had a nice sweet little ting going. That's over, fam. Gotta go big league, now. Like it or not. That's blood, sweat and tears. Ain't baby stuff.

One Ton *emerges from the bedroom, looking pretty calm. They turn, surprised to see him back so soon. He wanders over and takes the joint off* **Skanka**. *He looks around.*

One Ton I like this girl. (*He looks around. Chooses . . .* **Nico**.) You like this girl? (*He nods in the direction of the bedroom*).

Nico Do I like her? . . .

One Ton *waits for his answer.* **Tirella** *emerges from the next room.*

One Ton Course you fucking like her. Look at her. Now go do it.

Nico *just stands there, open-mouthed.* **Tirella** *makes an effort . . .*

Tirella One Ton . . . Come . . .

One Ton What belongs to man belongs to the mandem innit? This how we mek the ting strong.

Nico Yeah but . . .

One Ton (*to* **Nico**) You got a dick, or what? Go do it. (*He points at* **Skanka**, **Gizzy**.) Then you, then you. (*Points to* **Little Psyche**.) You . . . You don't touch my gyal. (*To* **Nico**.) Go.

Nico *walks over to* **Tirella**. *Nods his head for her to go back into the room.*

Tirella (*desperate*) Look, One Ton . . . what's the matter? Did I do something wrong? You and me again, yeah? You and me all day. Anyhow. Yeah?

Nico *walks through to the bedroom.*

Tirella (*pointing to* **Nadia**) Can she stop taking pictures?

One Ton Yeah. . . . Ah, the pictures, we put them on Insta, innit? . . . (*Pretending to change his mind.*) Ah, no we don't. We don't 'cos yuh gonna work for man now innit? No more eating the food for free.

One Ton *walks back to* **Tirella**. *Embraces her tenderly. Wipes away a tear.*

'Cos you family, now. I tell you what. Nadia, delete dem pictures. Do it now. This gyal good, she gonna run up and down country for us, I know dat.

Tirella I'll do that, I'll do that. . . . But not this –

One Ton Shhhh. Man come seckle you, make sure the mandem behave . . .

He lifts her up, almost romantically, and carries her into the bedroom. **Little Psyche** *exits unable to cope.*

Nadia (*laughing*) Ras. Gyal is gonna suffer in dere. Gyal is gonna get ruined. She gonna serve it up for all of yous. Dat what she want. Dat what every gyal want. Ain't dat right, Bumper? (*No answer.*) Bumper fam? Gyal is talking to you . . .

Bumper *stands, takes the gun out from under the sofa cushion, exits.*

Skanka (*to* **Bumper**) Easy

Shaznay Gyal, where you a go with dat?

Skanka Bumper!

Scene Ten: Outside The Trap House

Little Psyche *is standing outside. Still and silent.* **Bumper** *stops when she sees him. No words at first. Then,* **Psyche** *decides to go . . .*

Psyche I see you later.

Bumper Psyche . . . (**Psyche** *stops.*) You gotta stay. (*No response from* **Psyche**.) Man is testing you. Don't fail the test. Go back in there, get fucking high. Bust your noggin off, fam. Till you don't feel nothing.

Little Psyche *drags himself back in. Sees* **Skanka** *in the doorway. They look at each other. Nothing to say.* **Little Psyche** *pushes past* . . .

Skanka You alright?

Bumper Course.

Skanka Dat is fucked up, fam

Bumper She didn't have to fucking do it. She coulda run out, put up a fight. Cha gyal a pussy-o.

Skanka Put the gun back in there.

Bumper The whole thing changed up, Skanka.

Skanka No. Psyche and Gizzy raiding that crib, alright, we needed One Ton off our back. But no more of that shit.

Bumper Ain't a fucking game fam, you don't just tap out when it gets brutal.

Skanka That ain't what we is, Bumper. You and me.

Bumper You don't know me then, fam. Since young I always been the same. I'm a fucking winner. 'Cos I see the way the game go.

Skanka Dis what you really want, fam? Touch a gun, stroke a gun, wave a gun around – that's all cool. You really wanna put a bullet in some yout?

She takes the gun out. Feels its weight. Imagines doing it.

Bumper Some opps, fucking yeah! I watch him die.

Skanka The fucking opps is *us*. Yeah? Another mandem just like us. Gyal ain't dumb, gyal know that. And if we gotta gun, they get a gun. A bullet with your name on it.

Bumper That's destiny, innit?

Skanka We fucked this up.

Bumper If you don't wanna change up . . .

Skanka It ain't up, it's down, down. . . . It's outa fucking control.

Bumper (*total contempt*) Cha.

Skanka (*a bit feeble*) Bumper?

Bumper What?

Skanka Man could tell them I got kidnapped.

Bumper What?

Skanka I'll fucking like disappear and shit.

Bumper I ain't hearing dis.

Skanka You tell Mandem someone pulled a gun, threw me in a Beemer.

Bumper Nah, nah, you shook now, alright? I forget this.

Skanka Listen. I could get you out.

Bumper What the fuck?

Skanka Out. . . . For real. My sister can do it.

Bumper I don't want out. What fucking sister? The Manchester one?

Skanka *hesitates.*

Skanka She joined the feds down here.

Bumper Fuck you, Skanka.

Skanka She ain't like . . .

Bumper Fuck you tell me that for?

Bumper *starts to leave. Seriously freaked.*

Skanka I love you like a sister. But mandem ain't never gonna care about you.

Bumper What you talking about?

Skanka You're a fucking girl. Just a girl. Straight up, nuff said. Man can't fucking respect you.

Bumper Fuck you, fuck you, fuck you . . .

Bumper *exits.* **Skanka** *is left alone, paces a bit, rubs his head etc. – all stressed out.*

Yasmin *and* **Marlon** *enter.* **Marlon** *walks in front, beaming, shows* **Skanka** *the money in his pocket.*

Marlon This girl good as gold, fam.

Skanka (*to* **Yasmin**) Wait there.

Yasmin Where's my camera. I need to get my camera.

Skanka (*gestures at the bedroom*) You can't. One Ton's in there.

Marlon *freezes.*

Yasmin Come on guys, my camera!

Skanka Shut up, you stupid gyal. I should let you go in, get fucking raped. (*To* **Marlon**.) He's . . . he's got Tirella. Says we all gotta do her.

Marlon All?

Skanka 'Cept Psyche.

Marlon So if I go in?

Skanka I dunno. He's a proper madman.

Marlon Maybe if we give him the scroll we got, he'll go.

Skanka We gave him the full five. Psyche and Gizzy got it.

Marlon Shi-i-i-it . . .

Skanka (*to* **Yasmin**) I'll get your camera . . .

Skanka *disappears inside.*

Yasmin *breaths hard, looks stressed.*

Yasmin What's he talking about?

Marlon Things just got a bit real. You better keep away.

Yasmin Is something happening to one of those girls? Where's Bumper?

Marlon *is about to lead her away when* **Skanka** *reappears, holding the camera and tripod.*

Skanka Don't ever come back here.

He hands over the camera and tripod to her.

Yasmin Can you please explain what is –

Skanka (*interrupting*) Bumper fucked up bringing you.

Yasmin I wanted to see for myself how you all . . .

Skanka (*interrupting*) You didn't see nothing. You should thank God you didn't. Ain't no place for a tourist in the war zone.

Yasmin *exits.*

Little Psyche *wanders out, coming up fast on whatever drugs he took.*

Little Psyche My mandem. My people. My blood. My bones.

They all look at each other.

Skanka What we gonna fucking do?!

Little Psyche (*elated, high on the thoughts* . . .) You *know* what we gonna do. Do what One Ton say, right on point. Till the day come . . . when we fix everything. We fix One Ton. That day a-come. That . . . day . . . is . . . *promised.*

Scene Twelve: Yasmin's flat

TRANSITION: Sound of crying.

SCENE: **Mad Mick** *and* **Yasmin** *on the sofa. She is upset. He's comforting her.*

Yasmin What the fuck was I doing? Jesus.

Mad Mick I told you don't do it!

Yasmin Shit. . . .

Mad Mick Ya alright?

Yasmin That fucking Seb better buy this interview. After what I went through to get it. And why me, huh? Why am I the one to go in there? All the fucking producers want from me is Windrush, Grenfell, gangs. And I'm, like, they're not even my people. I spent my life trying to get a distance between me and them. But going my own way, there's nobody there for me 'cos I don't belong mainstream either. Just float free.

Mad Mick Free is the only way to be.

Yasmin For you maybe. But I don't want to be alone.

Mad Mick There's an upside to being alone.

Yasmin Not for me. I can't be alone. That's why I brought you here. I mean . . . you're alright. You're funny and that. But you could be my dad.

Mad Mick (*horrified*) Fucking hope not!

Yasmin Not literally!

Mad Mick Don't let me meet your mum, jus' in case I recognise her from way back!

Yasmin She's dead, remember?

Mad Mick (*talking across her line*) Yeah, yeah, sorry.

Yasmin (*sighing*) I need to figure out what to do with these recordings.

Mad Mick Ya get what ya want?

Yasmin And more. It's dynamite. They filmed themselves when I was gone.

Mad Mick So I set it up good for ya? Ya can thank me later.

Yasmin You better go.

Mad Mick Ya say ya no like to be alone.

Yasmin Sometimes you feel ten times more alone, if . . . if . . . you're with the wrong person.

Mad Mick (*deep breath, shrug*) When de bee no like de honey, me find another bee.

Mick *turns to leave.* **Bumper** *staggers in, looking wild. Wet face and shoulders.*

Yasmin Oh my God.

Mad Mick Jesus, gyal.

Yasmin I'm so glad to see you. What happened?

Bumper Shut ya stupid mouth.

Mad Mick   Hey! Don't bring ya madness in here.

Bumper   Ya don't want my madness? (*She pulls out the gun.*) How about this?

Mad Mick   Alright . . .

Bumper   So many fucking women. Everywhere. Why you come to my mama, again and again. Not leave her be. We was a family. All fucking shouting and fighting and wrong but that's family to me. And you bleed us dry like a vampire.

Yasmin   He cares for you. The way he talks about you . . .

Bumper   You hear me say open ya mouth? You just wanted this prick to get close to *me* – you wanted *me* to get close to Mandem . . .

Yasmin   You're the one I'm most interested in . . .

Bumper   You silence me. You wipe me away. You call me Lisa, put a mask on me. You don't want me to even sit with Mandem – 'cos there ain't no chicks in Mandem – just kidnap chicks, sticking needles and sucking dicks and getting passed around, that's how you *want* us.

Mad Mick   What you want now?

Bumper   You come back to the house.

Mad Mick   For what?

Bumper   Move your sel'

Mad Mick   You don't belong in that . . .

Bumper (*interrupting, bringing the gun closer to him*)   After today you won't never try tell gyal what to do.

Yasmin   Please, just wait.

Bumper   Get to your car.

Mad Mick   Car ain't close by.

Bumper   Don't try lie to me, fool. It's right out there.

Mad Mick   Bumper . . .

Bumper   Walk.

Mad Mick *stands with the gun to his head. Lights down.*

Scene Thirteen: Prison Classroom

TRANSITION: **Hawk** *sits in a chair drumming his fingers on a table, really listening to his own beat, almost in a trance. Eventually* **Julian** *enters, with a clipboard.* **Julian** *is nervous and ineffectual but upbeat to begin with.*

Julian   I'm so glad they let me see you.

Hawk   (*shaking his head, amused*)   I'm gonna miss you, Julian.

Julian   Uh . . . thank you. I'll miss you too. I hope I never see you again though.

Hawk   We ain't gonna bump into each other.

Julian   Promise me you won't end up back inside.

Hawk   I can't promise that. Unless you're on the parole board and then I'll promise you fucking anything.

Julian   I mean it. I don't want you to waste your life.

Hawk   Cool. They must have brought me to see you for some other reason, not just the bye-byes.

Julian   This! To finish off the course . . . I need you to fill in this questionnaire. Can you read it yourself? (**Hawk** *nods*.) Brilliant. Amazing. So . . . just choose an answer from 1 to 5, there are no right or wrong answers, OK . . . why are you laughing?

Hawk   No right or wrong answers . . .

Julian   There aren't, honestly . . .

Hawk   Respect me, man, and I respect you. The other inmates, they told me, when I start this course . . .

Julian   Told you what?

Hawk   First day of the course, they reckon, you tick all the answers down this side, yeah? 'Do you sometimes feel unable to control yourself physically? Has your anger affected your family or personal relationships?' Tick 'Strongly Agree' every time. Then, end of the course, you tick all the Strongly *Disagree* answers. Boom. Anger management course changed me. I am less likely to reoffend. Parole.

Julian   This is just a monitoring form. It doesn't affect your parole.

Hawk   I'm just telling you, 'cos I like you. You're alright.

Julian   Hopefully the course has helped you.

Hawk   With what? I ain't in here 'cos I get angry. I don't need Anger Management. I don't need Drug Counselling. I don't need Literacy. I'll tell you what I need. I'll let you in on the secret. I'll tell you the one thing that will stop me ever offending again. You wanna know what that is? Come close . . . (**Julian** *leans in, unsure.* **Hawk** *pronounces the word slowly and clearly.*) Mo-ney!

Julian   Sorry?. .

Hawk   Yeah. . . . That's what I need. The moment I get out of here, I'm gonna go stand at the bus stop. What do I need for the bus? Money. Look for a job – what do I need? Money. To print a CV, take a tube, credit for the phone. Money. Walk past a shop full of food – what do I need? Money. I wanna see one person – one other person – my sister – anyone – where we gonna sit? On my bed in my hostel? No. Go cafe – what do I need? Money. And if I spend money on cutting my hair, new shoes, a beer, a bit of weed, a computer game – if I can't bear the thought of life without those simple things . . . you shake your head and say I can't manage money. And I shouldn't go sell drugs to get those things. 'Cos someone like me ain't got the right to those things. Just what keeps me alive, that's it.

Julian   I know parole arrangements are far from perfect.

Hawk   Keep a dog in the yard. Never let it run. Or play. Or see another dog. Just food to keep it from starving. Let it look out on the street and the park but never escape and join the other dogs. Then what? Then listen to it howl – with all its little heart. See it chew its own leg and pull out its own fur. See it go for the first dog it sees when you open the door.

Julian   Prison's tough.

Hawk   I ain't talking about prison! I'm talking about living out there without money. Being in an invisible prison. You can't even imagine, innit?

Julian   I haven't got any money!

Hawk   Your idea of no money – that ain't *no money*. Fear, hunger, cold, shame – you don't feel them things for lack of money. Money's there all the time, holding you up – you just can't see it 'cos you grew up with it.

Julian *stands, prepares to leave, taking his clipboard. A bit sulky.*

Julian   I hope the course helped.

Hawk   Chill, boss. I'm just trying to explain the life. The life of the people you talk to. So you can hear them when they *howl*.

Julian *exits.* **Hawk** *stays where he is.*

Scene Fourteen:: The Trap House

TRANSITION: Music. Softer more soulful than the drill and rap we've heard.

SCENE: **Tirella** *sits on the sofa, upright, still as a statue, staring straight ahead. Looking beautiful, perfect, but vacant. The music is from her phone.*

Nico *has three packages. He takes out a condom, takes it out of the wrapping, pushes the three packages into it.*

Skanka *sits with his head back.* **Gizzy** *and* **Marlon** *enter together, looking at something on* **Marlon**'s *phone.*

Nico (*to* **Tirella**)   Hey. (**Tirella** *doesn't look round.*) Tirella . . .

Tirella   I wanna listen to the music.

Nico (*gentle warning*)   T?

Tirella *stands gracefully, turns off the music, and turns to him.*

Nico   Dere is the ticket for the train. (*Hands her a ticket. Then shows her his phone screen.*) Dis the number of the car. I tex' it to you now. When you get off the train, you go in the car park, he'll be waiting, you just give him dis. (*Shows the condom.*) Turn round, next train back. Easy.

She takes the condom. Steps towards the bedroom.

Nico   Wait. Gyal can't go in there.

Gizzy   Why's she all shy? Man knows where she gonna put it, mandem all been there. Even Skanka. Innnit, Skanka? Skanka! Was you crying when you fucked her?

Skanka *is on his feet. Goes straight for* **Gizzy**.

Marlon   Chill, fam.

Skanka   Fuck you.

Marlon   Jokes, Skanka, jokes.

Nico (*to* **Gizzy**)   Should let him batter you, fam.

There is a tussle during the dialogue above, **Marlon** *stepping between.* **Nico** *pulling* **Skanka** *back.*

Into the melee, **Mad Mick** *comes tumbling into the room, pushed sideways. Hands done with gaffer tape, and tape over his mouth. Blood on his face and shirt. Falls into the middle of the room.*

Nico   What the fuck?!

Marlon   Shit . . .

Bumper *enters, hyped, pointing the gun at* **Mad Mick**. *Walks straight to the middle of the room and gives him a kick.*

Bumper   Get in there. Get down. Film this.

Marlon   Film what?

Gizzy *takes* **Tirella**'s *phone, starts to film. We see the live recording projected on the wall.*

Bumper (*to* **Mick**)   Start begging. (*Bringing the gun closer and closer.*) Beg for it. Beg I don't end you right here, come on!!

Skanka   Bumper, Shit . . .

Nico   Wha' pen?! Who dis bwoy?

Bumper   Turn the music up! (*To* **Mad Mick**.) We gonna do you up proper. Put it out on the internet. Get on the table. (*He does so.*) Now dance, you cunt. (*Points the gun at* **Mad Mick**'s *feet, looking like she might do it.*) Fucking dance!

Mad Mick *starts to hop from foot to foot.*

Nico   He's doing it!

Bumper   That's shit. You ain't gonna get good comments for this video . . . this pussy dancing like baby gyal. Get sexy!

She kicks **Mad Mick**. *Others start to laugh and enjoy it as* **Mad Mick** *starts to dance properly. A couple of them give him a casual kick, making him totter.*

Bumper   Strip, mother fucker.

Marlon   Ah, nooooo!

Bumper   Ease dem' garms down slow, slow . . .

Mad Mick *starts to take his trousers down.*

Bumper   Film his face. So everyone recognise the dancing boy. We mash ya face up later, yeah? Big fat red closed up eyes, ya gonna have. Ya mother won't know ya, she won't let ya fuck her no more. Now turn round. . TURN ROUND . . . shake ya little booty for the camera. Shake it like batty man waiting for cock . . .

Little Psyche *appears at the door to the other room, a bit bleary.*

Little Psyche   Da fuck man . . . What you even doin'?

Bumper   Put this up, world see what happen.

Little Psyche *grabs* **Tirella***'s phone, stops the music and the filming. Tosses the phone to* **Tirella**. **Mad Mick** *goes still.*

Little Psyche   What happen *what*?

Bumper   World see what we do. No opps gonna mess with us.

Little Psyche   What opps you talking about?

Bumper   Any! Dey see how we roll.

Little Psyche (*pointing at* **Mad Mick**)   Man ain't opps,

Tirella   What you drag him in here for?

Skanka   Bumper, man . . .

Little Psyche   He ain't nobody.

Shaznay   Me a tell ya. De gyal head gone.

Bumper *is desperate for a way out . . . it's not going how she thought.*

Bumper   We supposed to be changing up. More than just shotters and runners now. We put up a video say what we do –

Nico   Yeah but he's random.

Bumper (*madder*)   Nobody gonna care who the fuck it is, they see what we do!

Little Psyche   Get him out of here.

Bumper   We fuck him up!

Little Psyche You fuck him up. If you want. He never mess with us.

Bumper (*quiet*) He mess with me. Back when man was thirteen. He fucking my mum just to get close to children, innit?

Shaznay My God . . .

Marlon Dat true? (*To* **Mad Mick**.) You a nasty pervert? You like lickle gyallies?

Marlon *steps forward and pulls the gaffer tape off.*

Mad Mick Bumper . . .

Nico He's a paedo right? He messed with you?

Mad Mick Bumper . . .

Little Psyche Shut up.

Bumper Jus' found him sexing up some young girl. Listen, we post a video of us fucking someone up proper. Serious. Not jigging round, making gang signs. (*Sees she's losing them.*) Fuck's sake . . . we is one mandem, innit? We do this or not?

Shaznay *steps forward, dead certain.*

Shaznay Gyal. . . . De man neffa touch ya. Ya na fi say dat. Ya na fi mek di mandem believe it.

Mad Mick (*to* **Bumper**) What's the matter with you?

Bumper *lashes out at him, he falls back. But she's lost this one.*

Shaznay Obea. The gun a mess with yah head. Evil spirit de inna di ting.

Bumper Shut up. There ain't no obea. No witches and duppies and shit.

Little Psyche (*to* **Mad Mick**) Cha. Pick up your panties and run.

Mad Mick *picks up his clothes. Scrambles to the exit but waits there.*

Bumper I say he done it.

Little Psyche (*just shakes his head*) Nah.

Bumper You calling me a liar?!

She raises the gun to face level.

Marlon Chill . . . chill . . .

Little Psyche Put the gun in my hand.

Bumper What?

Little Psyche It's mine.

Bumper You think what? Fucking leader? Big Badman? Man's bigger and badder and more of a man.

Little Psyche Give me my gun, or pull the trigger.

Marlon Don't . . . say things like that. Come, fam, blud, easy.

Mad Mick Bumper . . .

Bumper Shut up.

Mad Mick Who you trying' to be? One of dese? You ain't one of dese . . . I know you.

Gizzy Give him the gun. Fuck's sake . . .

Skanka Bumper. Think.

Bumper *and* **Little Psyche** *face off.* **Tirella** *stares intensely. The others look around – what now?*

Mad Mick That bullet in that chamber . . . you let it fly, you can't never get the bullet back in the barrel.

Bumper All of you, just shut up! Shut the fuck up!

Little Psyche I always liked you, Bumper. True say, you're lucky I do. Any of these put a gun in my face, I kill them. For sure. But you get one chance. So give me my gun.

Bumper This gyal's burning now, raging . . . can't go back.

Tirella *slowly walks forward. Steps in front of* **Little Psyche** *so she's facing the gun.*

Tirella Yeah. Pull the trigger. Bullet'll go right through me. Carry my blood and bone and scraps of what I ate . . . and through his T-shirt, through his skin, right inside him. Just rest there. Yeah.

Tirella *backs right up to* **Little Psyche**. **Bumper** *looks baffled.* **Tirella** *straightens herself as if for a photo. Lifts her top to reveal her belly to give* **Bumper** *a target.*

Tirella I'm ready.

Nothing happens.

Tirella *drops her T-shirt and lifts both hands up to the gun. Very slowly, for a moment they're both holding it. Then* **Bumper** *lets go.* **Tirella** *is holding it, but still pointed at herself. Then she spins it, so that it points at* **Bumper**.

Tirella Anyone who wants to get out, get out and never come back. (*No-one moves. To* **Bumper**.) Get out. Go.

Bumper *backs towards the door, still dumbfounded.* **Tirella** *points the gun at each person in turn, gets to* **Skanka**.

Tirella (*to* **Skanka**) Get out.

Skanka Why?

Tirella 'Cos that's what you want. Now you got no choice. Move.

Puzzled, **Skanka** *moves towards the door.*

Tirella Now!!

Skanka, **Mad Mick** *and* **Bumper** *back out. . . Exit.*

Tirella *is still holding the gun, facing away from the Mandem.*

Shaznay   Now what you gonna do?

Tirella   I wanna listen to the music for a bit.

She switches her music back on

Scene Fifteen: Outside the Trap House

TRANSITION: Long howl from **Mad Mick**, *maybe two.*

SCENE: **Mad Mick** *is on his knees howling in frustration, relief, fury – everything.* **Skanka** *is stunned.* **Bumper** *is breaking down.*

Mad Mick   Aaaaaaaaaaaaaagh! Whaaaaaaaaaaa – the fuck were you doing?!

Skanka   Fucking hell. . . .

Mad Mick   What is the matter with you?

Bumper   I'm sorry! I'm sorry, OK. I-I-I-I . . .

Skanka   You're sorry!

Mad Mick   You're sorry that you put a gun to man's head?!

Bumper   Yeah! Yeah!

Mad Mick   You tell those kids I messed with you and fucking strip me and threaten to smack me till my eyes close over. You SORRY about that?!

Bumper   I had to do something. You don't even know.

Mad Mick   A GUN TO MY HEAD?!

Bumper   YOU KNEW I WOULDN'T PULL THE TRIGGER!

Mad Mick   Let me put a shooter in your face, see how much you know, see how close you feel to fucking death.

Bumper   You know what? You could do it now! I swear! Death ain't no threat to me. I . . . don't . . . fucking . . . care . . . if you die . . . or I die . . . or he die (*meaning* **Skanka**) . . . or anybody die. Because . . . my mum die . . . OK? And for one whole year I just been waiting to do the same, and tell you the truth . . . I'll welcome death. When that boy come to get me, I open my arms, and I say lift me up and thank you.

Mad Mick   You think that's what your mum want?

Bumper   Don't talk about her. (*She grabs his clothes and hits him with them. Then keeps hitting him. Over and over again, but tearfully, like a child.*) You didn't know nuffin about her. All you did was take her away and take what she had till there was nothing left. Two years! (*Pushes, slaps, scratches.*) Last two years of her life she dashed dem in the fucking drain 'cos of you. Waiting on you. Getting wasted with you. Getting vex with you, and you ain't worth nuffin, you ain't shit, you ain't shit, you ain't nuffin' at all, and you're still standing there and she's fucking gone. She's GONE!

Bumper *stops clawing and just hangs off him. She slides down him into a crumpled heap. Defeated.*

Pause.

Skanka Bumper. What did you tell dem? What did you say about me? (**Bumper** *slowly turns to look at him, not focused on him yet.*) Why did she tell me to go?

Bumper *shakes her head.*

Bumper You wanted out.

Skanka Out where? Now what I got? Mandem is the only thing between me and the opps. I'll get ate out there. You know that.

Bumper I swear I didn't say nothing. Maybe Tirella just see it in your eyes.

Skanka Shit, man. Shit. I know what I need. I need to get arrested. That's better. I'll go fucking jail.

Bumper That ain't no solution. Jail? Without protection? No-one is watching your back. You need to walk back in there, man. (*She points back to the Trap.*)

Mad Mick Son . . . Don't go back in there.

Skanka Fuck d'you care?

Mad Mick That life is not the answer.

Skanka I ain't got a question, fam. I know. I know what my fucking life is.

Mad Mick You don't. You're a kid. You're all just kids. Kids with a gun.

Scene Sixteen: Yasmin's flat

TRANSITION: TV news bulletin. Seen\heard as the audience move. **Yasmin***'s dialogue is over it.*

News Victoria Carson, the schoolgirl who went missing eleven days ago in Eastbourne, sparking a massive police operation across the South East, has been found alive and well – just a few miles from where she was last seen.

Yasmin Aaaaaaaaa, Jesus Shit!

News Police arrived at a derelict house in Eastbourne this morning and discovered her during a search. There were four arrests, and two other girls have been taken into emergency care, according to a local police spokesman.

Yasmin Why, why . . . why now?!

News The news came as controversy broke out over the case, after reports that Victoria had repeatedly been reported missing over the last year as her behaviour became more and more erratic and she ran away from home. Victoria's parents, Martin and Lisa, are understood to have been reunited with their daughter but have not commented on claims that this was the latest in a series of police searches for the missing teenager. The high level of media coverage has also been criticised, with experts from homeless and children charities claiming that the wider problem has been overlooked for some time. In this interview, Susan Barrowclough of the NSPCC, told us of the problems faced by forces up and down the country in connection with so-called County Lines drug dealing and the frequent disappearance of school children whereby young children from countryside towns are being groomed by youths from city gangs to get involved in illegal activity.

SCENE: **Yasmin** *refills her wine glass and picks up the phone. Looking stressed. She says the lines below over the news report above.*

Yasmin Hello Steve. Yes . . . listen, I can edit my thing up for tomorrow evening. Tomorrow! It'll still be in people's minds. You guys could do a 'she's reunited with her family' thing, and then run my film about how – . . . No, I'm not telling you how to do your job. . . I just have ideas, sometimes. . . you can't let this go . . . I don't wanna take it elsewhere, you're my – . . . I do understand . . . yeah, yeah . . . wait, we've gotta sort out how we're gonna use this stuff. . . . Really? Come on, Steve . . . Steve, don't be – . . . I'm not . . . I'm . . . Steve! (*Steve has put the phone down.*)

She hears someone is coming into the flat.

Yasmin Mick?

Bumper *enters.*

Yasmin Where's Mick?

Bumper He's alright.

Yasmin What did you do?

Bumper We let him go. Sorry – about before. Can I come in?

Yasmin What do you want?

Bumper *empties her pockets of a couple of trinkets she stole from the flat before. She drops them on the sofa.*

Yasmin What – They're mine? What were you doing with them?

Bumper I took them before. When I came.

Yasmin You know what? I don't get you.

Bumper *sits on the sofa.*

Bumper You know Harry Potter?

Yasmin   What?

Bumper   Harry Potter. You lot is the Muggles, we is the Wizards. We from dis whole other world. It's right in front of you, but you can't see. We walk among you. We know each other. We make families, and armies, and wars and shit.

Yasmin   Right, but you know what? . . . I'm not even a Muggle. I'm an alien everywhere I go. They think I'm one of you. You think I'm one of them.

Bumper (*looking around*)   This your house? D'you like own it?

Yasmin   My dad owns it. Lives in Ghana.

Bumper   In fucking Africa.

Yasmin   In fucking Africa, correct . . .

Bumper   Huh, I like how you people get yourselves this peng house for big family and lock it up and fly over the ocean and the house sit here all quiet and still and empty. With all the rage and ruin going on outside 'cos the youth got nowhere to go. Jus' rot in some mouldy room with people that hate them and hit them and starve them. They can't come in. Not to the quiet and peaceful, 'cos they don't own it. If they freeze to death on the doorstep they good people, if they break in through the window, they bad, 'cos it's wrong to get anything if you don't own it.

Yasmin   Yeah! Yeah it is! It's wrong to steal mopeds and grab phones and handbags and sell drugs that kill people.

Bumper   So why you wanna talk to us?

Yasmin   'Cos gangs were in the news.

Bumper   Why you keep me out of it? Silence me.

Yasmin   My guy said make it scary, keep the girls out of it 'cos they're not scary.

Bumper   You want scary? I'm the scariest motherfucker you ever seen.

Yasmin   I know that now. Jesus . . .

Bumper   Film me now. Film my flow.

Yasmin   Too late.

Bumper   What?

Yasmin   That girl? They found her.

Bumper   Why you always on about her?

Yasmin   That's the angle. That's . . . the only reason anyone gave a shit about young people and gangs for a few days. Now they won't, so I'm told.

Bumper   I'll burn that camera out, believe.

Yasmin   No editor's gonna be interested –

Bumper Switch it on, I'll show you.

Yasmin Bumper, it's . . . not . . . happening . . .

Bumper *goes to the camera on the tripod, checks it, switches it on. Sits in front of it.*

Bumper (*into camera*) Rasss Yessy! Fucking rass yes fam! Is what I am saying! Fucking rass man Fucking (*faltering*) . . Fucking no man badder than me. (*Silence. To herself.*) What? . . . What? (*Silence. There's nothing there. Frustration about everything starts to build up and up . . .*). Aaaaargh!

Yasmin What?

Bumper I can't find the fucking words. The *right* words. The meanings that I wanna make. I open my mouth in front of the camera and . . . what comes out is something that's always getting said. Like . . . like . . . like you wanna put on your own clothes – then look in the mirror and they're just somebody else's clothes on you.

Yasmin Doesn't matter now, I told you. You wanna glass?

Yasmin *gets her a glass and pours a big slug of wine. Hands it over.*

Yasmin You think my life is peachy, I see that, but I'm in shit. I've always been in shit. Sometimes you wonder if the reason you're always in the shit is that you *are* shit.

Bumper Look around. It ain't too shit.

Yasmin I run around trying to prove to everyone I'm a journalist. Trying to prove it to myself. Spending money I haven't got, hoping to make it big and make it back. Every morning I wake up and wish I could be someone else.

Bumper Maybe if I stare that camera down, the words will come.

They both sit drinking their wine. **Bumper** *necks hers and stands.*

Bumper (*casually*) Thanks. I'm gonna need this. (*She takes the camera.*) And this. (*She takes the laptop.*)

Yasmin Wait . . . No.

Bumper When you first saw me . . . you saw something you needed, innit? Now I seen something I need. Thank you very much.

Yasmin You're just gonna walk off with my stuff – steal it?!

Bumper I can't do that, 'cos you *own* it. You'll be alright.

Yasmin You won't get much for selling that and I can't afford to –

Bumper I ain't gonna sell it, gyallie.

Yasmin I need it.

Bumper I pay you.

She pulls out the bag of gear from her pocket.

Yasmin   You think you can pay me with crack and heroin?

Bumper *tosses over the bag.*

Bumper   *Reality*'s what you *say* you looking for. Nice dose of reality right there. Take that down to the junkies on the street. Go film yourself.

Yasmin   Wait, wait, the memory stick – there! Give me that, yeah, at least!

Bumper *looks*

Bumper   What's on there so precious?

Yasmin   Everything I shot. Everything your friends made me pay a thousand pounds for.

Bumper *plucks out the memory stick, tosses it to* **Yasmin**.

Bumper *exits.* **Yasmin** *slumps. Hurls the drugs across the room. Pours wine into her glass until it overflows. Looks at the memory stick. Holds it up. Glances over her shoulder, thinking of* **Bumper**. *Picks up the phone.*

Yasmin   Steve. . . . Listen. . . . What if there's a gun? What if I got footage of some teenagers waving a gun? . . . (*Grinning.*) I thought it might. . . . They shot it themselves when I was out of the room. . . . *How* interested? It'll go viral, for sure. Do I need to take it to an agency and see what – . . . OK, OK. . . . (*Smiles, looking at the memory stick.*) Then make me an offer. . .

Scene Seventeen: Eastbourne, caravans

TRANSITION: **Mad Mick** *singing. Tuneless but joyful. Like the caravan scene at the beginning but not as manic. Audience arrive to find* **Mad Mick** *at the barbecue again, and* **Bumper** *sitting on a chair in front of the caravan. Like* **Yasmin** *was in the first scene but* **Bumper**'s *on her own side of the hedge. She is tapping intensely into* **Yasmin**'s *laptop (which we recognise from the stickers), totally consumed by what she's doing.*

Skanka, **Celine** *and* **Imani** *arrive, walking up uncertainly.* **Imani** *is carrying a sports bag.* **Mad Mick** *notices them.*

Mad Mick   Aaaaah. Skanka. AKA . . . ?

Imani   AKA Kelvin. I'm Imani.

Mad Mick *shakes* **Imani**'s *hand and holds onto it for as long as possible.*

Mad Mick   That's such a beautiful name. Imani. Man just gotta feel that name in the mouth one more time – *Imani* . . . Mmmm.

Imani (*pointing to the caravan*)   Is this it?

Mad Mick (*to* **Skanka**, *pointing to the other caravan*)   Your residence is here.

Imani   Do you own it?

Mad Mick   No, not own it, no.

Imani   Who owns it?

Mad Mick   We're waiting for confirmation of the owner. Till then, we found a key, and . . . I don't think no-one's gonna wanna use it. It's getting proper cold these days. What kind of crazy man wants to stay in a caravan by the sea in winter, you know?

Imani (*to* **Skanka**)   This is what you want? (*He shrugs.*) You call me, yeah? If . . . if anything at all.

Mad Mick   Stop teasing. Pretending you're gonna go when you just got here and got me all interested in ya . . .

Imani   Nice to meet you.

Mad Mick   Come stand between me and the barbecue all cosy warm and shit. We going . . . *tropical* tonight!!!

Mad Mick *holds up a pineapple with a flourish.*

Celine   I'm Celine.

Mad Mick   Pleased to meet you. I don't wanna hurt ya feelings but I'm more interested in ya friend –

Celine (*interrupting*)   I don't wanna hurt ya bollocks but I'll rip them off if you move to my friend.

Mad Mick (*to* **Skanka**)   What's the use of being a gentleman when the ladies are all rude these days?

Imani *hands* **Skanka** *the sports bag.*

Celine   Don't fuck this up, man. That window is nailed shut now. No way in.

Imani   Except through the front door.

Celine *and* **Imani** *exit.* **Mad Mick** *cracks a beer for* **Skanka**.

Mad Mick   Skanka. . . . Kelvin. . . . Blood. You can't believe I'm here, innit? Last time this gyal fixing to shoot man. Thing is . . . this gyal (*waves at* **Bumper**.) She temperamental. You know why she temperamental?? (**Skanka** *shrugs.*) Genius. She's a fucking gee-ni-arse. You see this shit she posting on YouTube. You see how many followers. That's mad.

Skanka   We seen Hawk. He's just coming.

At last, **Bumper** *looks up.*

Mad Mick   Ay, ay . . .

Skanka   He was on the same train. Our cab drove past him back there.

Mad Mick (*cracking another beer ready for* **Hawk**)   Hawk. Right. . There's two ways that could go. One way is . . . OK. Other way is . . . Badly. You get me, son?

Skanka Don't he like you?

Mad Mick Like me? The guy fucking love me. He just don't know it yet. Go check out your crib, innit?

Skanka *steps that way, sizing up his caravan, unsure.*

Hawk *arrives. Looks at* **Mad Mick**. **Mad Mick** *holds out the beer.*

Hawk You. Here.

Bumper He fixed up the place. Got food in.

Hawk And now?

Mad Mick (*puts the beer down*) I been sleeping in this one (*points to* **Skanka**'s *caravan*) . . . but now the young fella is taking up residence and all that, so now . . . I'm back to London. This your gaff.

Hawk I don't wanna see you round here again.

Mad Mick I kep' it clean and cosy for ya.

Hawk You gotta go.

Mad Mick One thing. It's in the whip, I'll get it.

Mad Mick *exits.* **Hawk** *looks at* **Skanka** *and* **Bumper**.

Bumper Good to see you out. In ya own garms.

Hawk Yeah . . . (*To* **Skanka**.) So . . . you our neighbour?

Skanka (*shrugs*) I suppose.

Hawk Hidin' out, yeah? Cool.

Mad Mick *re-enters with a big, battered, cardboard box. Puts it down in front of* **Hawk** *and* **Bumper**. *There's just random stuff you get when you clear someone's room out: pair of glasses, accessories, deodorant, a phone charger, a glass jar with cotton wool balls in it . . .*

Mad Mick Dunno which things is important, so I kep' it all.

Bumper *stares, steps towards the box.*

Bumper This is Mum's. All Mum's . . .

She kneels and just plunges her hands into the box, to feel the possessions . . . each random item a priceless treasure.

Hawk Where's her ring?

Mad Mick (*nervously*) Aaah, yeah. Couple months back, I had this chick . . . she wake up all rise and shine one morning and walk out with my phone, my Oyster card, my watch and she find your mama's ring and take it.

Hawk (*controlling his anger*) Go on, go.

Mad Mick I ain't bona fide family and that. And I know you think I'm an arsehole. And . . . you kinda right about that. But you know what they say about arseholes? . . . Everybody needs *one*.

Mad Mick *exits with a grin to everyone.* **Bumper** *takes the glasses from the box. Tries them on. Makes the other two laugh. Then picks up her stuff, ready to follow* **Mad Mick**.

Hawk What you doing?

Bumper Mad Mick's driving me back to London.

Hawk We're living here, right?

Bumper *You're* living here. I go back to the endz.

Hawk That ain't safe.

Bumper I need to be where I belong. Stuff to do. Argh!

Skanka What?

Bumper These glasses give me bare *eye ache*.

Hawk They're Mum's. You see different from her, innit?

Bumper True dat, brother.

She takes the glasses off. **Bumper** *exits.*

Skanka *looks at* **Hawk***, slightly freaked.* **Hawk** *picks up the beer* **Mick** *offered him.*

Hawk You're Skanka.

Skanka Yeah. You're Hawk.

Hawk Brandon. Good to meet ya.

Shake hands.

Skanka (*both looking out at the horizon*) Where the fuck is this?

Hawk (*cheerful*) This, my son, is the bottom.

Skanka What?

Hawk The bottom. It's where you start . . . when you start all over again.

They clink beer bottles.

TRANSITION: **Bumper** *sets up her camera.*

Scene Eighteen: Bumper's place now

Bumper *speaks to the camera. Behind her, there is a projection of views and angles of the urban landscape. It includes the places she refers to, but only empty, not with* *people in them. She is recording a voiceover for these images. The live camera image is superimposed on the landscape shots as she starts to speak.*

Bumper (*into camera*)   Clouds cut across the sky like butterfly.

High rise flats lick 'em

Reggae music plays . . .

And I can smell old Angela's cooking from number 28.

And right now, right now, that's old man Derik. Legend. Like man can still bust some moves at raves, and aww . . . look someone offers to help him with his shopping.

And I can hear stolen mopeds ripping up the place and sirens wail . . .

Like don't get man wrong. I am not gonna paint you some rosy cupcake picnic view of it all, there is roughness, madness, *badness*, ruthlessness.

I see the mandem out on road serving up drugs, smell the piss on the stairwells. Like fam, I can see the smashed bottles, wrappers, needles, dirty nappies . . . You're right – I am mad to come back.

I am gonna level with you. Everyone round here knows who I am and what I done.

Don't get man wrong I am shook just a little.

So why this mad love for the endz?

In this life, you live, and you die. You breathe and you bleed and you cry. And you laugh and you lie. You fuck and you fight.

Normal rules don't apply.

We build ourselves a business, you know that? A whole economy on the back of yours. We medicate the population. This population turned sick by the legit economy. We know what we is, and where we is. And the only thing we got, that we make for ourselves, our deadly, beautiful industry . . . you wanna shut it down????

I had people say they see something in me.

You know what they think. If only she could get away. See the right path. Like go college and uni and shit and learn to turn my back on the streets I grew up on.

Da ya think?

Or maybe you think I could like go and be calm with my family by the sea, work some nicey nicey little job in Tesco. Beep. Beep. Beep.

Da ya think?

Shit, though. I wanna go legit. I wanna join your game. But I ain't gonna sit at the bottom and hold the whole thing up for all of yous. So if that's the offer, I ain't on it. I ain't gonna wipe your plate so you can eat off it and sweep the pavement for you to walk on it. I ain't gonna stand at the bus stop while you drive past and tell myself that you deserve it more than me. I ain't gonna sit shivering in the park while your plane slices the silent, peaceful sky to take you to play in some foreign land where maybe your grandad's grandad stripped mine of his home, his kin, his name, his dreams, and everything but his skin.

That's why I don't listen to none of that.

Like I got this little voice deep inside me, like a mouse's heartbeat and it got louder like a drum . . .

You see this voice kept asking me this.

Maybe there's a different way?

Are we more than this?

Is there a different way?

Can I do it different?

And when I stand looking out at man's heartical estate

I think . . . I think maybe I fucking can, maybe I FUCKING CAN . . .

Coz this is my endz and my blood runs thick red through it and

I want to shout and stomp and rip up your view of it

I just want to show you my endz

I want grab *myself* a camera

I wanna use my voice.

I am going to use man's *voice* to speak.

I wanna show you all, lift the hood on my estate right back, let its little eyes sparkle.

This girl want to take you by the ears and eyes and show you.

I am gonna unzip the silence on it, show you, show you

Carve a new thing, a new life.

I'm gonna fucking try.

I am gonna use this bullet tongue voice of mine.

Blasting out.

Bringing life.

Bullet tongue girl gonna show you now.

Bullet tongue gonna tell you TRUE.

In conversation with director Maggie Norris

BP *Where did the initial idea for* Bullet Tongue *come from?*

MN It came from a discussion at a drop in. One young person expressed her frustration with the response of most middle class people to the gangs that were making money from county lines. She expressed her frustration for them wanting to dismantle those gangs. She felt that was naive and I felt that she was right. And actually, that was a really interesting view to challenge the audience with. On the surface, when you hear about the violence and the exploitation of the young people involved in county lines, the immediate and easy conclusion to come to is to dismantle those gangs. But the point that the member was making is that the people who are involved in those gangs are extremely bright which is how they've developed this booming alternative economy as a result of never having been given legitimate opportunities. And if you close them down, they will just emerge in a different form somewhere else because they need money and are, of course, endlessly enterprising. Again, she was right, and we thought this was really interesting to look at in the play. To challenge the audience. To challenge their views.

BP *And when you first thought of it, did you imagine it in promenade?*

MN Yes, I think we did. Because Bumper was on the run. She wasn't living anywhere in particular. She was living sometimes with the gang, sometimes in Eastbourne. And we were in so many different locations for the different scenes, it seemed like we needed to go on Bumper's journey with her.

BP *You've told me before about how you involved the audience in scene changes as they moved through the building. Can you describe some of those?*

MN I thought it might be interesting if the audience experienced being on the other end of a drug deal – to experience what that felt like. And so we laced that in as they moved from scene to scene. And we actually started the show with dealing on the street outside the building. We had people coming in before the show start complaining that there was dealing going on at the gate. It was great to see their faces when the play started and they saw the dealers in the play.

BP Bullet Tongue Reloaded *was very popular: it was popular with the public, but also it means a lot to many of the members. I was just wondering why you thought it struck such a chord.*

MN It was an exciting show and there was a brilliant central performance from Shonagh Marie and a great cast, both times. The audience doesn't like Bumper in the first third of the play. She's a bully. And so when you actually start to fall in love with her, it's a real surprise. We go on quite an emotional journey with this character. The audience were close to the action. It was very immersive and so powerful to watch. I also think the material was particularly easy to access for the young people because it reflected their experience so accurately.

BP *How did the cast respond to the immersive form?*

MN The young people that we work with generally haven't done much theatre before and having the audience so close can be quite intimidating, although they all grow to love it. However, when a young group comes in to see the play, who've never been to the theatre before, that can create friction with the cast because suddenly you've got a fourteen-year-old taking photos on their phone or chatting to a friend, or laughing too loudly. That can be difficult for an inexperienced performer. But those are the youngsters that love the show the most and are impacted by it the most. And so I always make sure to tell the cast that the reason that they're talking is because they are so engaged with the play and they're sharing that with their friend. They are the people that stay and want to talk to the cast afterwards and often want to join The Big House. The experience is unlike anything they've ever had before.

BP *Can you talk to us about the presence of the journalist in the story?*

MN I think what was interesting about Bumper's story is that the media wouldn't be interested in it. Many adolescents, who don't fit the criteria that the media have decided will elicit public sympathy, don't really feature in their stories. That's shocking. So one of the themes running through *Bullet Tongue* was the journalist's search for a young teenager from a middle-class background, who did fit the media's criteria, juxtaposed with Bumper's story.

BP *Is there anything else you'd like to add?*

MN *Bullet Tongue Reloaded* was also funny, and I think we forget that. Although it's quite a harrowing subject, the audience really enjoyed watching it. They didn't come out traumatised, they came out uplifted. They saw the vulnerabilities of the gang members, their hearts, their loyalty and their resilience in the face of adversity. There was real learning in the play for the audience about young people who get involved in county lines and the complex reasons why. They also realised that dismantling the gangs was not an easy solution as the gangs will re-emerge until those young people are given the opportunities and support that they need to survive and flourish.

Maggie Norris interviewed by Bel Parker
9 August 2022

The Ballad of Corona V (The Remix)

David Watson

Interview with writer David Watson

First of all, this is a socially distanced play. How did you achieve that?

Well, the play was conceived to accommodate multiple audience 'bubbles', who promenaded through a series of five scenes staged in different parts of the building. When each scene finished, that bubble would troop out to the next scene and the next one would immediately replace them, with the scene being replayed. So, in effect, the cast played the show about four times a night! This meant each scene had to be self-contained, with actors appearing in only one scene each, so it immediately lent itself to the form of vignettes, with a linking kind of leitmotif of the coronavirus hunting for his next victim, who we meet at the end.

What were the main challenges in writing for this format?

It was a challenge to make the scenes all the same length . . . but the timings were probably more of a headache for the Big House team on the actual nights, shepherding people around without causing bottlenecks! I find structuring plays in a strictly linear way the most difficult aspect, really, so this more fragmented, episodic style actually suited me.

The Remix is an evolution of the original piece – The Ballad of Corona V – restaged half a year later. What were the main differences between the two versions, and why did you feel the need to change the content so soon after?

The biggest change was the first scene. In the initial version we had a feverish, stream of conscious monologue by the virus, sort of spitting out this vomit of contemporary news and pop culture, which gave way to a New Year's party with people happily looking forward to 2020 and all it would bring . . . I liked all that, but in the intervening months I had this idea about a nurse who has died of Covid, finding herself at this cocktail party populated by people who have all died as a result of government negligence or ineptitude, from down the ages. It struck more of an angry note, and maybe reflected better where we were at with everything, eighteen months into Covid.

'The Panic Buy Dance', the fever dream of BoJo . . . we definitely experience the events and concerns of the pandemic in this piece but you go so much further than that . . . What were the other things you wanted to address?

In early 2020 I had started talking to Maggie about doing a Big House show with a big apocalyptic event at the heart of it, and a care-leaver character navigating that . . . the idea was that losing your parents or home-life kind of feels like the end of the world, and just running with that . . . and then when Covid happened, that idea felt a bit overshadowed, and it really felt like the thing to do was look at the pandemic head-on, through the prism of how the members were experiencing it. It was a bit like: care-leavers; that voice is generally not going to register very loudly in the mix, let's get them heard.

But then, when we got people together on Zoom, there was actually quite a big sense of indifference to Covid, and all the shenanigans around it. I was really struck by someone saying their life was pretty socially distanced anyway, never mind Covid, and that became the heart of the final scene. And then this was at the beginning of the Black Lives Matter protests, and that felt like a much more charged topic for the group.... There was universal anger about the death of George Floyd, but also quite a diversity of opinion about BLM and how that was playing out ... so I thought 'make it about everything, not just Covid!...Maybe this is all symptomatic of the beginning of the end of capitalism!'

Do you think that this show is limited to the context of the last couple of years or do you think there will be other opportunities to put it on?

I think it has probably had its (very singular) moment. But you never know. I'll never forget the surrealness of putting together a show at that time, particularly the first version in that wintry partial-lockdown. I used to stand out in the dark yard and see all the different scenes playing out through the windows, like some strange doll's house.

Black Boris. . . . That was a development between the first and second versions. Can you talk to us about that?

James had played it brilliantly in the first run, but then there was a new cast coming in. Really it wasn't a conscious decision to make him Black, it was just that, out of that new cohort, Sam was the one who fitted that part. That obviously added to the surreal nature of it, and the fact that Boris has been on record making these throwaway racist remarks obviously gave it an extra edge.

You referred to quite a few conspiracy theories in this show. . . . Why did this feel like such an important thing to explore?

There were a few of those buzzing around the group. Someone on the periphery of The Big House was into some quite outlandish stuff which was easy to dismiss, and some of that is played for comedy in the Boris scene ... but I didn't want to just dismiss that mistrust of authority; it felt right to put that in there. Traditional politics has failed to deliver for young people in so many ways that you can see where this reaching out for other narratives comes from.

How did you come to imagine the coronavirus as a cowboy sitting on a little rocking horse?

The rocking horse was Maggie's idea, I think they sourced it from a shop a few doors down the Essex Road ... As for the Virus as a cowboy, I think I'd always wanted to write something in that voice, and I could see Taurean doing it brilliantly. It seemed to fit the idea of the virus as this smooth, deadly outlaw.

Who would you most like to see this show?

It would be a good show to put in a time capsule and then dig up once the Covid pandemic has passed into history. Hopefully it would stand up as a record of what it felt like, from a particular perspective, to live through that particular moment in time.

The Ballad of Corona V (The Remix) was first performed at The Big House, London, on 2 June 2021, with the following cast:

Lorna	Laura Thompson
Agatha	Tia Shillito-Radicic
Fauzia	Iman El Naser
Clive	Geromme Allen-Dunkley
Mark	Abdulai Kakay
Jamila	Yohanna Yohanis
The Virus	Taurean Steele
The Mannequin	Dorivaldo Ernesto
Kayleigh	Megan Samuel
Rochelle *(screen only)*	Melissa Madden
Relative *(screen only)*	Ruth Oyediran
Friend *(screen only)*	Safina Simpson
Zoom Date *(screen only)*	Osman Enver
Fiona	Safina Simpson
Drey	Jermaine Freeman
Arabella	Eleanor Wyld
Doctor Sarm	Tayo Odesanya
Nurse Pereira	Najma Sharif
Boris Johnson	Samuel Kyi
Boris Johnson *(on screen)*	James Atwell
Seema	Fatima Abukar
Sade	Hannah Sonde
Stefan	Romario Splatt
Police Officer	James Atwell

Creative Team

Writer	David Watson
Director	Maggie Norris
Assistant Director	Bel Parker
Producer	Sarah Stallwood-Hall
Musical Director and Composer	Jammz
Sound Designer	Ed Clarke
Video Designer	Ben Bull
Lighting Designer	Ryan Day
Associate Lighting Designer	Sean Laing
Costume, Set and Props Designer	Eleanor Campbell
Production Manager	Jack Boissieux
Stage Manager	Leyla Percival
Chalk Installations	KEELERTORNERO
Lyrics	David Watson and Jammz
Movement Direction	Jammz and Osman Enver

Characters

Lorna
Agatha
Fauzia
Clive
Mark
Jamila
The Virus
The Mannequin
Kayleigh
Rochelle *(screen only)*
Relative *(screen only)*
Friend *(screen only)*
Zoom Date *(screen only)*
Fiona
Drey
Arabella
Doctor Sarm
Nurse Pereira
Boris Johnson
Boris Johnson *(screen)*
Seema
Sade
Stefan
Police Officer

A / slash indicates the point where the next speaker interrupts, and overlaps with the first.

Author's Note

This play was written and originally performed in 2020, at the height of Covid-19 restrictions. With social distancing rules limiting the number of spectators we could accommodate, it was decided that, rather than mounting a show in the traditional way, smaller audience groups – four or five 'bubbles' per night – would be invited to promenade through a series of connected scenes or vignettes. Each scene was repeated for each bubble, meaning the play was, in effect, performed several times each evening. Actors could therefore not appear in multiple scenes, which were also all the same length, to accommodate the timing of each audience group moving through the space.

In the summer of 2021, an updated 'remix' of the play was performed under the same restrictions; that is the version published here.

Pre-show

The audience mingle, out in the yard. Some kind of party or gathering seems to be taking place inside – the sound of chatter and laughter, and also the occasional more dissonant sound of someone shouting. There is music being played – popular songs from the 1910s.

As the audience mingle, one or two of them are approached by **Lorna**. *She wears her contemporary nurse's uniform. She seems a little bit hesitant and unsure as to where she has found herself.*

After a bit, she approaches a couple of audience members.

Lorna   Excuse me? . . . Sorry, excuse me, do you know what time it is?

Think my phone's died . . . Thanks, thank you.

On being told the time, she seems a bit surprised.

It's . . .? Oh, right.

She nods. A beat. Smiles –

Thank you.

She moves away a bit. After a while, she approaches the same, or different, audience members.

Sorry, are you here for the erm. . . . What are you here for?

They (hopefully) engage. . . .

Oh right. Oh right.

A pause. She still seems slightly disorientated.

I just came from work.

Yeah, I wasn't sure . . . what to expect actually, sort of thing . . .

Scene One

Lorna *still amongst the audience, as the door to the performance space opens –*

Fauzia *comes out. She appears to be having a mild panic attack.* **Agatha** *follows – she is wearing a nurse's uniform from 1918, and has a cocktail in hand.*

Agatha (*as they come out*)   Oops-a-daisy, where are you off to, Fauzia? (*Quickly, sotto voce, to audience.*) – Hello! – (*Double-taking, recognising* **Lorna**.) – Oh!

Fauzia   Agatha?

Agatha (*to* **Fauzia**)   It's alright, me darling, I'm here. I thought you were running away!

Fauzia (*breathless*) I'm –

Agatha Why don't you come back inside with me? (*Sotto, to* **Lorna** *and audience.*) Come in! –

Agatha *leads* **Fauzia** *back in, with* **Lorna** *and the audience following. Inside, there is party food on the table, and the walls are decorated with* **Fauzia**'s *artwork.*

(*to* **Fauzia**) Now, watch your step. And chin up! It prevents drooling! That's just a joke of mine –

Fauzia (*smiling, humouring* **Agatha**) Yeah.

Agatha I'm a proper old joss at the best of times.

Fauzia I know, right? –

Agatha That's what the girls on the ward used to say; 'Our Aggy's as merry as a grig, don't you know, but she's always liked for her manner at bedside'!

Fauzia OK –

Agatha Or did they mean to say I've always a *like,* for a *man* at me bedside!

Lorna (*approaching*) Excuse me –

Agatha Hello!

Lorna Sorry –

Fauzia Agatha?

Agatha (*to* **Lorna**) Would you give me one sec?

Fauzia Can you –

Agatha Yes, dear?

Fauzia Can you –

Agatha Get another glass of water? –

Fauzia (*offering her phone*) Can you stream this on my Instagram?

Agatha Of course I can, my darling –

Agatha *turns to* **Clive***, as he passes. He wears tattered clothes from the early 1980s, and moves around in a Zen, chilled, almost catatonic state.*

(*Passing* **Fauzia**'s *phone.*) Clive, sweetheart, would you mind? Because Fauzia wants to- to steam this on her . . . itsy-gram.

Fauzia Steam –

Agatha I mean –

Fauzia Stream it –

Agatha On her insadam, you know what she means by that.

Clive (*to* **Fauzia**) I told you it doesn't work in here, fire-child . . .

Agatha She's feeling out of sorts.

Fauzia Can you smell –?

Agatha What's that, dear?

Fauzia . . . Thought I could smell burning.

Clive (*to* **Fauzia**) Maybe it's you.

As he moves away, **Clive** *flicks his cigarette lighter on –* **Fauzia** *flinches.*

Agatha (*warning* **Clive**) Clivey. (*Softly.*) Fauzia, my love, we have talked about this –

Lorna (*to* **Agatha**) Hi –

Agatha (*to* **Lorna**) Oh! Yes! You must be Lorna!

Lorna . . . Yeah –

Agatha I've a cloth-head for names; Lorna . . . Brennan!

Lorna (*confused*) That's right –

Agatha (*offering her hand*) Agatha Pearson. Pleased to meet you, I'm sure.

Lorna Yeah – Oh – (*withdrawing her hand*) I dunno if – 'Hands.' 'Covid.'

Agatha What's that? Oh yes! Oh you poor love!

Lorna Sorry?

Agatha Oh – pair of us with our scrubs on, look – Snap!

Mark *emerges in the doorway. He wears a British army uniform from 2006. He carries a bottle of beer, holding it up to* **Agatha**.

Mark Ags.

Agatha Alright Markie, now you want me to find you an opener don't you, but are you really sure you need another drink now?

Mark Ags!

Agatha (*to* **Lorna**) Would you excuse me?

Fauzia (*to* **Lorna**, *referring to her phone*) Is that an i-phone 8?

Lorna Sorry? Oh. Yeah. I think so. (*She is disinfecting her hands.*) I'm just . . . with the Covid . . .

Fauzia What's Covid?

Agatha (*to* **Lorna**) Help yourself to anything you like. Drinks are over there, the food's here. You'll see it's always strawberry season in these parts! And we've some crisps, if that's what they're called, and – and well Mark's laid out most of his ration pack for us, haven't you, sweetheart?

Mark (*impatient*)   Yeah you done know.

Agatha   And Fauzia's brought some – what was the name of it, dear?

Fauzia   Samosas.

Agatha   'Samosas.' And where are they from?

Fauzia   Tesco.

Agatha   'Tesco.' Samosas from Tesco, if you're at all partial – (*having opened beer bottle*) – And now Markie this is your last drink for now, and that's doctor's orders –

Clive   'Doctor Foster went to Gloucester . . .

Agatha (*to* **Lorna***, referring to* **Clive**)   Here he goes . . .

Clive   'And I shoulda been a foster child, but they called me too wild . . .

Agatha (*to* **Lorna**)   He's awfully lyrical, you see. Could have been a poet, our Clive, I shouldn't wonder –

Clive (*opening the fridge*)   'Said I take the biscuit. . . . But now they just can't fluster me – (*With a pot of custard, grinning at* **Agatha**.) . . . 'Cos I'm in safe *custody*. . . .

Agatha (*to* **Clive**)   That'll fatten you up! –

Agatha *quickly turns to* **Jamila**, *who is sat quietly with a blanket, her hair wet.*

Agatha   Are you sure you're quite comfortable there, my love?

Jamila   Can you see the land?

Agatha   The land? You're not on the boat anymore now, are you?

Lorna   Excuse me – Sorry –

Agatha   Yes. Lorna. Tell me about your work.

Lorna   . . . Oh. Right.

Agatha   Because I would be fascinated, I'm sure, to know about all the changes, and all the things that have stayed the same and, and well we could swap notes I suppose, couldn't we?

Lorna   Yeah –

Mark   You from London?

Fauzia   I'm from London.

Mark (*to* **Lorna**)   Whereabouts?

Lorna   Erm – sort of Forest Gate?

Mark   East? Oi that's East innit.

Agatha Markie, give her a chance to catch her breath.

Mark It's by Stratford, innit. It's by what's-it – Westfield. Is it called Westfield?

Lorna That's right.

Mark Is it open now, yeah?

Agatha (*indicating* **Lorna**) The year two-thousand-and-twenty, Lorna's from.

Mark It's open, innit. I swear it's open by then like, it's mad. (*Shaking his head in disbelief.*) I'm from Hackney like; fucking – uptown shops all up in East London like – crazy.

Lorna (*not quite understanding*) Yeah.

Fauzia I'm from West.

Agatha (*to* **Fauzia**) Now *you* were born in – (*Referring to* **Fauzia**, **Lorna** *and* **Mark**.) Well, you three are all from almost the same –

Jamila Maybe she can help us.

Mark (*laughs, dismissive*) Jokes . . .

Jamila Look at her clothes.

Mark She can't help us.

Clive (*offering* **Lorna** *food*) Gotta help herself.

Agatha (*jollying them along*) We don't need any help here, do we?

Fauzia Where did you work?

Lorna Erm . . . St Thomas's?

Agatha Tell us what you do.

Lorna Well . . . (*Bit self-conscious.*) So I'm a ward sister?

Agatha Oooh.

Lorna So . . . every day's a bit of everything, really. Except . . . what with everything's happening and that, I mean I was in the ICU for the last few months –

Agatha You've been awfully brave.

Lorna . . . Er . . . Yeah it has been a bit full-on. Took us a while, d'you know what I mean, to learn all the protocols and, and what we were dealing with, really –

Clive (*referring to a karaoke machine*) Agatha.

Agatha Yes! Oh!

Clive Just run the riddim, mek me tear down the whole place.

Agatha (*to* **Lorna**, *moving to the karaoke machine*) When he talks all that mumbo-jumbo I don't know what he's at, but I *do* know we're all potty about the – 'okey-dokey' . . . 'hokey-cokey' . . . what's the thing called?

All (*except* **Lorna**)   Karaoke!

Agatha   That's the chappie. Now, how did you get it to work the last time . . .

Lorna (*half to herself*)   I feel like I should call my daughter but my phone's . . .

As the others busy themselves around the karaoke machine, **Fauzia** *approaches* **Lorna**.

Fauzia (*to* **Lorna**)   Do you know WK, the college?

Lorna *looking blank.*

Lorna   Erm –

Fauzia   Westminster Kingsway?

Lorna   OK.

Fauzia   That's where I was at.

Lorna   Oh right.

Fauzia   I was studying art?

Lorna   Oh right?

Fauzia   Yeah I wanna – wanted to be an artist. Like . . . or maybe not artist, but . . . (*Indicating the pictures around the room.*)   I done these, but . . .

Lorna   . . . Oh wow.

Agatha (*shouting over*)   Yes! Aren't they wonderful? Those are all Fauzia's!

Lorna   Yeah.

Agatha   We're a talented bunch, and no mistake! Well, I'm not.

Clive (*into mic*)   One two? . . .

Agatha (*back to the karaoke machine*)   Now –

Lorna (*to* **Fauzia**)   My daughter's into acting.

Fauzia   Is she really?

Lorna   Yeah, she's done a few bits and bobs . . .

Fauzia   That's cool.

Lorna (*referring to her artworks*)   I'm loving the look of these though, they're blinding.

Fauzia   I died at Grenfell.

Lorna (*to* **Fauzia**)   . . . You what, sorry?

Fauzia   I died at Grenfell?

Clive (*into mic*)   Good evening . . .

Fauzia There was a –. There was a fire? Was it on the news?

Agatha (*in preparation for* **Clive**'s *performance*) Right . . .

Jamila (*distant*) The wind's coming again . . .

Mark (*with karaoke machine*) Oi where's the menu thing?

A backing track is starting.

Clive (*into mic*) Everybody with their musical ears in gear . . .

Jamila I hear the ocean.

Mark Where's the menu?

Agatha One at a time, eh Markie.

Lorna (*pursuing* **Fauzia**) Sorry –

Clive *launches into his karaoke performance – it is a song from his 'time' – 'Sing, Baby, Sing' by The Stylistics.*

Clive (*singing*)

> Sing, baby, sing
> The world is getting better
> It's something else since we're together
> Let's have a ball, let's do it all and sing
> Ain't we got it made
> (Sing, baby, sing)
> Ain't we got it made.
> (Sing, baby, sing)

> Dance, baby, dance
> And let the sun shine on us
> There ain't a blessed thing to stop us
> Let's live it up, fill up a cup and dance
> Ain't we got it made
> (Dance, baby dance)

Lorna (*shouting over the music*) Excuse me? –

> Ain't we got it made
> (Dance, baby dance)

Clive Ain't we got it made

Lorna Sorry, excuse me, can I just have a word with somebody please? –

Agatha Lorna?

Mark (*roughly taking the mic from* **Clive**) Oi done this, done this.

Clive Oh, I love a man in uniform –

Mark Fuck you.

Lorna I don't wanna be a party pooper and that –

Clive (*referring to* **Lorna**)   Uh-oh.

Agatha   Of course you don't –

Lorna   But Christ –

Clive   Uh-oh.

Agatha   Come and have a samosa.

Lorna   I was at *work*. Right? And then the next minute. . . .

Agatha   It's discombobulating, I know –

Lorna (*thinking*)   Except I wasn't *at* work. . . .

Mark *opens another beer.*

Lorna   'Cos I was in a bed. At work. I was in a bed in the ICU –

Agatha   Now –

Lorna   I've gotta speak to my daughter –

Agatha   Lorna –

Lorna   Can someone tell me. . . . – (*Referring to* **Fauzia**.) – She's on about she died at fucking Grenfell –

Jamila   It's dark on the beach when we touch the shoreline.

Lorna   I –

Jamila   It's very hard. Lights on the ocean . . . don't know basically if it's fishing boats or . . . thing. England.

Clive *idly hums/sings the tune of 'Rule Britannia', the chorus line.*

Fauzia (*to* **Clive**)   Ssh.

Jamila   It's very hard . . . to do this thing. To cross. Four countries. It's hard to say in English. (*Realising.*) I can speak English. Now I'm here, I can speak English.

Agatha   You see, it's not all bad!

Jamila   What language is it in France?

Mark   French.

Clive   Français.

Jamila   Montez dans le bateau.

Agatha   Oh – I should know this –

Jamila   'Get in the fucking boat.' (*Starting to shake.*) You don't feel the water when you drown.

Mark (*searching the drinks table*)   Oi let me get a JDs and Coke out here man

Agatha (*going to her*)   Jamila, dearie –

Lorna   She needs help –

Clive (*staring at* **Lorna**)   You need help. That's why you're here. That's why you're in here, Sambo. It's Royal bloody wedding Day 1981, and the rest of the country's out having a pint in the sunshine, except for muggings here, cosy indoors with you. You, and all the other ingrate, lowlife pieces of shit, who nobody wants, nobody loves, and nobody gives a flying fuck about. . . . Except for me. Except for me, Clivey-boy. 'Cos I can help you –

Jamila *suddenly vomits water.*

Jamila   Can you touch me?

Agatha   Shh . . .

Jamila (*trying to move* **Agatha**'s *hand to her crotch*)   There.

Agatha (*warning*)   Jamila . . .

Jamila   No-one ever touched me. Now it's too late.

Clive (*tenderly running his hand through* **Jamila**'s *hair*)   We can help each other. . . .

Lorna   I'm not fucking dead!

Mark   Finally.

Lorna   What, you're saying what? Covid? You're saying I caught fucking Covid and then –

Fauzia   Check your notes.

Lorna   Check what?

Clive *takes a script out of her pocket and hands it to her. A beat.*

Lorna (*reading from the script*)   Finally she gets it.

Agatha   That's you, Mark.

Mark   Finally she gets it.

A beat.

Agatha   Lorna?

Fauzia (*prompting, over her shoulder*)   I remember now . . .

Lorna   I remember now.

Fauzia   I never caught the thing at work.

Lorna   I never caught the thing at work.

Fauzia   Even though I was floating about without / a mask on –

Lorna   Even though I was floating about without – that's it, no proper mask for about two fucking weeks – this is *after* all the stuff with the PPE –

Fauzia (*prompting*)   I get it now –

Agatha   Alright, Fauz.

Lorna   I get it now.

A beat.

Fauzia (*to* **Jamila**, *prompting*)   It's you.

Jamila (*to* **Lorna**)   It was Eat Out to fucking help out.

Lorna   It was Eat Out to fucking help out. With my daughter. . . .

A beat.

Agatha   Lorna. . . .

Lorna   Kayleigh. . . . Is she alright?

Agatha   I know, / you –

Lorna   We'd only just buried my bloody mum, d'you know what I mean – and she got it in a care home!

Agatha   I know you're angry, sweetheart –

Lorna   – A *care* home, d'you know what I mean, like the clue's in the fucking name –

Mark (*in agreement*)   Yes!

Agatha   Have a samosa, dear, there's no point being angry –

Mark   Yes there is!

Agatha   Look at me! There I was . . . August the 5th, nineteen-hundred and eighteen, and plucky as a bell-boy's button, I don't mind telling you; I was in the field camp, at Picardy, when a dirty great jerry bomb . . . (*A beat.*) I've been here for longer than all of us. I try to make do. I try to make the best of things! But I didn't realise, you see! I didn't cotton on to the fact that me buying it – (*Corrects herself.*)   . . . that my . . . 'death' . . . well, that it was the same as everyone else's here; an example of, of, of –

Jamila   Systemic institutional injustice.

Agatha   Thank you, dear. You see I thought we were fighting the war to end all wars! But Markie here tells me it wasn't the war to end all wars –

Mark (*shaking his head*)   Nn-nn.

Agatha (*checking with* **Fauzia**)   And the – *Google?* –

Fauzia (*nodding*)   Mm-mm.

Agatha   – The *Google* was telling that it was in fact . . . a 'war for markets'!

Mark   Deep.

Agatha   A 'war for markets' it says! And so . . . and you'll have to pardon my French . . . but if it wasn't the war to end all wars . . . and if it was in fact a war for markets then it rather begs the question –

Lorna   You're all . . .

Mark   Fuck this! –

Agatha   – it begs the question what the bloody hell were we doing there?! –

Mark (*picking up the mic and taking the 'stage'*)   Fuck this –

Agatha   – dying there?! –

Mark   – Who's ready for the fact-check piece?

Clive   Preach, sister –

Fauzia (*to* **Lorna**)   He's got this thing –

Lorna   Eh?

Mark   My time now –

Fauzia (*to* **Lorna**)   It's like a speech, he's gonna read to the government? –

Mark   Listen –

Fauzia   Except obviously he can't read it –

Mark   First of all –

Lorna (*dazed*)   He can't – ?

Clive   Because he's dead.

Mark   This one goes out – to Bush, and Blair, and the full coalition – of the born-corrupted leaders across the globe, yeah? I would like to say – I would like to ask the question: – *What* – is the mentality – that leads a leader – a *leader* –

Fauzia (*to* **Lorna**)   I like your hair colour.

Mark   – Right: –

Fauzia (*suddenly, to* **Lorna**)   Did thing become the President yet?

Lorna   What?

Fauzia (*remembering the name*)   Corbyn.

Mark   – You're sending Red Caps into the dead zone, yeah? And we're putting on our flaks. . . .and we're ready to go to war for yous –

Clive (*singing*)   Buffalo / Soldier . . .

Mark   I'm saying we're ready to go to war for yous lot; We enter the north-east quadrant of the square . . .

Agatha   Markie –

Military sounds start envelope **Mark**; *a helicopter; gunfire. . .*

Mark   . . . The heat's on our faces! . . . I can taste blood and sand, mate. . . . Blood and sand; We're ready to go to war and we got fifty rounds of ammunition each yeah, and no radios!

Agatha   Lance Corporal –

Mark   I'm saying fifty rounds –

Lorna   It's –

Mark (*to* **Lorna**)   It was a war! We were fighting a war!

And they should have protected us.

Jamila *has started to sing softly, a religious lament. A beat.*

Mark   Incoming!

He is getting his hand-gun out.

Lorna   Is he –

Agatha   He always does this –

Mark   Fuck this –

He puts the gun in his mouth.

Lorna   Don't! –

Mark *pulls the trigger – nothing happens.*

Mark   Incoming!

He tries again.

Mark   Incoming!

He repeatedly tries to shoot himself, to no avail. **Jamila** *still singing. After a bit –*

Agatha (*to audience*)   If I might suggest –

The voice of an old-school Texan cowboy, from the stairs. It is the **Virus**.

Virus   Well, I ain't a betting man, but I'd put a punt on us pushing on through to the Ballad section, up the wooden hill; what say you, folks, come on now. . . .

The **Virus** *leads the audience to the next scene.*

Scene Two

Music is playing – the instrumental of 'The Ballad of Corona V'. Once the audience are assembled, the **Virus** *raises a remote control. He abruptly shuts the music off and launches straight into –*

Virus Roundabout the 1300s, a pestilence came to good ol' Europa. Constantinople was the point of origin; layed out North of five thousand locals in the first one week. Some folks took to whipping theirselves in the streets, in an effort to I don't know – 'appease the Gods' or something. . . . Others thought a particular minority group was to blame, and –

Well would you look at me justa rabbitin on like a sunstruck prairie goat – Permit me to introduce myself. Couple weeks from now folks'll start to call me 'Covid-19', but . . . I find that moniker sits kinda ugly on the tongue. I prefer 'Corona.' Lone Ranger – though I do like company. Femme Fatale – though I can be of both the female and the male persuasions; non-binary, I believe is the term, a shapeshifter. Certain times I'm of the South African variation. . . . Other times I can give you a Brazilian! I can be here, there and everywhere – going forwards in time, backwards in time – But enough about me. How's about we try and break the ice up in here just a little? Would anybody care, metaphorically speaking of course, just to lower-down the mask they're a-wearing and share with the group the name by which they tend to go?

(*To audience.* . . .) Yes Sir/Madam? (*Name?*) Well, that's a pretty name, who give it you? (. . .)

Oh your Mother and your Father; (*Chuckles to himself),* god-dammit, I always forget that you all are the products of a primary and secondary reproductive cycle, as opposed to parthenogenesis! I bet you all have some fun with that procedure, hey [Name]. Well I don't know about you all but I feel the atmosphere in here has improved ten-fold!

Did you ever think that this is all a bad dream?

If it is, then when did it start?

Was it when they closed the schoolhouses, the restaurants? Was it the part when they said wear a face-cover every god-damn place you go, except don't do that, except do, except don't again.

Was it before that. When they told you 'many a' the older folks are gon' die.' Was it when they started saying 'Build the wall.'

Was it when they said 'Brexit means Brexit.' Was it when they took back control.

Was it before that even. Was it when the police started covering up their badge numbers. Was it when the ice caps all a' shrunk again, hundred-odd gigatonnes year on year. Was it when they started running folks over on the bridges. Was it when they started drop the bombs; Damascus, Tripoli; Was it when Prince died? Bowie?

Was it when the Homo-Sapien first rose himself up out of the oceans and learned to walk.

The point I seek to make is we'll never know when it started – but I'll tell you when it's done – and it ain't done yet! And even when it is – I'm go' be all up on your minds a long while after. You gonna recall . . . how I made the birds sing somehow sweeter up in the trees. How I made the sky blue again; the air clean. And the things I taught you. How to appreciate the smaller things in life. The taste of a well-cooked meal; the touch of loved one's hand, maybe up in the midst of a busy restaurant, maybe Christmas time. . . . Maybe I helped you remember how to live again. How to hope.

Now, Hope, of course, is not a promise I can make to everyone. Least of all those upon my list; the list of those I am called upon to visit with and who will be, I'm afraid, morbidly inconvenienced.

Is there a Stefan Prince in here tonight?

Nope?

Some of you all been hiding out all quarantined and playing hard to get!

Do you suppose I could, metaphorically speaking, saddle up on my stallion . . . and shapeshift my way through a series a' scenarios in search of this Stefan Prince?

And thus provide something in the way of a 'story arc', for those who covet such things?

You do?

Well then – let's buckle up, hold on tight, and we may even find ourselves a happy ending.

(*Consulting his list again.*) It appears, in advance of Mr Prince, that one 'Lorna Brennan', mother of one, and health-care worker is the next-up item upon this sorry roll-call.

Well, with a heavy heart, and a degree of deviousness – I believe I will see to her presently.

*The **Virus** presses a button on a remote – a burst of static, and then suddenly – a talking shop-window **Mannequin** appears on screen –*

Mann   – as we begin 2020!

Virus   What the – ?

*The **Virus** has been trying to 'change the channel' – he finally succeeds, and **Kayleigh** appears on screen. Stylised – various copies of her face all projected around the room. She is a usually energetic, slightly off-beat young Londoner, but is now looking drained. She sits in darkness.*

*The **Virus** watches, although **Kayleigh** is obviously unaware of his presence.*

Kayleigh   I feel old.

Virus   Brennan? Lorna Brennan?

The **Virus** *presses the remote and the footage jumps to –* **Kayleigh** *at home. Less stylised, more naturalistic style (probably just one of her now.) Still sat in the dark. March 2021. (It should be decided whether the dates in the following sequence are shown for the audience or not.) (The March 2021 section we will keep returning to is all part of the same Zoom call –* **Kayleigh** *is on a Zoom date.)*

Kayleigh   Basically I'm just tired. I guess. But it's all good. I'm good. Considering. . . . This whole messed up –

Footage jumps again – **Kayleigh** *at home. January 2020.* **Kayleigh** *is now full of energy, recording a self-tape audition.*

Kayleigh   Hi. Hello.

Virus   Hey now.

Kayleigh   Er, Kayleigh Brennan, and I'm reading for the part of – 'Girl.' Appropriately.

The footage suddenly jumps again –

Virus (*to audience*)   Looks like we got ourselves a few gremlins up in the mix –

– to another audition.

Kayleigh   Hello, I'm Kayleigh Brennan –

Virus   Brennan! –

Another jump, to another audition –

Kayleigh   . . . Kayleigh Brennan –

Another jump, to another audition –

Kayleigh   Kayleigh Brennan.

Virus   This must be the daughter –

The footage jumps back to **Kayleigh** *in the darkness, March 2021.*

Kayleigh   – 2021, like, I'm thinking it can only be better, though, right?

Virus   You think?

Kayleigh   I miss so many things . . . I wanna get back to acting –

Footage jumps – stylised **Kayleigh**.

Kayleigh   – I just wanna be real.

Footage jumps – back to the darkness, March 2021.

Kayleigh   . . . llike Algarve or Majorca, I don't give a fuck right now, pardon my –

Footage jumps – an audition –

Kayleigh (*wearing a beret*)   Mystique.

*The **Virus** is increasingly exasperated as the video speeds through a series of jumps between different auditions –*

Kayleigh   The new fragrance from –

Another –

Kayleigh   London and the south

Another –

Kayleigh   east Asia report –

Another –

Kayleigh   – ting bruv, dunno what's real like, I swear all –

Back to the darkness, March 2021 –

Kayleigh   – I'm good though.

Another audition –

Kayleigh   I don't believe –

March 2021 –

Kayleigh   – I'm really good; I'm lucky.

Another audition –

Kayleigh   – like –

March 2021 –

Kayleigh   – other people had it much –

Another audition –

Kayleigh   I am Astrid, Queen of the Metatraxi –

March 2021 –

Kayleigh (*remembering something*)   – Yes!

Virus (*taken aback*)   What?!

Kayleigh   – That's the other thing about this whole thing as well –

Another audition –

Kayleigh   My name is Kayleigh Brennan, and I would like to give my music component –

Song: 'The Ballad of Corona V'

*The **Virus** defiantly presses the remote – the footage jumps again. As it does so, an underscore begins – 'The Ballad of Corona V.' The **Virus** makes the footage jump again. (It's still not right, but he gives up, moving to his box of props and searching through it, preparing himself.)*

At this point, some of the above footage is dipped into again, ultra-elliptically, with key phrases echoing in time with the music – 'running down my – whole messed up – Girl – bruv, dunno what's real' sort of thing.

Then the **Virus** *starts to sing/rap. Whilst he does so, footage jumps to – montage of* **Kayleigh** *out jogging, on different occasions. She has her headphones in.*

Virus

    You thought that it was done but I'm back again. . . .
    Made the furloughed fella get the sack again . . .
    I'm bugging out like the software's hacked again.
    So watch your back before the next wave attacks again.

    The song sung yet?
    Nah, it's pending.
    It's like a ballad but it doesn't have a ending.
    We ain't done yet.
    It's embedded, man.
    It ain't over 'til the fat lady's said Man –

In one of the jogging scenarios, an indistinct male voice behind **Kayleigh**.

Kayleigh   Can you go away please? . . .

Indistinct shouts.

Kayleigh   . . . Yeah, I've got a boyfriend?

Footage jumps – January 2021. **Kayleigh** *on a Zoom call with an NHS* **Therapist**.

Therapist   . . . and obviously it's been a really challenging year for everyone . . .

Kayleigh   Yeah.

Therapist   And so yeah; I'd just like to check in, really; see where you're at with things, and what you'd like to talk about.

Kayleigh   . . . Yeah.

The footage jumps forward a little –

Kayleigh   Like you say . . . 'New Year' . . . everyone wishing for a better one . . .

Therapist   Sure.

Kayleigh   . . . And Christmas obviously weren't exactly –

The footage jumps – a Zoom call in November 2020. A glum-looking **Kayleigh**, *along with other* **Relatives** *in separate chat boxes. Others trying to put on a brave face.*

Rochelle   – Christmas . . . it'll be a weird one, obviously . . .

Relative (*baby crying in the background*)   Of course it will.

Rochelle   . . . But, you know, we'll make the best of it, that's the only thing we can do, although I know, obviously I know. . . .we'll be without some special things – and it won't be the same, you know . . . without . . .

Kayleigh Without Mum.

Relative (*not hearing*)   What's that?

Kayleigh You can just say it. You can just say without Mum.

Footage jumps – **Kayleigh** *jogging in the dark.*

Virus

It's like a Ballad, but you can't stop the sound.
It's Corona V, heavy lies the crown.
'Cos what goes around comes back around
Baddest of the badness, I'm world renowned
The song sung yet? Nah it's pending.
Its like a ballad but it doesn't have an ending
We aint done yet. Still hear the sound? –

Footage jumps back to **Kayleigh** *and* **Lorna** *on the Zoom call in March 2020, now joined by* **Rochelle**. *There is a blank chat box marked '***Nan**.*'*

Kayleigh So what's it like at work then, Mum?

Virus Lorna?

Lorna (*considers*)   . . . Erm. What's it like at work. . . .

Rochelle Have you got enough masks?

Lorna . . . Well at the moment it's like the quiet before the storm, I suppose . . . I mean we've closed two wards, which are gonna be designated Covid wards and all that –

Footage jumps – **Kayleigh** *jogging.*

Virus

The song sung yet?
It's pending.
It's like a ballad but it don't have a ending.
The ting done yet?
Still hear the sound –

Mann

But you know you ain't the only badness up in town
True you ain't the only badness around

Footage jumps – June 2020. **Kayleigh** *is on a Zoom call with two friends.*

Fiona   – like 'Oh my God – it's not the only thing going on!' – but all you hear is 'Covid, Covid, Covid' – and then a whole lot of other bad stuff they can just sweep under the carpet, until *finally*, when the flipping like *news* cycle *starts* to get sick of it, then they switch it up to like 'Black Lives Matter', like was George Floyd the first Black man to get killed by police, but anyway –

Kayleigh And this is what you said to Boris, yeah?

Friend Boris?

Fiona   I shoulda done.

Friend   Hold on, what?

Kayleigh   Yeah, Fi met Boris, and basically ambushed him.

Fiona   Boris come to my work yeah; I was screwing. Like 'From you come down here, for your little photo op, you better know I'm gonna tell you how it's fully all a scamdemic mate, and you're just training us to be all mask-wearing sheeples like they done in China –'

Kayleigh   . . . And so as you're being ushered away –

Fiona   . . . as I'm being ushered away, I swear to God, he says to me (*Boris impression.*) 'In ten years time you'll probably be my, my special adviser, ha ha ha'.

Friend   Did he say that?

Fiona   I'm saying 'Jokes mate, in ten years time we're all dead; it's the great re-set –'

Footage jumps – **Kayleigh** *jogging.*

Mann

   20
   21 Vision we take the specs off, Zoom
   In on the disease and take the Hex off
   Thought you were viral? It's all bets off, so
   Don't get gassed with your little death cough

   Death's BEEN around and it will be after;
   Just hit the food bank and choose a starter
   You might have the shine, but you're shining darker and the
   Ballad that your singing just gained a partner. .

   . . . See I'm the type to expose the mad ting . . .
   You got the gossip and the media reacting
   To fake news, you don't even know what fact is;
   Nobody knows if it's real or –

To the **Virus**'s *annoyance, the music abruptly cuts out. Simultaneously, the footage jumps into another speed through split-seconds of different auditions and Zoom calls –*

Kayleigh (*an audition intro*)   – acting, has always been a passion of –

Kayleigh (*tearful, with other chat boxes full of other* **Relatives** *and a comatose* **Lorna**)   Mum?

Kayleigh (*March 2021*)   – don't get me wrong –

Kayleigh (*singing, an audition*)   'All I want for Chris –

Kayleigh (*an audition*)   Cross

Kayleigh (*Zoom call*)   Mum?

Kayleigh (*March 2021*)   – the whole 'Sarah' thing like don't get me wrong, I feel properly bad for the family?, and also the fact it was a fucking police man who –

Kayleigh (*an audition*)   Done it!

Fiona   'Covid, Covid, Covid' –

The footage jumps to March 2021.

Kayleigh   – But did it really take a pretty white girl for it to happen to, for it to get things moving like, And did it really take a globalised pandemic to like . . . done the news cycle for long enough so the media take notice? – That's if it is a pandemic. Which it is. Obviously. Is it? Basically I'm just tired. I guess. But it's all good. I'm good. Considering. . . . This whole messed up – I miss so many things! I miss . . . cocktails; oh my God, there's this place in – (*she grimaces*) – 'Shoreditch'; I admit, I'm a basic bitch – (*remembering something*) I was out for a run the other day you know and this guy – I kinda even missed that, like, bit of street harassment mate, walking home, grabbing up my keys; I miss so many things! . . . I miss my mum . . . 'cos I buried my mum three weeks ago . . . except I couldn't be there . . . She never got no 1 per cent pay rise . . . 'Clap for carers'. . . .

A beat.

Sorry. (*A beat.*) Oh. . . . Hello? Are you there?

Zoom Date   Hello?

Kayleigh   . . . Oh. . . . Hello?

Zoom Date   Sorry. . . Yeah, my wi-fi –

Kayleigh   Yeah. Yeah no worries. . . . 'Zoom dates.'

Zoom Date   What's happened to my camera, man –

Kayleigh (*limply*)   I was just saying about, erm . . .

Cocktails –

The footage jumps back into March 2020 Zoom call – **Kayleigh**, **Rochelle**, **Lorna** *and the* '*NAN*' *chat box.* **Kayleigh** *is walking down a street.*

Rochelle (*to* **Lorna**)   Have you got enough PPE?

Kayleigh (*to* **Lorna**)   Mum?

Lorna   Oh, I can hear you now.

Kayleigh   What's PPE?

Rochelle   They're saying you ain't got enough masks?

Lorna   . . . Er, I'm not entirely sure to be honest with you . . . I mean having said that, I was looking for one the other day, a mask, and the thing, like the cupboard they're usually kept in it was yeah, completely empty . . . so yeah . . .

Kayleigh   What's happened to Nan, anyway?

Rochelle   I know, where's Suse? Does she know how to work this thing?

Lorna   Well there's someone in the home, one of the carers, who helps her do it, that nice one, Rahila?

Rochelle   Oh yeah?

Lorna   . . . but maybe she's not around –

*The **Virus** speaks to them, but Nan's chat window remains blank. **Virus** continues to speak in his usual accent.*

Virus (*having donned an old woman's bonnet*)   Hello?

Lorna   . . . Oh!

Kayleigh   Nan?

Rochelle   Alright, Suse?

Virus   Can you all hear me OK?

Rochelle   We can hear you but we can't see you!

Lorna   Turn your camera on, Mum.

Virus (*winking at the audience*)   My what?

Kayleigh   You have to click the camera thing.

Virus   . . . I'm afraid I have no idea what you all are talking about.

Lorna   Is that Rahila there?

Virus   It's just me.

Rochelle   Oh well.

Kayleigh   We'll have to talk to you but not see you, Nan.

Virus   I guess we will.

Lorna   Are you OK?

Virus   Me?

Lorna   . . . Your voice sounds a bit funny

Kayleigh (*smiling*)   Yeah bit deeper like . . .

Lorna   Mum?

Virus   My voice?

Lorna   Yeah.

Virus   . . . Well, all the better for conversating with you all about how well I'm doing, how the sun is in the sky, and how sociable I'm feeling!

Rochelle   Yes, Suse, that's what I'm talking about.

Lorna   Are you sure you're OK?

Virus   I surely am, honey. I just wish that I could see my daughter in the flesh, and for you all to come and visit with me.

Lorna   . . . Oh, I know. . . .

Rochelle   We all do.

Virus   I surely hope for that.

Lorna   It's tricky, Mum –

Kayleigh   I could come and see you, Nan.

Virus   Yes!

Lorna (*warning*)   Kayleigh!

Kayleigh   Just put on a mask on, and –

Virus   You wouldn't need to wear a mask would you?

Rochelle   It's a tough one, Suse.

Lorna   It's risky at the moment, Mum –

Virus   Surely one little visit with one or all of you would just help spread some love around – and you can spread love even asymptomatically you know –

Lorna   But, Mum, think about it –

Kayleigh   Anyway, listen I gotta go, I'm at the supermarket now

Lorna   You're what?

Kayleigh   Later man, look at this queue.

Virus   Can you all hear me?

Rochelle   You stay safe, Kayleigh.

Kayleigh   Alright; I love yous, yeah? I love you!

Lorna   Kay –

The **Virus** *suddenly disappears, as do* **Lorna** *and* **Rochelle** *on the screen –* **Kayleigh** *enters the space – 'live' – holding her phone in front of her.*

Kayleigh (*looking at audience*)   Rah, why there so much people in here man, look at these dudes all buying up their toilet rolls –

Suddenly, the **Mannequin** *turns and talks to her.*

Mann   Welcome to Asda.

Kayleigh   Shit!

Mann   You good?

Kayleigh   . . . Yeah.

Mann   That's great. Look a bit jumpy though.

Kayleigh   Yeah well . . . not too good with crowds. Bit panicky as well, like with the virus?

Mann   I am the virus.

Kayleigh (*stepping back*)   OK.

Mann   Not Corona though.

Kayleigh   OK.

Mann   I'm worse than that. I'm the virus of capitalism.

She stares at him.

Kayleigh   . . . The virus of . . . ?

Mann   When you check it, it's deep.

Kayleigh   OK.

Mann   I am the group-think.

The craze.

Set the trend that others follow.

Kayleigh (*starting to understand*)   OK.

Mann   Whisper in the ear, now they're all happy-slapping. Or ice bucketing. Or rumour munching.
Whisper it – 'They're gonna close the shops.'
'They're turning on the 5G' –

Kayleigh   5G! – Is that a true story?

Mann   It's true that it is a story.

Kayleigh   . . . Right.

Mann   Let's pray.
Dear Drake, who art in Toronto.
And dear Murdoch. And Putin.
In this time of no God, it falls to popular culture to provide our moral sustenance.
It falls to comfort food to provide comfort.

Kayleigh   . . . Deep –

Mann   Things with no value have become most valuable; The hunt for commodity a co-morbidity.

And when the world's going down . . . the planet buys.

Kayleigh (*looking around her*)   . . . Panic buys . . .

Mann   These people have been panic-buying since they first gained the power to consume.

I just put a foot on the gas. . . .

And led the dance.

Kayleigh   The dance?

Mann   The panic-buy dance. The new talk taking over.

Kayleigh   Yeah?

Song: Panic Buy Dance

*The **Mannequin** launches into a song/dance routine –*

Mann   It's the Panic Buy Dance *X4*

Everybody buss a Panic Buy dance.
Could be furloughed, could be freelance
Could be road, could be middle-class
Don't stand still, stand up inna prance
And nobody's gonna get a free pass
Don't stand still, stand up inna trance
Everybody buss a Panic-Buy Dance

2020-bring-a-new-way-to-die
But keep follow that impulse to buy,
We're all vexed with the system, a' lie?
But true-say we *are* the system, now fly

2020 just buss a new year – eh
Everybody got their plans in gear – eh
Competition, that's real out here – eh
Foot-forward, face no fear – eh
'Cos you gotta get yours while you're able
You know you gotta put the food on a table
You gotta keep tings strong keep stable
Best-before-use-by-check-label.

You gotta get that shopping in a bag
Five-a-day-all-fruits-ripe, that's swag
Funds for shopping all good, that's a bly
You coulda been at the food bank, a' lie?

Everybody buss a Panic Buy Dance.
Could be furloughed, could be freelance
Could be road, could be middle-class
Don't stand still, stand up inna prance
And nobody's gonna get a free pass
Don't stand still, stand up inna trance
Everybody buss a Panic-Buy Dance

Virus

> True you never quite know wha' go happen
> Life don't really follow one pattern
> 2020 you was gonna get rich but
> 2020 lef' all your plan them flatten

Kayleigh

> Get your protein shake 'ca your dench – true
> Get your toothbrush-paste for your dental
> Get your sanitary product for your menstrual
> Cycle, don't take the bus, are you mental?

Mann

> Boris sayin' face cover not essential
> No wait there – it's essential
> No wait there – nah it's not essential
> No wait there – it's essential
>
> Everybody buss a Panic Buy Dance.
> Could be furloughed, could be freelance
> Could be road, could be middle-class
> Don't stand still, stand up inna prance
> And nobody's gonna get a free pass
> Don't stand still, stand up inna trance
> Everybody buss a Panic-Buy Dance

Scene Three

April 2020.

A street corner. Rows of houses and shops; the shops all closed. Among them is an electrical/TV shop; a TV inside is showing a news channel, without audio.

Windows and pavement are decorated with rainbows, etc.

Drey – *A young man, dressed in a postman's uniform, complete with postal bag. He is taking a break.*

As the audience file in, he answers a call on a hands-free phone.

Drey (*speaking on call*)   . . . Yeah?
. . . Oi relax yeah, from I said I'm gonna be there, I'll be there.
. . . Course man, weed, anything, say nuttin.

He is distracted by another call. He looks at the number. **Drey** *seems to hesitate around this new call, unsure whether he wants to take it or not.*

. . . Oi listen. . . . Oi shut the fuck up anyway I'll come.

(*New call.*) . . . Yeah what you saying, what's happening?
. . . Ah?
What's happening with *me*? . . . Fucking nothing like, just busy . . . ain't never *been* this busy like, I dunno what they really chattin 'bout globalised pandemical-whatever like, I'm shottin' in broad daylight, making *money*.

(*Laughs to himself*) 'Cos I'm dressed like a postman fam!
. . . Why you care where I get the clothes? . . .
. . . Yeah whatever like, cats gonna always need their drugs like, don't watch no virus. . . .

Drey *stops moving.*

. . . What?
. . . The funeral?
. . . Yeah 'cos I never talked to *no-one* at the funeral, what you talking about?
. . . 'Cos I didn't feel to. Like he's dead yeah, that's done.
. . . Yeah, it's done.
. . . 'Feel suttin?' –

Suddenly, on the TV screen, the **Virus**, *complete with cowboy hat, cuts into the broadcast – with sound –*

Virus   Stefan Prince?

Drey (*on phone*)   What you mean 'feel suttin' –

Virus   Partner?

Drey (*to TV screen, in disbelief*)   What? Nah . . . (*On phone.*) What?

Virus   Are you Stefan Prince?

Drey (*to TV*)   Nah man – is this for real? – (*To phone.*) Not you –

Virus   God darn it –

The TV screen cuts into static, then cuts dead.

Drey (*staring at the TV screen, still on phone*)   . . . Yeah you know what – . . .

Un-noticed by **Drey**, **Arabella** *has entered. She is a wealthy local resident. She carries something in a gift bag.*

. . . (*Back on phone.*) Oi what you talking about 'feel suttin' anyway like, I feel to fucking just – Fuck it, I gotta go.

As he ends the call –

Arabella   I am so sorry! –

Drey (*taken by surprise*)   – Shit –

Arabella – Because I know you must be so busy –

Drey What?

Arabella – Because I know everyone's sort of – I know *we're* just ordering absolutely *everything* online and – I mean they said on the news it's like *Christmas!* –

Drey Yeah?

Arabella – I mean it's like *Christmas*, they said, the level of, of *demand* I mean not just in terms of the Royal Mail but –
We try not to use Amazon.

Drey Nah.

Arabella . . . We use it very rarely. I mean we've used it once or twice, we've – I'm going to cancel Prime.

Drey Real.

Arabella I'm going to cancel it. Because it's not fair, it's just not fair, is it, that level of, of *pressure* on, on *workers*, and – I mean let's face it do I really need another lamp-shade or exercise bike or – That reminds me –

Drey . . . Yeah?

Arabella (*to herself*) . . . Incense. Incense, I was just going to order a – Well actually I'm not gonna – (*Back to him.*) Because it's all just *stuff* isn't it, d'you know what I mean, it's just *things* and *stuff* and, and: –

Anyway! (*She brandishes the bag.*) . . . We've been a bit worried. About Errol.

I mean we haven't seen him now for what, for two weeks!? You know? I mean since this whole awful thing started up, and – Of course he's been doing this this, this what-do-you-call-it, What do postmans . . . post-people call their . . . 'walk'? . . .

Drey . . . Yeah –

Arabella . . . Their 'round?'. . . .

Drey Yeah we just basically – I dunno you know.

Arabella I mean Errol's been the postman here for *years!*

Drey OK.

Arabella I mean longer than *we've* been here!

Drey Big man out here, yeah?

Arabella Every day he says to me 'Morning, darling' he says. 'Keep smiling, it costs nothing' he says, in his funny . . . accent, And obviously with the virus we did worry . . . (*She hesitates.*) . . . Because I know it does seem to be affecting . . . disproportionately . . . I mean people like yourself. . . . .

Drey . . . Postmen, yeah?

Arabella . . . No! I don't know! Is it? No I mean BME . . . the BME . . . the BAME, er, community –

Drey . . . OK –

Arabella But, I – Presumably he's a colleague of yours –

Drey Yeah –

Arabella – and if you *were* able to get this –

Drey You see –

Arabella – It's just a little something, for him –

Drey Yeah Errol –

Arabella – because we just love love love love love him –

Drey Errol got sick.

Arabella *staring at him.*

Arabella . . . Oh my *God!* –

Drey Yeah not Corona though!

Arabella No?

Drey Nah.

Arabella Oh thank goodness for / that

Drey Yeah, just a minor . . .

Arabella Oh thank God.

Drey . . . Or maybe . . . like I think he's on his like holiday you know.

Arabella . . . Oh right?

Drey Yeah. That's it. My man just . . . took a minute like –

Arabella He's gone on holiday in the er . . . ?

Drey Yeah.

Arabella In the er . . . ?

Drey In the . . . aeroplane.

Arabella In the lockdown?

Drey . . . Nah. Nah not . . . 'on' on holiday like, just . . .

Arabella He's on leave?

Drey Yeah leave.

Arabella Oh I see!

Drey Yeah, leave. . . . Yeah he's on that, still, so –

Arabella   Oh lovely Errol.

Drey (*moving towards the gift*)   – What I'm gonna do . . . Let me take this now, take it back to like . . . base, the Postman base, and then. . . .

Arabella   Would you?

Drey   Let me make sure I get that to him, when he reach back from. . . .

Arabella   His leave.

Drey   Yeah.

Arabella (*staring at him*)   . . . Thank you so much.

Drey (*to himself*)   Yeah whatever like, fuckin eediot.

Arabella (*still staring at him*)   Thank you, gorgeous man. (*Getting her phone out.*) Perhaps . . . Do you think we should take a selfie together –

Drey   What?

Arabella   – with the present, just to help show my daughter –

Drey (*suddenly stern*)   Oi what I ain't taking no photo like what's wrong with you?

Arabella   – No – Sorry.

Sorry.

Drey *softens a little.*

Drey   . . . I ain't taking no photo. . . .

A pause.

Arabella   . . . I didn't catch your name.

Drey *staring at her, hesitates.*

Drey   . . . Nah. . . . Nah. . . . Drey, man.

Arabella   . . . Drey-man.

Drey   Nah. . . . Drey.

Arabella   . . . Arabella.

She offers her hand to shake, then stops, then does an awkward sort 'bow' of introduction. **Drey** *nods.*

Drey   . . . OK.

Arabella (*having noticed something*)   . . . Oh . . . I don't know if you've . . . My daughter and I, we did a little. . .

He looks at her, blankly.

. . . Just a little: . . .

Drey   . . . Ah?

On the pavement, alongside all the rainbows and 'Thank you NHS's, she indicates a quite elaborate chalked decoration, in honour of the Royal Mail – 'Thank you.'

Arabella   . . . The postman there.

Drey   OK.

Arabella   We just wanted to say, you know. I mean it probably seems so silly to you!

Drey   Nah, that's –

Arabella   I mean because it's, everyone loves the NHS, *we* love the NHS, but what about *you!*, you know, and the dustmen, and the, there's a milkman who comes round, and the delivery workers –

Drey   Yeah.

Arabella   I mean I'm just in advertising – for my sins! – which is just – I mean everything about me is just ridiculous, but *you!* . . . You're a key worker!

Drey   You know that.

Arabella   On the frontline!

Drey   Yeah it's real out here.

Arabella (*indicating the drawings*)   I mean you probably think it's so silly! Don't you!

A beat.

. . . I mean you probably just think, do you ever just think . . . FUCK these CUNTS, with their fucking . . . RAINBOWS, oh GOD. . . .

Arabella *puts her head in her hands.* **Drey** *stares at her. A pause.* **Drey** *looks around. Turns back to* **Arabella***. He hesitates.*

Drey   . . . Yeah . . . Yeah. . . .

Drey*'s ringtone goes off again – he cancels the call. A pause.*

Arabella   . . . I'm sorry.

Drey   . . . Yeah. . . .

Arabella   . . . I, erm . . . (*Clears her throat.*)

My husband sort of erm, lost his job this morning. I mean he's freelance, but he . . . .all of his contracts just . . .

We were so *close*, to paying off the *mortgage!* I mean 'first world fucking problems' but . . . I mean we're fine. But it just sort of . . . it just sort of brought things home, a little bit, yeah it sort of . . . it brought things home.

. . . And it's all so frightening! Isn't it? Is it frightening?

Drey   . . . Boy . . .

Arabella   A friend of ours . . . Luca . . .

Drey (*half-recognising the name*)   . . . Luca? –

Arabella   . . . He had to self-isolate, because he'd come back from – (*bit embarrassed*) of course, a skiing holiday – cringe! – in the north of Italy somewhere and. . . . He's so funny, he's got a very dry sense of humour, he said. . . . 'We've all got blood on our hands.'

He said 'The international middle class . . . with our insatiable appetite for travel, and for goods and for useless commodities we've spread this virus around the world', and I . . .

I refute that, actually.

I mean the level of . . . of self-hatred within that sentiment is actually . . .

Drey *hesitates. Then he seems to want to ask* **Arabella** *something.*

Drey   . . . Yeah: –

Arabella   But it just feels so important, doesn't it, to feel . . .

Drey   . . . 'Feel suttin' . . .

Arabella   . . . at a time like this, to feel connected . . . to one another. . . .

Drey   . . . Yeah –

Arabella   Is there anything I can do? For you? As a . . .

Drey   What?

Arabella   I mean I don't know. Anything. I mean. . . .

Arabella *notices another child's drawing, on a wall. She smiles, a little embarrassed again.*

. . . Oh . . .

She eyes him.

(*indicating the drawing*) . . . I don't know if you. . . . My daughter again, we just wanted to . . .

Drey (*looking the wrong way*)   . . . Yeah?

She shows him the drawing she means – a little doodle surrounding a 'Black Lives Matter' hashtag.

Arabella   I just think it's so important. You know? Because. . . . Well . . . 'Black lives matter.' I mean it's as simple as that. They matter. And we should say it. We just need to say it.
. . . Don't you think?

Drey *hesitates.*

Drey   . . . Yeah. . . Better know I'm living *my* life out here. . . .

Arabella (*not quite hearing/understanding*)   . . .Yes!

Drey   . . . But . . . crackheads on my phone like I swear . . . take their Black lives and fucking bounce bruv. Jarrin.

. . . That's what I feel.

Arabella *hesitates.*

Arabella   . . . Sorry?

Drey *looks at her. He hesitates, then says the thing he's been wanting to say –*

Drey   . . . Nah. . . . You was sent to me though innit.

Arabella   . . . What?

Drey   You was sent to me. (*Smiles, looks at the sky.*) . . . Fucking . . . messed up suttin playing games with me like. . . .

(*to her*) 'The Vision', yeah?

Arabella   The vision?

Drey   It's a what's-it like, a book, like you know that piece there?

Arabella   The Vision!

Drey   Yeah?

Arabella   No.

Drey   It's a book about the . . . about the self.

Arabella   Mm! Mm-mm.

Drey (*he is embarrassed*)   Fuck it. You gonna meet someone. It says, yeah?

Arabella   Right.

Drey   . . . It says you're gonna meet someone, and they're gonna show the truth to you – not 'the' truth – like 'a' truth – *their* truth.

Arabella   . . . OK.

Drey   . . . And through that truth, you're gonna feel your own truth, which is *the* truth. To you.

Arabella   . . . Right.

Drey (*embarrassed*)   . . . Nah . . . Fuck it.

Arabella   No! –

Drey (*with sudden anger*)   Fuck it. Fuck it anyway.

A pause. She hesitates. He seems to soften again.

Drey   ... Everyone's a ... a messenger.

Arabella   ... Right!

Drey   Even though you don't know it, we're *all* the messenger, with our own truth, like to feel.

Arabella   Oh my God yes of course, and of course you're a *postman!* –

Drey   What? Yeah.

Arabella   Yes, oh my God –

Drey   Fuck that anyway like – Who cares? Fucking ... 'feel' –

Arabella (*not listening*)   ... OK –

Drey (*not listening*)   Man ain't got time to feel out here, you get me?

Arabella   This is going to be very raw –

Drey   What is?

Arabella   We're working on something for Skype. OK? Because they've become a bit ... Well they've had the carpet whipped from under them by Zoom and, so the brand has become a bit toxic overall, but, so anyway –

Here's the pitch. ...

A pathway. Snaking, through a sunlit ... woodland.

We creep along. ... Through the leaves. ... The birds singing, and the ... nature ... things.

We find ... a Postman.

A BAME Postman. Possibly.

He's carrying his bag ... full of letters and parcels, and ... as he walks along the wooded path. ...

Voiceover –

'... oh ... something-something, bla bla bla ...: In times like these, we all need to stay connected.'

The postman smiles.

... We pan out ... and above...

... to reveal that he is walking through a woodland which itself, from above, seems to form the shape of a face ... a Black face – possibly – ... And the face ... Smiles.

 'Skype. Hashtag – make connections. Hashtag – BLM.

 Hashtag –

 You are the messenger.'

A pause.

... I know it's fucking shit, but I mean it's pretty fucking good! Isn't it?

... Do you think?

Drey   ... You done this, yeah?

Arabella   ... What? Oh ...

She realises he is looking again at the 'BLM' drawing.

... Yes. Yeah – Well I mean my daughter –

Drey   Yeah.

It's kinda good you know.

Arabella   ... Yes! –

Drey   It's a little bit shit though.

Arabella   ... It's? ...

Drey   I don't wanna be like disrespectful –

Arabella   No –

Drey   ... Edges are kinda messy like –

Arabella   I know –

Drey   Smudged.

Arabella   Sorry.

Drey (*half-laughs*)   You sorry?

Arabella   ... I don't know.

Drey   ... Fuck's sake, I swear I've met you before –

Arabella   I know, I feel like that, I feel a very deep ...

Drey   Nah ...

Arabella   ... connection –

Drey   You're lying to me though innit.

You ain't giving me the truth.

Arabella   ... I don't know what / you mean –

Drey   Oi. ... Advertiser, yeah? Arabella.

Arabella   ... Yes –

Drey   Arabella the seller. ...

Arabella (*laughing politely*)   Yes –

Drey   Let me pitch *my* ting now yeah?

Arabella   ... OK –

Drey   You see that park?

You go to that park innit. Most probably you take your kid to that park, it's a very . . . 'it's a very pleasant park', as one might say, You might say it's a 'nice . . . spot, to take one's doggy for a walk', but also as well . . . interestingly, my brother got stabbed in that park. Yeah. Yeah basically –

Arabella   Oh God –

Drey   – that's what happened to him, inside that park, And don't get it twisted like, 'cos me personally, I'm saying 'Fuck the police' all day long, but also as well; we got Black people are killing Black people out here. Yeah? But I don't really see no advert for . . . for 'make that shit right', hashtag, whatever. And anyway like, from some ute try come for me and me and mines – I'm gonna be the next one killing it!

Arabella (*softly*)   No . . .

Drey   And furthermore . . . that's a problem yeah and also . . . shit don't matter! Yeah? What matters is money! What matters is me for me, and fucking . . . So how do you like that kinda hashtag, yeah? (*laughs*) 'Shit don't matter.' You making that what . . . connection?

Arabella   Drey –

Drey   Stop chat to me –

Arabella   Why?

Drey   'Cos I don't wanna hear it. Yeah? I don't care.

Arabella   I think you do care, Drey.

Drey   No fuck what you think, (*half-laughs*) you think I'm a postman like –

Arabella   When I . . . I don't know about you but –

Drey   No you don't know about me –

Arabella   . . . Luca was saying –

Drey   Luca, where do I know this fucking name –

Arabella   But anyway, with all this going on I mean you *should* care!

Drey   What, BLM yeah? Why?

Arabella   Because we all care about it now! I mean not just 'now' –

Drey   No-one don't care –

Arabella   Everyone cares, I mean it's a hashtag! I mean, not because it's a hashtag but because. . . . Everyone cares because it's a hashtag, and – it's a hashtag because everyone cares!

Drey (*touching the drawing*)   What they care, and they can't even get the shading right –

Arabella   But that's just a drawing –

Drey   Yeah.

Yeah that's what it is.

It's just a drawing, bruv.

A beat. He prepares to leave.

. . . (*to himself*) Fuck am I doing out here –

Arabella   I just feel so . . . impotent –

Drey   It's done.

Arabella   Let me help you.

Drey   What?

Arabella   I could – I don't know, at a time like this – with your deliveries! –

Drey (*preparing to leave*)   – the fuck away from me man, I'm gone. Postman, yeah? Do my ting.

Arabella   You're not just a postman, Drey.

Drey   Yeah, real –

Arabella   You're a prince.

Drey   I ain't a postman.

Arabella   You're a poet.

Drey   I ain't a postman bruv.

Arabella   I remember something Luca said –

Drey (*remembering the name*)   Luca!

He lives in them flats, the warehouse flats.

She is staring at him.

Has parties. My guy. Yeah. Big parties.

Arabella   . . . Yes –

Drey   That's where we met. That's where I seen you.

Arabella   . . . What do you –

Drey (*laughs*)   Yeah; yeah it's not no. . . 'connection.'

I'm not no postman, I'm a drug dealer.

Arabella   . . . You're not a drug dealer, Drey, you're a Prince! –

Drey   Yeah literally I – (*Stops, checking himself.*) . . . I got a bag full a' drugs like, that's how I know you.

Arabella   . . . Yes.

A beat.

Drey   So what, you wanna buy?

Arabella   . . . No!

Drey   What, you said you wanna help me yeah?

Arabella   Yes! No! . . .

I mean we said we'd. . . . We said we'd be very strict, with that sort of thing . . . I mean during the lockdown . . .

Drey   I'm gone yeah –

Arabella   I'm sorry!

Drey   Why you sorry?

Arabella   . . . I don't know.

Drey   What don't you know?

Arabella   . . . Tell me about your brother.

Please.

He stares at her.

Drey   My brother? . . .

He was a dickhead man, I swear –

Arabella   Dickheads . . . matter.

I should know.

A pause.

Drey   He was kinda . . . kinda smudged. Yeah? That's how he was. That's how he moved. Kinda blurry.

. . . I said to him you know . . . 'Can't really move like that, you gotta be *one* thing. . . .'

You gotta be one thing.

Drey*'s phone rings – he answers.*

(*on phone*) Yeah?

Yeah alright. Yeah five minutes.

He hangs up. Prepares to go.

Arabella   I'm going to re-think the pitch.

Thank you, for this conversation, Drey.

. . . I'm going to make it much better, make . . . Make things better.

I just need . . . to take some time.

Drey (*flatly*)   . . . Ain't got no time.

Scene Four

We appear to be in a plush meeting room at the House of Commons – a view through the window of the river. A TV screen is silently jumping from news clips circa April 2020 to bits of the Panic Buy Dance, and other excerpts from previous video bits.

Amongst the audience sits **Errol**, *the postman talked about in the last scene. He is in his uniform, and on a drip, somewhat out-of-it.*

A **Deputy Stage Manager** *sits with a script, wearing a medical uniform.*

A pair of transparent doors separates the room from a corridor. In one corner, a female patient lies in a hospital bed. There is a tense and fearful atmosphere. As the audience enter, a **Doctor** *and* **Nurse** *are busy around the patient.*

Noises and beeps of the medical equipment throughout the scene.

Doctor   OK, blood pressure now?

Nurse   She's . . . 68 systolic.

Doctor (*under her breath*)   Fucking hell. OK. Can you get me the most recent ARG?

Nurse (*searching*)   Yes . . . I put it –

Doctor   So PO2 was still six, twenty minutes ago . . .

Nurse (*with paper*)   This was 16.02.

Doctor   . . . And the shadowing on the X-Rays . . . yeah it was quite pronounced. OK, I think we're talking bilateral consolidation and I think she's still in septic shock.

Nurse   SATS are . . . 80 per cent, heart rate is 106.

Doctor   We may need an arterial line.

Nurse   OK.

Doctor   And let's give her a litre of Hartmans over an hour, and let's also say . . . 12mg of Norad over an hour.

Nurse   Right.

Meanwhile, at **Nurse**'*s line* '*Sats are . . .*' *the bathroom door opens, and* **Boris Johnson** *enters. He wears his usual suit, but looks a bit dishevelled and disorientated. As the nurse and doctor talk, he dodders into the room.*

Boris   . . . Right. Good. Right . . .

He watches the medical team working.

. . . Splendid. Excellent, ah, Teamwork! Team . . .

He is approaching the audience.

. . . Team GB . . . (*to audience members*) Hello, Boris Johnson . . .

He begins to procrastinate around hand-shaking etiquette.

. . . I won't shake your– . . . I, I, Well I feel a *compulsion*, to ah, to shake everyone's – In fact I *will* shake – I won't shake anyone's ah. . . .anyone's hand, but ah –

Fiona, *a senior political advisor suddenly enters and approaches* **Boris**. *She carries a red ministerial despatch box, and a McDonald's bag.*

Fiona   Good morning, Prime Minister.

Boris   Good morning. Prime Minister. (*Correcting himself.*) I mean – Yes. What?

Fiona   How are you today?

Boris   Ah, Hugely! Hugely **revived**, thank you for asking, Miss? –

Fiona   Egg McMuffin.

Boris   – Miss Egg McMuffin. What? I mean Yes. Thank you, I've, I've I've always said the ah, the McMuffin is the corner stone of –

Seema *has appeared on screen. She is high, and in a state of agitation. She is the female patient's daughter. She bangs on the doors.*

Seema   Oi FUCKS!

Boris   – of any nutritious, ah –

Seema   You ain't, gonna do this, yeah; I swear you ain't gonna pull the wool, over my third-fucking-eye!

Nurse (*shouting to* **Seema**)   Excuse me? –

Boris   – Breakfast!

Seema *goes, slamming the doors as she does so.*

Seema (*exiting*)   FUCK!

Fiona (*having produced papers from the despatch box*)   Are you ready for a briefing?

Boris   Yes! Excellent, yes, please – brief away!

Fiona   The weekend's ONS data is just in, and the good news is that National Compliance levels remain at 60 per cent.

Boris   Excellent – (*with egg McMuffin*) – This is very good –

Fiona   There has been, however, some low level disturbance centred mostly on the West Midlands.

The **Nurse** *appears on screen.*

Nurse (*on screen*)   Mr Johnson?

Boris   What kind of disturbance?

Nurse (*on screen*)   Mr Johnson?

Fiona   An activist affiliated with the 'New Reclaim' party staged an attack on a vaccine lab in Nuneaton.

Boris   I see.

Fiona   There was also an incident at Walthamstow; a trio of sisters of the order of the Blessed Virgin Mary of Mount Carmel set fire to a pile of face coverings, shouting – (*reading*) 'Fuck this endless shit for a game of soldiers, we'd rather be dead than living two metres apart; Joe Wicks is a Heathenite.'

Boris   I see.

Nurse (*on screen*)   Mr Johnson can you hear me?

Fiona   The MOD are advising postponement of the joint Brexit-Covid tenth anniversary celebrations, and suggesting we leak rumours of a twenty-sixth national lockdown.

Boris   I see. What do I normally do in these situations –

Fiona   Order a non-opt-out booster vaccination to sedate the population.

Boris   Excellent.

Fiona (*producing a syringe*)   Speaking of which – time for your next shot.

Boris   For my? –

Fiona   Bend over please, Prime Minister.

Boris (*doing so*)   Right you are.

Fiona   Mr Gates was hoping to administer the dose in person, but found himself otherwise detained. (*Producing her phone.*) He did ask for a selfie though –

Boris   Mr ah – Gates? –

Fiona *takes a photo of* **Boris** *as she injects him. At the same instant, the* **Doctor** *with* **Nurse** *appear on screen –*

Nurse (*on screen*)   His hand moved at the sound of my voice earlier on –

Doctor (*on screen*)   Even on the vents they can hear, sometimes.

Boris   Listen –

Doctor (*on screen*)   We can probably up the Norad a touch, and change the bags.

Nurse (*on screen*)   Yes.

Boris   – What I'd like to do is prepare a press conference, with, with Paddy Vallance, and ah . . . name of the chap who doesn't blink? –

On the TV screen, Chris Whitty pops up, mid-government information advert –

That's him!

Boris   Another press conference, that's what we need; a Churchillian, booster-jab of, of raised morale, putting the word out to everybody that if everybody simply follows the rules – of Hands, Face . . . Ace of Base, then we'll all be out of this in time to, to protect the NHS, and save Pancake Day.

Doctor   Mr Johnson?

Boris (*suddenly becoming aware of the* **Doctor**)   Yes – (*To* **Doctor**, *as if inviting a press question.*) The lady here from ITN –

Doctor   How are you feeling?

Boris   Ah, Hugely! Hugely revived –

Doctor   Good.

Boris   – thank you for asking, Doctor –

DSM   Sarm.

Boris   Sarm. Thank you. (*Double-taking at* **DSM**.) What?

Doctor   When you arrived with us, Mr Johnson, you were very seriously ill.

Fiona   Mr Johnson –

Boris   Right. Yes. Crikey.

Doctor   And, if I can be frank with you, you still are.

Boris   I see.

Fiona (*to* **Doctor**)   If I can borrow the Prime Minister very briefly –

Doctor (*ignoring her*)   Your lungs, are working now to about 40 per cent of their usual capacity –

Boris   OK –

Doctor   Yesterday we administered broad-spectrum antibiotics –

Boris   Right.

Doctor   – We're also being alert for any signs of inflammation in your lungs, which would be a very serious outcome.

Boris   OK.

Doctor   We're also –

Boris   To be quite honest –

Doctor   Yes?

Fiona   Mr Johnson?

Boris   . . . I'm not too keen on the idea of ah –

Doctor   . . . on? –

Boris   the idea of ah –

Doctor   The idea? –

Fiona   Prime Minister?

Boris Of dying. I rather feel like I'm . . .

Nurse (*with the female ventilated patient*) Doctor Sarm?

Boris Especially having so recently . . . 'nabbed the top job', so to speak –

Seema *is back at the doors.*

Seema Mum!

Boris Not to mention my girlfriend – my fiance! – cripes! – is ah –

Nurse Doctor Sarm I think we need you here.

Boris Well she's ah . . . She's a little bit ah –

Seema Oi FUCKS!

Nurse (*to* **Seema**) Keep back.

Doctor She's? –

Boris Pregnant. So I mean with all that in mind –

Fiona Prime Minister, are you with us?

Doctor (*on screen*) Mr Johnson, can you hear me?

Fiona Another egg McMuffin?

Boris I ah –

Doctor Mr Johnson –

Boris (*to* **Doctor**) McMuffin.

Seema (*storming in*) Listen yeah –

Nurse (*to* **Seema**) Excuse me –

Seema Excuse you fucking what, mate, let me come through!

Nurse This is an active Covid ward, you need to understand the protocols we have in place!

Seema Oh my God, that's what I'm fucking say though bruv – That's what I'm saying that you put my *mum*, on a active Covid ward, you dickheads; you snakes in the fucking grass!

On screen, the **Virus** *suddenly appears.*

Virus Good evening –

Boris (*as if inviting a question again*) Ah – yes, Hugh Pym from the BBC –

Virus (*on screen*) May I ask could Stefan Prince please contact the nursing station?

Seema Listen! –

Doctor Madam, I'm going to ask you to please calm down –

Seema   I'm gonna show you fucking calm! – (*Exits*.)

Virus (*on screen*)   Could Stefan Prince –

Doctor (*dismissively, to* **Virus**)   There's nobody here of that name.

Fiona   Prime Minister?

There is a change in the light, and the deep, rumbling sounds of a ventilator. **Boris** *becomes further disorientated.*

Boris   ....Something about all this doesn't seem quite –

Fiona   Yes?

Boris   You look familiar.

Fiona   Of course. I'm your senior political advisor.

Boris   I've met you before . . .

Fiona   We met at my former workplace, on the 15 of June 2020. You told me –

Suddenly, on screen, another **Boris** *(played by a different actor), in the midst of a media scrum –*

Boris (*on screen, talking to* **Fiona**, *who is out of shot*)   In ten years time . . . you'll probably be my, my special advisor! –

Fiona   Now ten years have past, and here we are.

Boris   Here we are! (*unsure*) Are we?

Nurse   Mr Johnson?

Boris   What?

Nurse (*stern*)   I have something I'd like to say to you . . . (*looks around*) . . . in confidence.

Boris (*nervous*)   Ah –

Nurse   I would like to say thank you.

Boris (*encouraged*)   Ah.

Nurse (*with packet of cigarettes*)   You smoke?

Boris   . . . Do . . . ? –

Boris *looks sheepishly at the audience . . .*

Well I'm not entirely sure we're supposed to ah –

. . . Well . . . Well yes, in fact I will have a – I don't see why a few pesky rules and –

Nurse   Please.

Boris   – restrictions should put the stoppers on a cheeky cigarette –

Nurse Thank you, Mr Johnson.

Boris (*with cigarette*)   Well – thank *you* –

Nurse   I woke up this morning before the dawn. As I'm walking to the bus stop, I see the sun rise over the silent rooftops of Canning Town . . .

Boris   . . . Well I've always said that ah, that Canning Town is the beating heart of –

Nurse   Thank you, Mr Johnson, for this Coronavirus lockdown, which has brought a time of peace and contemplation for so many.

Boris   . . . Well, I mean. . . . Well I suppose it has.

Nurse   Thank you for your complacency, in contracting the infection yourself.

Boris   . . . Yes, well . . .

Boris *looking around, at the audience etc., can't quite believe this is real.*

Nurse   The nation has watched you conquer this disease, emboldened by your strength.

Boris   Have I? Has it?

Nurse   And thank you, Prime Minister, for the roll-out of the vaccine programme.

Boris (*as if this is news to him*)   . . . Yes. Oh good. Excellent!

Nurse   With the population implanted, we shall all be willing servants.

Boris   Quite. Servants to whom?

Nurse   The fear-based, lower-vibrational secret elite who hold sway over all of us.

Boris   What?

Nurse   Hail, the great re-set!

Fiona (*warning, to* **Nurse**)   Miss Pereira?

Virus (*on screen*)   The great re-set!

Boris   The what?

Virus (*on screen*)   Hell, I don't know, I'm just here to get up in your hands, face, space –

The **Doctor** *presses a button and the* **Virus** *cuts out.*

Fiona   Prime Minister, I'm not sure that Miss Pereira is following protocols?

Nurse (*to* **Boris**)   You are showing us the way!

Boris   Well I mean of course I went into politics to . . . I went into politics to. . . Why *did* I go into politics? –

Nurse Your bigotry and incompetence is but a small price to pay, for the gift of freedom.

Fiona Miss Pereira?

Nurse Yes?

Fiona Sorry my love, I know you're busy-busy –

Nurse Actually I'm just in the middle / of –

Fiona I just need to know why you're on an active Covid ward and not wearing appropriate PPE?

Boris . . . Ah –

Nurse I'm in the middle of a discussion with the Prime Minister –

Boris Well I did think – I did rather wonder why she wasn't wearing ah –

Fiona Miss Pereira –

Boris – why she wasn't wearing ah –

DSM '. . . why she wasn't wearing any / PPE.'

Boris (*suddenly accusing* **Nurse**)   – why she wasn't wearing – (*he double-takes, at the* **DSM**) – yes, any PPE, I mean we can't have people ignoring ah, protocols –

On screen, the **Virus** *coughs – perhaps this is a sound effect.* **Nurse** *coughs – again perhaps a sound effect.*

Boris Ah – Line?

The **Virus** *coughs again.*

Boris Line?!

DSM She also gave me a cigarette.

Boris She also gave me a cigarette!

Fiona Miss Pereira, I'm going to have to suspend you now in advance of a disciplinary hearing –

Virus (*coughs*)

Nurse (*coughs more violently*)

Fiona Miss Pereira?

Nurse You don't understand –

Seema (*off*)   OI!

Doctor Nina, I'm going to have to isolate you –

Nurse The great re-set!

Virus (*coughs*)

The **Nurse** *explodes. A shocked pause.*

Boris (*becoming light-headed, lying back down in his bed*)   Now there's something about all this that doesn't seem quite –

Doctor   A cleaner here now please. (*To* **DSM**, *Referring to* **Boris**.) And let's take his stats.

Boris (*dazed*)   What is this place?

Doctor (*on screen*)   You're being treated in St Thomas's Hospital.

Boris   Who . . .

Doctor (*on screen*)   Can you hear me?

Nurse (*re-entering, seemingly re-born*)   How are you feeling today?

Boris   Ah, Hugely! (*staring at her*) Hugely revived . . .

Doctor   Two days ago you were admitted here, and placed in Intensive Care.

Nurse   Your pregnant partner waits at home.

On another TV screen, **Boris** *appears, in press conference mode, played by another actor.*

Boris   Carrie . . .

Screen Boris   Carrie . . .

Boris   Help me!

Fiona   You're in a coma, Prime Minister.

Boris   I'm? . . .

Seema   Mum!

Fiona   It was felt best not to inform the public as yet –

Boris (*having found his reflection in a mirror*)   My God.

Nurse   Mr Johnson?

Boris (*looking at his reflection, touching his face*)   Well I'm also –

Nurse   Yes?

Boris   Well I don't want to say the wrong thing but I appear to be a –

Screen Boris   What?

Boris   A –

Nurse   'Piccanninies, with their watermelon smiles?'

Screen Boris   / Well that is taken out of context . . .

Boris   Well now you're taking me completely out of context I mean –

Fiona   And these physicians –

Nurse   'A flood of unskilled workers, treating the United Kingdom as part of their own countries'? . . .

Screen Boris   As soon as I got out of here I said –

Boris   I'm going to fight!

Screen Boris   Quite right!

Boris   I'm going to fight to protect the NHS with, with renewed vigour!

Screen Boris   I'm a changed man!

Boris   I *am* a changed man, I mean a brush with, with / death

Screen Boris   death, I mean it –

Boris   changes a man.

Screen Boris   It does.

Nurse   A change that comes too late for some.

Fiona *moves to* **Errol**.

Fiona   This is Errol Lester, Prime Minister, a postman. A husband, and a grandfather. He was admitted to hospital ten days ago. He has two days to live.

Boris   . . . Well look –

Audio cuts in, echoing around – a clip of Boris Johnson's speech from 3 March 2020 –

Boris Audio   'I'm shaking hands continuously, I was at a hospital the other night where – I think there were actually a few coronavirus patients and I shook hands with everybody –'

Errol *suddenly speaks, making* **Boris** *jump.*

Errol   Morning, darling. Keep smiling. It don't cost nothing.

Boris (*To* **Errol**, *introducing himsel*f)   . . . Hello, Boris – I'll shake your hand – I won't shake your hand –

Errol   We gotta take back control of the borders, mate.

Boris   I'm sorry?

Errol   It's the Bulgarians.

Semma (*re-entering*)   Mum!

In silent slo-mo, **Seema** *remonstrates with the* **Nurse**. *Meanwhile,* **Errol** *suddenly stands and approaches* **Boris**. *Music plays – 'Still Alive' by Frank Sinatra.* **Errol** *begins to lead* **Boris** *in a dance.*

Boris (*To* **Errol.**)   Right, what are you - I see . . .

Errol *begins to lip-sync along to the song* –

Errol (*lip-syncing*)   This was a triumph!

> I'm making a note here. Huge success!
> It's hard to overstate my satisfaction
> Aperture science:
> We do what we must
> Because we can
>
> For the good of all of us
> Except the ones who are dead
> But there's no sense crying over every mistake
> You just keep on trying til you run out of cake –

The song suddenly cuts out as **Seema** *bursts in* – *She approaches the medical team around the bed.*

Doctor (*to* **Seema**)   . . . Please –

Seema   Don't fucking touch me don't come close to me – (*to patient*) – Mum?

Doctor   You're her daughter?

Seema   Ask her! D'you get what I'm saying, you could even ask her, if it weren't for 'Whoops; got her on the fucking ventilator' –

Doctor   What's your name?

Seema   I'm not telling you my name –

Doctor   I'm afraid your mother is very seriously ill.

Seema   I know, she's fucking ill, you're tryina tell me about 'Corona Virus' –

Doctor   Please . . . –

Seema   – Or should I say *lie*-rus – yeah? –

Doctor   Why don't we go and –

Seema (*looking at the ventilated patient*)   Nah bruv, nah, no no; why've you got her like that?

Doctor   She's very peaceful.

Seema *staring at* **Doctor** *for a beat, then* –

Seema   . . . She came in here, with a broken leg, right; are you taking the piss? Then on the phone next thing you're on about pneumonia –

Doctor   Listen to / me –

Seema   – I'm an *addict!* Yeah? A-d-d-i-c-fucking-t, and my mum's an addict! And she stole fifty pound I was giving to my daughter but that's not even why I'm here for bruv! –

Doctor Let's –

Seema Fucking look at her though like, my name's Seema!

Boris (*to* **Nurse**) . . . Spirit . . .

Doctor Seema? –

Seema What?!

Doctor Your mum is in septic shock. We've done everything we can, but . . .

Seema I'm from Bethnal fucking Green mate, d'you know what I mean?!

Boris Spirit . . .

Seema – And she's not gonna fucking do this; she does *not* get to do this –

Doctor She –

Seema She doesn't get to fucking just die! Yeah? She needs to look at me first!

Boris Spirit . . .

Seema This bitch needs to look me in the eye –

Doctor Seema?

Seema Mum?

Boris Show me no more of this, spirit.

Seema Mum?! I'm begging you! Mum!

Boris Show me no more!

Seema Mum?!

Blackout suddenly, on all except the ghostly **Nurse** *and* **Boris**. *The* **Nurse** *stares at* **Boris**, *somewhat expectantly. A beat.*

Boris Look . . . I mean Look . . . I mean . . . What I would say. . . . As a government, any government, *of course*. . . .we have to be led by, we *have* been led by the science. . .

Any death is of course a tragedy, and what I would say . . . Of course any government is obliged to take . . . not obliged but . . . but any government of course makes . . . in the line of any response there are going to be. . . . What I *would* say . . .

. . . Line? . . .

. . . Line? . . .

. . . Line? . . .

. . . Line? . . .

. . . Line . . .?

The audience are ushered out, as **Boris** *continues to flail.*

Scene Five

April 2020.

A park. Late morning.

As the audience enter, **Sade** *is stood, talking on the phone.*

Sade (*on phone*)   . . . 'What's happening?' . . .

I dunno like, that's why I called to ask *you*.

. . . I said I called to ask *you*; What's happening with you?

. . . What?

. . . Swear down? . . . Nah, like I thought everything's fucked, no-one's making no money. . . .

. . . How?

. . . You dressed like a postman?

Stefan *has entered. He is wearing a mask, and probably some disposable gloves.* **Sade** *sees him and acknowledges him. At some point, whilst* **Sade** *is still on the phone,* **Stefan** *takes out some canned fizzy drinks. He cleans them with an anti-bacterial wipe, and places them on the ground, some distance away from* **Sade**. *Meanwhile –*

Sade   . . . What where d'you even get the clothes?

. . . That's some madness like, you're walking around in broad fucking daylight, drugs all up in your what, postbag?

Oi; you see last time I see you yeah. . . . (*She closes her eyes for a bit, then:*)

. . . At the funeral yeah, why you never talked to me?

Like just all sat up in the corner . . . just screwing.

. . . What d'you mean by that?

. . . Oh; OK yeah he's dead, that's over then; our brother's dead like, just move on then innit, basically; Don't you think you need to like examine what's in your brain, and really . . . *feel* suttin though?

. . . Ah?

. . . I dunno!

. . . Yeah whatever man I gotta go too.

She hangs up. She takes a moment. **Stefan** *hesitates.*

Stefan   . . . You good?

She looks at him. Stares at him. A beat.

Sade   Seriously?

He doesn't know what she means.

Sade   Are you a doctor now, yeah? Or what, you gonna rob a bank?

Stefan *smiles, acknowledging his mask.*

Stefan   ... Yeah. ...

He removes the mask so it hangs around his neck. A pause.

... My mum. ... She got diabetes and that. ...

(*indicates his chest*) I got a thing too like, my heart. ...

(*with the canned drinks*) I got your drink anyway.

... What's-it-called, last time ... couldn't remember if it's Fanta or Lilt, is the one, for you, like, so. ... Bought 'em both.

She is watching him, half-smiling. She steps towards him – he instinctively steps away. A beat.

Sade   ... What?

Stefan   ... Nah. ...

... Two metres. ...

... It's long.

She kisses her teeth. He hesitates.

... Human beings –

Sade   Ah?

He hesitates.

Stefan   ... We're erm. ... Social – like – creatures.

So. ... everything, with the lockdown. ...

On the news –

Sade   I don't watch no news.

Stefan   They're telling everybody keep away; hold your distance and that, but. ... It's unnatural. For humans, to be apart like that –

Sade   This how you normally chat to a girl?

Stefan   ... Why did you wanna hang with me?

She stares at him.

Sade   Stefan Prince.

Prince, of the fucking ... world, and the lockdown –

Stefan   Who was you on the phone to?

Sade (*ignoring him*)   ... Prince, of being the most random person at our school and Oh my God I just remembered suttin you know.

Are you still lighting fires?

Like remember when you burnt down the little fucking bike shed thingy?

Stefan *doesn't know what to say to this.*

Stefan   ... Nah –

Sade   Are you still doing that though? –

Stefan   Not any more ... or something like that. ...

Sade *half-smiles.*

Sade (*imitates*)   ... 'Not any more. ... or something like that' –

Stefan   What happened with the job?

Sade   Fuck's sake. ...

Stefan   ... Like, we don't have to talk about it like I just thought, if you wanted to talk about it –

Sade (*wearily*)   Nothing happened with the job, there is no job, basically; basically I spoke to her again, the first one, the OK one. ...

Stefan   OK.

Sade   ... and she's telling me about ... they don't really know anything, 'cos it's bad timing 'cos of the lockdown, all the staff on furlough and rey rey rey –

Stefan   OK –

He steps away from her a little as she veers a bit too close. She gives him a look.

Sade   ... And then it's what – two days later ... still haven't heard shit ...

and then the *other* one calls me, the bitch one. ...

Except for randomly she calls me on the *landline* I've had to give, so the call goes through to the *desk*, and it takes another two days for them to get the fucking message to me. ...

So I've phoned her back, she's like 'Yeah I phoned two days ago', I've had to say 'Yeah sorry, but I'm living in the YMCA, in fucking Old Street'. ... and from that point now she don't even to *need* to say nothing. ...

'Cos I can *hear* the change in her voice like from she knows my situation ... now anyway she's saying 'Oh yeah ... I should have spoke to you like two weeks ago because now we're not really in a place to be taking on new staff, it's a crazy time'. ... so I'm saying 'Why the fuck you never told me that two weeks ago, don't you know I been really waiting on this?', she starts swearing at me, I'm swearing at her. ... And now that's it, there's no job. Boom. End of.

A pause.

Stefan   ... That's deep –

Sade (*soulless*)   Yeah! . . .

Stefan   I know . . . it's hard out here, with the lockdown. . . . Like people suffering . . . even without the virus. At my work like . . . I don't know how long some people gonna keep their jobs. . . . And like you ain't even got a job. . . .

Sade *starts to laugh, softly, looking at* **Stefan**. *He smiles, unsure.*

Stefan   . . . What?

Sade   . . . With your little mask on. Chattin' 'bout 'lockdown' . . .

Stefan   What d'you mean?

Sade   I'm out here, man, this is my flex *anyway* bruv.

From January this year . . . I wake up in the morning . . . go eat . . . don't sit close to no-one 'cos they're jarring. . . . Go out, if I can be bothered . . . or more time I just stay in my yard. My 'yard.' My room.

So I don't watch no pandemic or lockdown, them things . . .

Come like. . . . 'Welcome to my fucking world.'

Stefan   . . . Boy –

Sade   I was gonna have a job! Yeah? This was gonna be my fucking . . . year! D'you know what I mean by that?

Stefan   . . . Hold out your hand.

She looks at him.

Sade   Dead ting, I ain't doing that again.

Stefan   I know how to do it this time –

Sade   You still write your little poems?

Stefan *says nothing.*

Sade   Yeah? You do though innit!

She opens his bag.

Oi what's he got in here man, Always carrying all them papers and pens like Oh my gosh he still is! –

She has found pen and notepaper.

Stefan   Nah –

Sade   You still are though, bruv, you got your little writing papers and everything –

Stefan   D'you think –

Sade   Are you writing suttin for me? –

Stefan   D'you think –

Sade   Ah?

Stefan D'you think I'm dumb?

She looks at him.

Yeah? You think I'm dumb though innit.

At school, did you think –

Sade You were dumb. I was dumb, everyone dumb at school –

Stefan Yeah what about just shut up for a minute.

A pause. **Stefan** *has surprised himself. She stares at him. A pause.*

Sade My brother was dumb. Dumb-arse couldn't even read, 'til he was like fifteen –

Stefan I heard, that he –

Sade And me and him got farmed, like to separate houses. . . . Ended up at our school for a bit; I knew he was dumb there, but not on road.

Yeah that's where he start get a little bit . . . 'wise'. That's where I guess he start to think 'I'm bigger than this. I could be making more money than x-y-z.'

That's where he got himself stabbed. Basically.

'Cos I guess he weren't quite dumb enough.

She looks away from him. She can't look at him. A pause.

Stefan . . . I'm sorry about your brother.

Sade . . . Why you sorry?

He used to beat you up.

Stefan . . . Like. . . .

Sade Are you dumb now yeah?

Can't you fucking see?

I want you to hold me.

I wanna hold someone.

But you're just being a pussy over some bullshit virus. . . .

Stefan Nah. . . . My mum's . . . shielding . . .

Sade Why *you* shielding?

A pause.

Stefan *hesitates, then begins to recite a poem he's composed.*

Stefan

'. . . Look out the window . . .

Hear the visions . . .
See the sounds . . .
The senses don't make sense.

She sells . . . sea shells . . .
Though she's not sure . . .
if the sounds that she selling
are just static
or straight symphonies.

But what fear?
But what for?
Buttered waffle world waffle on . . .

But don't listen to its actions.
Don't watch no noise.

She will sink above it all.'

She is watching him. A pause.

As if by a little magic trick, **Stefan** *produces some matches.*

Sade . . . You still a little firestarter?

Stefan (*smiles*) . . . Still carry them from work. . . .

He lights a little fire between them. He holds his hand above the fire, in its warmth. A beat.

Stefan . . . Hold out your hand.

Sade . . . I don't like no tricks man.

Stefan No, it's not that.

She holds her hand out, close to his. Both their hands in the warmth of the fire.

They stand there together.

For a bit, it is just the two of them, the crackling of the fire, and the sounds of the parkland.

Then there is the crackle of a radio.

A radio crackles again. A police radio.

A **Police Officer** *enters. They put their hands down, and tense up a bit.*

Officer (*into radio*) Yeah, Sierra two-four . . . I'm in Wenlock Park, attending, over. (*To* **Stefan** *and* **Sade**.) Hello guys.

Sade (*under her breath*) Fuck's sake.

Officer Gonna tell me what you're up to, yeah?

Sade (*softly*) Ain't up to nothing / mate

Officer (*into radio*)   Yeah IC3 one male, one female, currently engaging on foot – (*To* **Stefan**.) Don't walk that way, mate, 'cos we're having a conversation yeah?

Stefan   OK –

Officer   There's no fires, by the way, or barbecues allowed in the park –

Sade   Are you taking the piss?

Officer   I beg your pardon?

Stefan (*to* **Sade**)   / It's alright –

Sade   – I seen literally about five fucking hipster type a' people –

Officer   Listen –

Sade   – all got their barbecues down the other side man–

Officer   Listen to me – (*to* **Stefan**.) You stay where you are mate, yeah?

Stefan   Can you please keep your social distance please?

Sade   He's shielding.

Officer   I'm keeping my social distance – Yeah? – That's absolutely fine – The reason I wanna talk to you, is because someone matching your description, right?, has committed a robbery in this area. So obviously because of that I wanna have a quick chat with you – (*To* **Stefan**.) What's your name and address please mate?

Stefan   Stefan / Prince.

Sade   Jokes mate.

Officer   I can't hear you.

Stefan   Stefan Prince. 48 Holby Close, London N1 / 7LT.

Sade   I can't believe this like this is funny.

Officer (*to* **Sade**)   Listen – if you're gonna be – yeah? – the stereotypical . . . 'youth'. Right? Then I will be, the stereotypical . . . whatever I am.

Sade (*softly*)   Cunt.

Officer   Sorry?

Stefan   Nah . . .

Officer (*to* **Sade**)   Open your bag.

Sade   Open it for what though / like –

Stefan   Nah –

Officer (*to* **Sade**)   You're detained for a search

Sade   What, by you!?

Officer You keep still and wait for my colleague – (*To* **Stefan**.) You – I'm now gonna search you / OK?

Stefan Can you please keep your distance like you ain't got a mask! –

Sade For real / though –

Stefan You're speaking and you're coming too close!

Officer – Listen –

Stefan I got a heart condition.

Officer What?

Sade Did you hear that, he's got a fucking / heart condition –

Stefan I got a heart condition as well –

Officer (*to* **Sade**) – Right –

Stefan *is moving away – the* **Officer** *moves towards him again.*

(*To* **Stefan**.) Where are you going? –

Sade Oi . . .

Officer (*to* **Stefan**) You f– Come here!

Stefan Nah man –

The **Officer** *loses it – he lunges at* **Stefan**.

Sade OI!

Officer (*to* **Stefan**) You're under / arrest.

Stefan Get off me!

Officer Keep still!

Sade What you / DOING?!

Officer (*into radio*) Sierra two-four –

Stefan Help me.

Officer (*into radio*) – code zero –

Stefan Help me!

Suddenly blackout, and a TV screen turns on –

The TV screen shows police body-cam footage of the struggle continuing . . .

Indistinct and chaotic . . . **Sade** *shouts in the background. . . .*

Stefan *shouts. . . The* **Officer** *shouts 'Taser!'*

Sade *screams . . .*

The footage cuts out into –

Static.

Suddenly it cuts into –

Footage of a wooded pathway. . . . Serene music . . .

Reveal – a **Postman** *walking down the path. We are in the advert, as proposed by* **Arabella** *earlier on.*

A voiceover begins. . . .

Advert V/O   In times like these, we all need to stay connected. . . . .

Then we cut into –

Static.

Then, lights up on –

Stefan*, lying on the ground, dead. On the TV – the* **Virus***, looking down at* **Stefan***.*

Virus (*on screen*)   . . . Well, there he be. Stefan Emmanuel Prince. Finally found you.

He looks closer.

Although it appears our friend has died himself a death, of different causes. . . .

He picks up a spent taser and examines it.

Seems I *ain't* the only virus in town.

Ah, hell's bells. And I promised you all a happy ending.

Let me see what I can do.

The **Virus** *initiates a 'rewind'. . . A burst of sound and light, and then, lights up on –*

Stefan*,* **Sade** *and the* **Officer***.*

Officer (*to* **Sade**)   Listen – right? – I am carrying out a legitimate search. OK? 'Cos I've got reason to believe you've committed a robbery.

Sade   What, both of us or him?

Officer   – So if *you're* gonna be – yeah? – the stereotypical . . . 'youth'. Then I will be, the stereotypical . . . whatever . . . whatever I . . .

The **Officer** *stutters a bit.*

. . . What – . . . (*he coughs a little*)

Sea shells.

The **Officer** *coughs/splutters a little again. He seems confused.*

Sade   . . . What?

Officer (*to* **Sade**)   You stay there. Right?

Sade What did you just / say –

Officer Open your bag!

Stefan Nah –

Officer (*to* **Stefan**) No, where are you going. Where are you going? Where we going? . . .
Going . . .
Go in!

Sade Go in where?

Officer Please go in.
Keep going.
What?

Stefan Where?

Officer Forwards. Together. What?

Sade Oh my days what / is –

Officer Because you're walking away from me, you're going – Don't walk away from me!

Stefan Nah.

Officer (*softer*) Don't walk away from me?

Sade (*having started to film on her phone*) Swear down . . .

Officer . . . Can't go backwards, gotta go –

Stefan Gotta go –?

Officer We gotta go! Stand still! Don't stand still, move forward!

Stefan Always forward.

Officer See the sounds.

Stefan Hear the visions.

Sade (*in disbelief*) Nah . . .

Officer Express . . .

Sade Express . . . ?

Officer What's in your bag?

Stefan Express . . .

Officer What's in your mind?

Stefan (*to* **Sade**) Come with me.

Sade (*to* **Stefan**) . . . What's in *your* mind?

Officer Piece of . . . PC . . . PC Renton. (*On radio*.) PC Renton, reporting to –

Stefan (*to* **Sade**) Are you into . . .

Officer . . . 'porting to –

Sade (*to* **Stefan**) You?

Officer (*to* **Stefan**) You!

Stefan Me.

Officer Me! PC . . . Express . . . Pizza Express –

Sade (*to* **Stefan**) Be with me.

Officer (*to* **Stefan**) You be with me; we can either do this now, or you can come with me, and accompany me back to the, to the Pizza Express in Woking!

Stefan You waking?

Officer Woking. Waking. Wake up! I'm waking up!

Sade *is lowering her phone –*

Stefan (*to* **Sade**) I'll take your one bag of dark clouds, stormy nights
And buy a dress –

Officer Address –

Stefan A dress for you –

Officer Name and address for you –

Stefan – made up of bright new mornings.

Officer Holby Close –

Stefan Hold me close.

Officer Help me.

Sade (*to* **Stefan**, *without edge*) This how you normally chirpse?

Officer One . . . One second let's turn the light back on. Back on.

Stefan Beckon.

Officer Beckon me on. Beckon 'em. Beckenham I'm from.

Sade Yeah well I'm from Hackney, so –

Officer Hackney so . . . Need, so . . .

Stefan Need you so.

Sade (*to* **Stefan**, *softly*) I need you, so . . .

Officer . . . Change . . . what's happening here. What's happening here?! . . . Happy near? . . . Happiness near . . .

Stefan (*to* **Sade**) Happy new year.

Sade (*to* **Stefan**) Happy new year?

Officer Happy new year.

Near our . . .

Nearer . . .

Nearer now.

Stefan Here and now.

Officer Gotta all stay near to get far.

Sade To get . . .?

Officer To get far.

Stefan (*to* **Sade**) Together.

Officer Together.

Sade (*to* **Stefan**) . . . Together.

Together.

They stand there for a bit. **Stefan** *and* **Sade** *facing each other.*

Lorna *enters, still wearing her nurse's uniform. She addresses the audience. She hesitantly leads the audience out.*

Lorna D'you wanna? . . .

She has led the audience towards the exit.

Erm. Yeah I just wanted to say. . . . .

Because obviously it's too late for me.

But – I just feel like there could have been another way?

Couldn't there?

If we'd, you know, if they'd locked down earlier, or. . . .

I mean I get it, I do get it. . . . It's people's jobs, isn't it, and I do get that.

I feel like I might have. . . . What's the word? Grand. . . . Grandmother! I feel like I could have been a Gr–

She seems to become aware of something.

Oh. Hang on. I can . . . sort of taste again. (*Half-laughs.*) That's weird.

Bitter.

A beat. She starts to exit into the night, and vaguely indicates for the audience to follow.
The End.

In conversation with director Maggie Norris

BP So, Remix. *Well, first of all, the fact that The Big House was putting on shows when no one else was putting on shows is just kind of amazing. How did you do it?*

MN Well, I refused to let the pandemic shut us down. Until lockdown, and then it was illegal. So I was determined, absolutely determined to keep open for lots of different reasons, but primarily for the mental health of the young people. They wanted to come into the building. They desperately wanted to come into the building. And they didn't want to be isolated and they wanted to create work. So I thought, how can we do that? How can we do that safely – safely for them, safely for the audience? And that's when I thought up the idea of taking bubbles of six in the audience around a show where the characters only appeared in one scene. So there was no way that there could be risk. We rehearsed the play in separate groups and each scene had their own rehearsal day. We followed the guidelines but made them work for us!

BP *What kind of challenges came up through developing a play with such a form?*

MN It threw up lots of challenges for both David and I . . . how do we tell a story that is moving when you can only see each character once? Whose story do you follow? So we used video really carefully so that the central character appears in more than one scene, but only once in the flesh. And we made the characters' stories interconnect. So if you didn't see them in the next scene, you would perhaps hear them on the phone or seen them on Zoom or TV. So you did get those through stories and you did get the emotional impact.

BP *And the central ideas in the play, where did they come from?*

MN One of the triggers for doing the play was hearing everybody in the media constantly repeat 'we're all in this together'. And quite patently we weren't. The experience of our young people was hugely different. Seeing our young people queuing at foodbanks and struggling with their mental health, witnessing the lack of support as their council workers were put on furlough (we struggled to pick up the slack) whilst endless programmes on the TV were talking about baking sourdough and how to make banana bread – It made us want to tell their stories. One of my favourite storylines in *Ballad* was that of a young postman, who's not a postman but a drug dealer, who is actually making the most of the opportunity to make money in the pandemic and raking it in, whilst also dealing with some serious challenges in his own life.

BP *We were receiving a real glut of Covid-related content at the time, but when I saw* Ballad, *it was so far from being another Covid play. What was it that made it so unusual in your eyes?*

MN It was funny. Darkly funny. A moving but hilarious moment in the play was when the Cowboy Virus interacted with the Zoom call, pretending to be the granny that they hadn't heard from and were discussing. He then tried to infect them by getting them to go outside. It was really disturbing but – what David Watson does so brilliantly – it did make you laugh in the darkest of moments.

BP *Any other moments you'd like to speak about?*

MN Seeing the young daughter visiting her dying mother in an Intensive Care Unit, who she obviously had an incredibly complex relationship with, was a very powerful scene. The grief. The actress who played that part was gut wrenchingly moving. Feeling that grief in such close proximity and seeing the reality of a Covid death was profoundly upsetting, not just for me, but for every audience every night.

BP *I remember people coming out and saying, I lost my mum to Covid, or, I lost my aunt, and how much that scene had meant to them . . .*

MN A beautiful thing . . . somebody came out of that scene and rang their mother, whom they hadn't spoken to for ten years. They were so upset by the scene that it put into perspective the rift that they were having and they made the call.

BP *Can you tell us more about how the audience responded to being at The Big House and watching the show? In that moment, when live performance was such a different thing, and maybe a scary thing.*

MN Well we created a special atmosphere at The Big House for it. We couldn't have everybody standing in a bar because of restrictions so we stayed outside and had a fire pit and mulled wine. And that was so cosy and festive and the anticipation really built up amongst the audience waiting to go in as they could see all the different scenes happening in the different rooms. Our building is full of large windows and it was all lit up like a doll's house. That was magical. So we actually got a very, very warm response to staging the plays. People were delighted to be out and about. They were grateful for us keeping them safe. It was challenging for the cast to have an audience in masks, particularly a play that is not only dark, but funny. But the audience were more effusive as a result. They gave more. And they really showed their emotion through the mask. It was a unique and memorable trip to the theatre.

Maggie Norris interviewed by Bel Parker
9 August 2022

Redemption

James Meteyard

Interview with writer James Meteyard

What was the process of developing the original idea for the play?

I worked with Maggie on a previous production, *Bullet Tongue*, where I'd provided music support. We spoke a lot about music and its ability to engage nontraditional theatre audiences. Maggie was keen to create a piece which was very music driven and so we started from there as an idea. I was interested in exploring male suicide, connection through music, and the concept of family. Due to The Big House's core purpose as a charity, the care system was a key theme too. We settled on the leads being a fiery female rapper and a shy male singer connecting through making an album together. This opened up opportunities to explore the intense pressures faced by many young people in care as well as a rare tenderness in the private moments they shared together. The idea felt extremely raw and burned with so many qualities unique to The Big House.

What is unique about the process of writing a play for The Big House? Most enjoyable/ most challenging?

I was writing for seventeen performers, many of whom had never been onstage before. And although some of the older performers were staying on from the R&D workshop we did, I was writing for a lot of young people I'd never met. The most enjoyable aspect was working with the members who are just so full of life, emotion, heart and character. I could go on, but I think the most extraordinary thing is the intense personal support given to the members, combined with the impressive artistic ambition and execution of their productions. The journey for many of the members is truly monumental and unlike anything I've ever seen, and whilst the territory comes with turbulence, the result is authentic, raw and life changing work. It's been an absolute privilege to have been a part of this journey.

Songs or story first?

Story for me. Always. I see the music as an extension of the characters' experiences. What can we reveal here which we can't through words? When Maz raps her lyrics about her brother in the basement of the cinema where he used to bring her . . . that is a way of expressing something to Aaron which she simply can't say. Through her music she is able to be emotionally vulnerable in front of him for the first time. I couldn't have written those lyrics before I truly understood her struggle, her pain and her relationships, and subsequently what she needed to express through her music.

Play-with-music . . . What is that? Why isn't it a musical? Is it a piece of gig theatre?

This is a question I've wrestled with a lot throughout making work. To me, a play-with-music is a story driven piece in which music aids the story telling, but isn't necessarily present the whole way through. In the case of *Redemption*, all of the songs exist within the action of a scene, there is no breaking the fourth wall to sing thoughts and feelings; everything is justifiable within the world of the play. One interesting factor of a play-with-music is you can justify resting in the 'play bits' for longer without feeling the need to give the audience another song, this can allow the time for a greater exploration of difficult themes.

Were there any characters that you found more challenging to write for? How did you approach them?

Definitely. Due to the size of the original cast I found it extremely difficult to make sure every character had a strong arc and a purpose in the piece. Also, I was writing about the care system which fosters young people from a broad mix of ethnic backgrounds. Which, as a white middle class writer, felt exposing at times. I found myself asking, 'Is this a story I have the right to tell?' The process was one of listening, dialogue, research, observation and ultimately collaboration and I believe the outcome is authentic because of that.

Did the script change considerably in rehearsals? What were some of the most surprising changes?

Yes absolutely. For many reasons! I think the most surprising changes came out of the fact that it was originally written to be presented in one space but, due to the pandemic, we decided to present it at The Big House's Islington venue instead. The building is an old framing factory and so we chose a promenade form, with the audience walking from room to room to see different scenes. In the single space version, I had scenes which were only a few lines long. However, as I learnt mid-way through rehearsals, if you physically move an audience to a new location, you have to give them a scene complete enough to justify them having got up and moved. Which changed the feel of many of the scenes drastically! Also, due to the turbulent experiences many of the actors face in their day-to-day lives, it was inevitable that the group would shift and change, with some people dropping out and others joining. So it was essential that we had a story which was robust and malleable enough that changing pretty much any character's gender, age, relationships, profession, cultural background etc. didn't compromise the overarching piece and themes being explored. Which was a challenge, particularly with the rhymes . . . I think Michelle became Tyrell, then Chantelle before finally Darnell . . .

How did the audiences and critics respond to the piece?

The response was overwhelmingly positive from both the audiences and critics. I think the combination of the rawness of the story being told, by an extremely talented cast who all felt authentically connected to the world, whilst being so physically close to them in each scene was a special experience for many. Also, the themes which were explored are inherently emotional and they had a powerful effect on audience members.

What do you see for the future of this piece?

I'd like to revisit the single space version. I think the whole piece would have a pace and ferocity which would match Maz's emotional journey and force the audience to be an active participant in what that kind of a whirlwind might feel like. I'd also like to explore a screen version, as there is something which feels so cinematic about the locations around London. I'd love to capture shots of some of the iconic places which are underexplored on screen. There's beauty in the ugliness of their surroundings, much like in the experiences both Maz and Aaron face.

Can you talk to us about Maz, and talk to us about her relationship with the audience?

Maz is our protagonist and our narrator. She talks directly to the audience in rhyming verse as she guides us in and out of scenes. Right from the opening monologue we're met with her ferocious and explosive energy. But as the piece goes on, we gain a deeper understanding of Maz's extremely troubling and turbulent life, as her protective armour is disarmed by Aaron's gentle soul and genuine kindness. Through this poetic monologue form, Maz is able to express herself privately to the audience, sometimes alone, sometimes in the middle of a scene, and through these asides she shares her unique perspective revealing the complexity of what is truly going on for her.

What advice would you give to actors approaching this sort of rap/spoken word/ dialogue combination?

The rhythm is there. Find it first, then let go of it. It should support you, not become a focus over your intention in the scene or monologue. You don't need to hit the rhyming words with any kind of force, nor highlight any patterns or leave space at the end of every line. Rather, once you've found the rhythm, just speak it as natural text and allow the poetry to take care of itself. Then when you've got that, revisit the ends of lines and rhyme patterns and ask why this break, pattern or rhythm has been put there . . . more often than not, it's just the way the poetry has fallen, but a fair amount of times there is intention in why I've broken the line there, or left a big gap or used certain rhyme flow/ structure, which is connected to the character's emotional or psychological experience which I'm attempting to share. Every writer is different . . . so ask questions of the text and make choices. But always connect with and prioritise your character's intention over any kind of word play or 'doing the poetry' . . . keep it authentically in your character's voice, spoken naturally, and ask, what do you want? What do you need to overcome in order to get what you want? How are you using these words in order to do that?

Is there anything else you'd like to say that hasn't been raised by these questions?

Just that this has been a long and incredibly eye opening journey, working with some extraordinary people, from the cast to the creative team and the Big House staff. It's a truly special organisation and this play is a product and reflection of all of those people's work, openness and passion. It's a piece we're all extremely proud of and I hope you enjoy reading it as much as I enjoyed writing/making it.

Redemption was first performed at The Big House, London, on 17 November 2021, with the following cast:

Maz	Renaya Dennis
Joe	James Atwell
Darnell	Dymond X
Aaron (aka Tayo)	Shaquille Jack
Michael	Taurean Steele
Scratch	Tezlym Senior-Sakatu
Plots	Jermaine Freeman
Brenda	Shanice Logan
Carlos	James Atwell
Mum	Nadège René
Patricia	Tajah Workman-Jeffrey
Ensemble	Shaq Brown
	Alpha Menda
	Fawaz Adekunle
	Jayden Atuah-Hemaah
	Armani Morris

Creative Team

Writer and Lyricist	James Meteyard
Director	Maggie Norris
Dramaturgy	Maggie Norris
Composer	The Last Skeptik
Producer	Sarah Stallwood-Hall
Assistant Director	Bel Parker
Set and Costume Designer	Zoë Hurwitz
Assistant Designer	Ellie Roser
Lighting Designer	Martha Godfrey
Video Designer	Daniel Denton
Sound Designer	Jack Baxter
Musical Director	Jammz
Choreographer	Kendra Horsburgh
Props and Costume Assistant	Yohanna Yohanis
Production Manager	Sean Laing
Stage Manager	Leyla Percival

It was then restaged at The Big House the following year, 30 June 2022 with the following changes to the cast:

Darnell	Dymond X/Aaron Virciglio
Brenda	Victoria Nwaesei
Mum	Victoria Nwaesei

Creative Team 2022

Writer and Lyricist	James Meteyard
Director	Maggie Norris
Composer	The Last Skeptik
Producer	Sarah Stallwood-Hall
Assistant Director	Bel Parker
Set and Costume Co-Designer	Zoë Hurwitz
Set and Costume Co-Designer	Rachael Light
Lighting and Video Designer	Tyler Forward for Big Tele
Sound Designer	Benjamin Grant
Original Sound Design	Jack Baxter
Musical Director	Jammz
Choreographer	Kendra Horsburgh
Production Manager	Sean Laing
Deputy Production Manager	James Maginn
Stage Manager	Leyla Percival/Amy Blower/Ellie Roberts

Characters

Maz – *Aged seventeen. Female. Grown up in the care system in London. Has been rehomed four times due to running away from all of her placements. A rapper.*

Joe – *Early thirties. Male. An 'off-the-grid', London born and bred music producer living and making music in Hackney.*

Darnell – *Late twenties/early thirties. Male. A music manager working for a prolific music management company. Aaron's current music manager.*

Aaron (aka Tayo) – *Aged twenty-one. Male. Originally from Nigeria. Was sent to the UK aged six. Grew up in the care system in the North West of England. A singer/songwriter who has had some minor success. Working on a new album with Joe under a new name, Tayo.*

Michael – *Late twenties/early thirties. Male. A social worker working in the London Borough of Hackney. Used to be Maz's social worker when she lived there but isn't any more now she's moved placement. Has a soft spot for Maz.*

Scratch – *Early twenties. Drug dealer living in Hackney. One of Maz's friends from the roads. Smokes weed 24/7.*

Plots – *Mid twenties. Male. A rapper from East London. Used to be close friends with Jerome (Maz's brother).*

Brenda – *Thirties. Female. A worker in the unregistered care home where Maz is currently placed.*

Carlos – *Teens. Male. Another resident at Maz's placement who has psychosis and shows violent tendencies towards Maz.*

Mum – *Late thirties/early forties. Female. Maz's mum.*

Patricia – *Sixties. Female. Jamaican. A lady who works at the Rio Cinema Dalston. Worked there for years and likes Jerome and Maz.*

Notes on the Play

The action takes place over two weeks.

The piece should be more or less entirely underscored by music, played live or pre-recorded.

Spoken text is written on the left.

Songs are written on the right.

Tayo's music leans towards Soul. Definitely singer/songwriter style.

Maz's music is either Grime or HipHop. Although she sings some of Tayo's songs at times too.

. . .	Indicates a character trailing off or searching for a thought
–	Indicates an interruption
Beat	Indicates a shift in thought, action or emotion
Pause	A moment of space. Doesn't have to be a beat but may be . . .
Silence	A longer moment of space. Usually filled with some sort of feeling, thought or tension

Audience enters into **Joe**'s *studio. There's music playing pretty loudly. It's the preshow music to* **Joe**'s *live stream.* **Joe** *can be seen setting up the camera, making sure the tech is working.* **Plots** *is pacing up and down, practising his bars.* **Joe** *is half aware, every now and then giving him notes.* **Darnell** *is watching him, checking his phone from time to time. There's tense anticipation in the air.*

When the audience is settled **Maz** *bursts in, not in* **Joe**'s *studio, and speaks directly to the audience.*

Act One

The opening monologue is in silence until the music is cued.

Maz   Fam I can't even believe this!
Not even been here two days
and man punches a hole through my door!
Through my fuckin' door fam!
Are you actually serious?
This guy's has been actin' up
since the moment I got here.
Smashin' windows an that.

I come out like rah!
What the fuck are you doin' ?
But as soon as I open my mouth
he starts screamin' in my face
gripsin' me up an that.
So I start shoutin' back at him
and then my man just turns round
and starts screamin' at the fucking wall.
At the fucking wall!
Like what fuck!
He's psycho init!
How you menna feel safe
with a fuckin' psycho around?

Next ting,
Brenda comes out the kitchen.
Fuckin' Brenda man.
BRENDA!
Who the fuck is called Brenda anyway?
And for no reason
Brenda don't even like me init!
She's all like:

Brenda   Eh! What are you doing to Carlos?

Maz What am I doing to Carlos???
WHAT AM I DOING?
The fuckin' cunt just
grips me up and you ask me
WHAT AM I DOING?

Brenda You know he's not well!
You shouldn't provoke him like that!

Maz What so I ain't being provoked
when you keep tabs on me, Brenda?
I ain't being provoked
when man grabs me, Brenda?
But I tell you what BRENDA
I bet you'll be tellin' them
that he was provoked
when man stabs me, BRENDA!

Oi fuck this, run the track fam.

Music starts.

I need to get outa here man.
I know they're gonna come after me again
but I ain't hanging around
just to get shouted at by some cunt
Bustin' holes in my door
and when I retaliate I get blamed for it!

Are you takin' the piss?
I'm done with this shit.
I chuck a left down the road,
start marchin' quick,
take out my phone
and check how long it'll take me
to get to Joe's.

Great. I'm late.
Joe says this is some important day
And I'm seventy minutes and
three fuckin' buses away,
in the arse end of nowhere,
miles away from any of my mates
and no one even gives a shit!

The bus ride goes slow
but I write bars on the way
so the time fades quick.

I walk up to Joe's door
ring the bell,

And wait for a minute.

Joe You're late.

Maz I know, but I'm here init.

Joe What's wrong?

Maz This boy Carlos come at me. Punched a hole in my door.

Joe Fucks sake. Look, I wanna hear more. But right now you gotta focus on this shit.

Maz What even is this?

Joe It's big. That's why I said get here at six. Look just keep it calm, drop a bar . . . don't do some gang shit, just make sure it's raw.

Maz I push my way through the hanging beads
that Joe calls a bedroom door
and into his smokey half lit studio.
There's some moody lookin' guy
That I half know,
acting like he's in a movie.
It's a fucking joke.

We move into **Joe***'s smokey, half lit, relatively high quality home studio.* **Joe***'s decks are running a dirty grime beat.* **Plots** *is just about to drop some bars, hyping up the stream with an introduction.* **Joe** *is live streaming via a camera or phone which we can see projected on screens.* **Darnell** *is stood watching with an air of professionalism and quiet confidence. Clearly enjoying the vibe.*

Plots Yes, yes! We're live and direct. Hold tight all the mandem locked in on the stream, yeah. One, two. Get to know! Plots about to shut this ting down.

We drop into a heavy music section. We feel a slight difference here. Maybe it's lights. Maybe it's volume. But we slightly move away from the studio and are let into the boys' experience as they see it.

Plots

> *Man I move in the night*
> *With the ting at the waist,*
> *And the crew by my side.*
> *Blacked out*
> *Like hood and my Nikes*
> *Put the ting to your face*
> *'cause I'm loose in my mind.*
> *I'm rude not polite*
> *Don't think you could fuck with me*
> *'cause I shoot with the 9*
> *Man I roll up quick*
> *Like who's on a hype?*

If you stand up you'll be losing your life.

Like car, car,
Man I shoot with the 9
And guys don't wanna see me on a hype
Fuck losing my pride
So if it's beef then you might
lose a tooth in a fight
I know guys who are moving the white
'Cause they've got food to provide
Every day on the roadside I'm on the grind
But fuck that these days music's my life

Why you actin'
Like you got guts
if you're tryin' to slew me
Then you must be nuts
Like dickhead
I'll make your whole click dust
Rob all your shit
send you home on the bus
I'm not playing games
Like hide and seek
But guys wanna hide
When they see me
Are you dumb?
You know I'm merking the beat
And watch when I see you on the street.

It's the heavyweight psycho
I'm on the mic doe
In this game you're lyrically micro.
I'm lyrically tight bro
You could never fuck with me
on the mic doe
Spittin' on stage shows
I'm out to make dough
Only nineteen but don't watch my age though
So
You better take note
Bangs will lick back your head like canerow

Plots Yuh dun know!

Joe Maz jump on it.

Maz (*to* **Joe**) I thought I was doing this on my own?

Plots *laughs.*

Maz What the fuck are you laughing at?

Plots You must be joking fam. This bitch ain't got bars.

Maz My blood boils
but I'm frozen to the spot.
When I clock this boy
on the sofa in the corner
Not saying much
Just staring at me.

Plots Oi get the fuck outta here. Deadin' up the stream, you know. Just like your wasteman brother, init. Oi you know what . . .

Plots *grabs the phone and turns the camera on* **Maz**, *walking up to her slowly so she can be seen on the live stream.*

Plots All the mandem locked in take note. This little pussy hole hoodrat thought she had bars. She ain't got BARS. She's just a fucking joke. Just like her pussyhole brother who couldn't even – oi what the fuck –

Maz *suddenly turns around, pushes past* **Plots**, *grabs the mic and wheels up the deck.*

Maz I don't need BARS. I'll murder you on a freestyle.

Maz *spits a freestyle verse with venom.* **Maz** *dominates the stage, directly addressing* **Plots**.

Maz

> *You don't wanna hear*
> *from me anyway*
> *'cause when I lay it down*
> *you fall back*

Joe *hits play on the decks.*

> *Your vibe is dead*
> *man I hate that*
> *So I turn up my sound*
> *and you rate that*
> *Don't answer to you*
> *so stay back*
> *'cause man I got bars*
> *since way back.*

> *You're not a heavyweight*
> *You're just bare fat*
> *Walk gassed up*
> *Air Max*
> *You couldn't rack up*
> *100 views*

> *When I post my tunes*
> *They share that*
>
> *I ain't no hood rat bitch*
> *I'm a killer on the mic*
> *Bringing venom when I spit*
> *And if you ever try*
> *move to this*
> *I'll send you away*
> *with a busted lip*
>
> *I don't wanna rise to this kid*
> *This little man ting*
> *With his little man click*
> *Talk about 9s and shit*
> *The only shots you fire*
> *when you bust too quick.*

Joe *wheels up the decks.*

Joe   Oiii! Big up!!

Plots   Nah, nah, nah that was dead fam.

Maz *goes right up to the camera. Her face is projected on the stream.*

Maz   Run that on your fucking stream you CUNT.

Joe   That was hard, you know.

Plots   Oi put the beat back on, lemme go in again.

Joe *goes to run the track.* **Darnell** *stops him before he does.*

Darnell   Nah, we're good.

Joe *turns off the music.* **Darnell** *is measured and controlled when he speaks. Exuding presence and a calm confidence.*

Darnell   You've got some serious talent, I can see that. (*Looking at* **Maz** *but addressing the room.*) I think we're onto something here, Joe.

Joe   For real. These two are pure fire.

Plots   You know that.

Darnell   What's Joe told you about me?

Slight pause

Plots   That you're some manager, init.

Plots *starts getting more and more gassed through this.*

Darnell   I am yeah. But I started out like you. Bashment mainly. I was at a rave nearly every fucking day, getting wavy and spitting bars. I set up my own label, had artists all over the world. Flying first class, festivals, parties, Kingston, LA, London, Montreal, Santa Catarina, Mexico City! Man, we were everywhere! But I fell outa love with Bashment for whatever reason . . . maybe I was just tired of getting on it so much. And I went over to Island Records to work on distribution for the likes of Dizzy Rascal, Kid Cudi an that. Then, one day, I see my man Aaron over here (*points to* **Aaron**) at this tiny bar in Bristol. And he blew my fucking mind. So I bring him to the table back at Island . . . and they do the same old shit, stringing him along. But I'm like, 'cool that's normal, it's no drama' . . . Then bam! They hit me with, 'He's not quite our vibe at the moment.' Like damn are you for real? So I say 'fuck you lot, you wouldn't know good music if it was handed to you on a platinum record. I'm out.' And as soon as I hit the pavement I had this urge, I swear it was like it was from God or some shit, and I knew . . . like I knew . . . I just needed to bell Aaron and offer to manage him there and then. And what did you say, Aaron?

Aaron   Let's go.

Darnell   Let's. Fucking. Go! So . . . we get some studio time, release a couple tunes, get some live shows going and things start moving in one direction only. Skyward. But I thought why stop there . . . when there's so many incredible artists out there who never get no chance 'cause cunts in glass offices, who don't know fuck all about what people actually want to listen to, get to decide.

Plots   Trust me!

Darnell   So I hit Joe up, said 'I want the best fuckin' artists you're working with.' And you know what he said?

Joe   I got that heat for you right here!

Plots   Dun know!

Darnell   I'm doing a night tomorrow in Hackney. Joe's gonna host. My boy Aaron's gonna do his ting. Got loads of press, industry, influencers down. Plots, you think you can handle an hour set?

Plots   Easy.

Darnell   Get there for 5. Maz, I want you to jump on Tayo's set.

Maz   Who's Tayo?

Aaron   That's me.

Maz   And he just carries on staring at me.

Aaron *smiles and half laughs.*

Maz   What the fuck you laughing at?

Aaron   You're just funny.

Maz   What the fuck's funny about this fam?

Joe   Calm it, man. You doing this or what?

Maz I'll think about it.

Joe (*aside to* **Maz**) Oi, this ain't suttin' to think about, Maz?

Maz I'll think about it.

I say again.
I ain't got time for Joe's stress
He thinks he's doing me a favour
But I'm bless, man I don't need this.

Joe Well when you've 'thought about it' . . . at least come down yeah? I'll put you on the guest list.

Maz I'll –

Darnell Think about it. Yeah?

Maz *exits. We transition to outside of* **Joe**'s *flat.*

Maz When I step outside
into the afternoon air,
I see Michael's waiting for me
at the end of the drive
with some bleak look on his face.

Michael I knew I'd find you here.

Maz Move from me, yeah?

Michael Maz what are you doing?

Maz Why you even here anyway?

Michael Brenda rang me.

Maz Fucking Brenda man.

Michael Why are you running away again?

Maz It doesn't concern you.

Michael You know they're gonna put you in Secure if you carry on like this?

Maz I don't care.

Michael You ever even seen a Secure Placement? Three locked doors between you and the outside world.

Maz Why do you even give a shit?

Michael *considers how he's gonna deliver the news. He decides to be direct.*

Michael Your mum rang me.

Maz She can fuck off!

Michael She wants to see you, Maz.

Maz   Bit late for that.

Michael   What shall I tell her?

Maz   Tell her to fuck off. Obviously.

Michael   She's different now, Maz. You know people can –

Maz   Michael. You ain't my social worker no more. Just fuck off out my life, yeah?

It's starting to get late.
And Brenda's been bellin'
my phone all day.
So I contemplate making my way
back to the house of horrors.

I get all the way to the front gate
when I notice a crack in my window
on the top floor. That means
not only has Carlos punched
a hole in my door,
he's now been smashing up
my fucking room too.

Music starts.

I sleep on a bus tonight.
Up top on the back seat.
I'm restless so I don't sleep easy
and the bright lights of the bus
keep me up.

I head to Spotify and search Tayo.
And funnily enough
only one song comes up.
I play the track and lie back
Along the six seats
as the smooth ride
of the night bus relaxes me.
And Tayo's tune drifts me off to sleep.

We see **Tayo** *sing this song alone at a microphone still in the studio space.*

Tayo

Frozen lake
Ice cold on my face.
Ambition fades from me.
Washed on the waves
floats another day
where I can be free.

Peace of mind

> is hard to find these days.
> When what is whole
> is made of two.
>
> And life seems fine
> when we run from the truth.
>
> Replace ourselves
> with whatever helps
> as liquor takes me through.
>
> But that don't help
> my sorry self
> when all I need is you.
>
> Frozen lake
> Ice cold on my face.
> Ambition fades from me.
> Washed on the waves
> floats another day
> where I can be free.

Maz   The sun rises up
to give the ugly arse buildings
that surround me an orange tint.
And to some people
it may look rough as fuck
but to me, this is where I been,
for the last couple years
so it looks like home.

I check the battery on my phone
One per cent. So I make a quick call
to one of my oldest friends,
Scratch.

Scratch (*on phone in a different space*)   My G! Long time no see! Where you been at?

Maz   Nowhere man. I'm about.

Scratch (*on phone*)   Come check me then, yeah?

Maz   Say no more. I'll be right there.

We move to **Scratch**'s *yard. A flat on a council estate in Hackney.*

Maz   I enter Scratch's yard
Which stinks of some strong bud
And through the thick smoke
I see Scratch sat on the sofa playing COD.

What's going on bruv?

Scratch (*heavily stoned, speaking slowly*)   Maz, I ain't see you in time!

Maz   It's been a madness recently. Not gonna lie.

Scratch   I saw you on Insta last night!

Maz   Shut up.

Scratch   For real, you were fuckin' live!

Maz   For real?

Scratch   A lie? You were sick! You gonna do a set tonight?

Maz   How'd you know about that?

Scratch   Joe posted online. I left you love in the comments, not gonna lie.

Maz   Rate that.

Scratch (*offering a joint*)   You wanna get high?

Maz   Nah man. I'm alright. I'm not really on that no more, init.

Scratch   Bro this is Stardawg. You bun one of these zoots you won't need another one for like . . . (*Long pause.*) twenty-five minutes.

Maz (*laughing*)   Nah I'm not on it.

Scratch   Alright, I guess you're on your focussed ting now init. You're a superstar, Maz, you know that. Don't let no one tell you nothing, cuzzy. When you gonna bring me through with this music shit?

Maz   What? You got bars?

Scratch   Does a wall have bricks? Oi turn that off quick. Listen to this.

Scratch *puts a beat on her phone and dramatically prepares herself before dropping this extremely aggressive and over the top song with absolute belief that it's amazing.*

                                Scratch

FUCK YOU BLUD
FUCK YOU BLUD
FUCK YOU BLUD
FUCK YOU BLUD

Fuck you you're a prick
You've got a small fuckin' dick
You couldn't ride with this chick
Why did you cry like a bitch

FUCK YOU BLUD
FUCK YOU BLUD
FUCK YOU BLUD
FUCK YOU BLUD

Maz *interrupts the song.*

Maz   Yo, yo, yo . . . Scratch! Stop I beg you!

Scratch   Yes yes! What do you think?

Maz   It's nice and . . . um . . . aggressive. Keep working on the . . . the bars and that. And next time I'm with Joe I'll definitely mention you.

Scratch *starts selecting another beat.*

Scratch   Let me show you this other song too. I've got a whole EP. Trust me it's live.

Maz   I'm actually wondering if you've got a supply?

Beat

Scratch   What to shot?

Maz   Yeah but not weed. White.

Scratch   What? Why?

Maz   I need the cash.

Scratch   Say no more. I got your back.

Maz   Scratch gets up
and goes over to her book case,
To grab her stash.

Scratch   How much do you want?

Maz   A zed.

Scratch   A zed?! I don't carry that. I got a Q and a ball. You got the pees?

Maz   Scratch looks at me.
She studies my face
and she can tell in a second
what I'm about to say.
So she jumps in quick.

Scratch   I ain't doing it on tick.

Maz   I'll have the money back in no time Scratch. Just sort me out man. How long we been family for?

Scratch contemplates this
for a moment or two,
over a couple of buns on her zoot.
Before she looks at me,
spliff between teeth
and says

Scratch   I need it in a week.

Maz Is that as long as you can do, bro?

Scratch I gotta get a reload. This is serious though. I got some mad people to pay back so don't fuck me about. Do you want it, or not?

Maz I want it.

And she slaps the food in my hand
and the deal is locked.

Scratch One week you got my pees, yeah?

Maz One week.

*We move away from **Scratch**'s flat.*

Maz I manage to shift a few packs
to a couple of German guys
Getting ready for the night life
of London's tourist town.
I think about whether I should head home
When I feel a vibration on my phone.
I take it out and see a call from Joe.

*A video call with **Joe** is projected.*

Joe Yo, Maz! What you saying, you alright?

Maz I'm fine.

Joe What'd you think of Darnell last night?

Maz I dunno, there was a weird vibe. . And from that other guy . . . Tayo.

Joe He's cool man.

Maz Why did he keep staring though?

Joe (*laughing*) I dunno. He's alright though and his music's sick. After you left we were busting tunes for a bit. Some of his hooks are big. I think you guys would really click.

Maz I said I'll think about it.

Joe Darnell's gonna be at the show tonight. He's well connected you know, like some of the people he knows are proper big time. I think this is a good opportunity for you, Maz. I just don't want you to regret turning it down.

Maz *doesn't respond.*

Joe Don't worry about Plots.

Maz I don't care about that guy.

Joe Aight. You know you blew up on that stream last night.

Maz Don't lie.

Joe   Trust me, bare people were hyped. I just sent you the link. Look for yourself if you like.

Maz   I head to YouTube
and search for their stream
And sure enough
My face pops up on the screen.

We see **Maz**'s *face from the day before projected on the screen behind her as she shouts into the camera:*

Maz (*on screen*)   Run that on your fucking stream you CUNT.

With loads of likes and emojis popping up in the comments: 'Oi that was fire' 'she went in', 'you man just got merked' *etc. Then we switch to a montage of Instagram Stories.*

Person 1   Oh my days all you lot need to check this video right now this girl is absolute fire

Person 2   Yo this guy was being a proper cunt to this girl yea and then she just goes HAAAAAMMMMMM.

Person 3   I mean like DESTROYS him. Made him look like a proper idiot fam!

Person 4 (*laughing uncontrollably*)   The only shots you fire . . . the only shots you fire's . . . the only shots you fire's when you bust too quick hahahahahhahahahaahhahahahaha.

Person 5   Yo people check out my girl Maz absolutely kill it last night. This one's a proper superstar so you better get to know. Destined for great things you heard it here first.

Person 6   Yo I ain't seen raw talent like that since the naughties fam. Rappers these days ain't cold like this no more.

Person 7   This girl goes in fam!

Person 8   Is she playing tomorrow?

Person 9   Where can I find more?

Person 10   She's fire!

Maz *looks up at the audience.*

Maz   I guess Joe wasn't lying. Maybe I'll check it out for a bit. See what the vibe is, you know . . . Not like I've got anywhere else to go.

Slowly the lights change and a grime beat comes in, filtered down at first, but gradually getting louder as we transition to a grimy club under a railway arch in Hackney. The place isn't huge but it's packed out. There's a big stage at one end of the room with a set of decks and some microphones.

Joe   Pull up my selector!

FX6 is wheeled up.

Yes yes! Here we go!
Are you lot having a good time?

SOMEBODY MAKE SOME NOISE!

Oh my days are you for real?
You lot must be dead or suttin'.

On the count of three.

    1
    2
    3

SOMEBODY MAKE SOME NOIIISE!

Alllright that's more like it.
Bit o'fire out there as well as up here
just so I know we ain't alone, init?

Hold tight all the man inside.
Hold tight all the galdem
out for the night of their lives
I'm here to bring the vibes
and take you all on a spiritual ride.

The opening to a DnB track sounds. Smooth synths/pads. It's got a spacey quality and an epicness to it.

See tonight!
Inside these four walls
we're gonna leave behind
the fucked up world outside.

We're gonna journey
together into the unknown.
So everyone take out your
phone and take note of this.

It's all love!
Tonight is a fight for your
freedom and for mine!
A fight against the system
that enslaves us.
And trust it ain't no lie!
So if you take one thing
away from tonight, take this.

Don't conform to a system
that will split us up in an instance.

Politicians always bitchin'
how the other party's less likely
to fix the shit we're left in!
Call me crazy I want to section
Half the people I should be respectin'
That's why I don't vote
in no fuckin' general election!

They wanna see us controlled.
Brainwashed into believing
that there ain't no life without the system
breeding mindless minions
who follow a path of life without living.

But fuck that! That ain't me.
That ain't us! So you lot inside
raise your hands to the sky
and join me as we rise up
and take control of our lives.
Take control of our time!
Take back the power for the people!

And if they resist us
I don't give a fuck!
'cause we ain't afraid to fight
for the righteous path tonight!
So are you lot ready
to get hype hype hyped!

Alright! Damn!

Run the track fam!

Joe

To all my
downtrodden sufferers
bass lovin' shufflers,
revolution warriors
and night time strugglers.

Trade goods smugglers
blue skin rustlers
this is for my geezers
my ravers, my hustlers
lighters to the sky
as we burn it down, raise it up
darkness all around
but never mind we'll shake it off
now pass me the mic
get hyped if you'll come with us

hyped if you'll come with us

hyped if you'll come with us

Rida rida rave it up
I'm out on the riddem
and I raise it up
from the road to the track
to the stage I'm up
When I'm back in the booth
man I blaze it up

You slack in the game
better straighten up
I'm thick in the skin
so I can't get cut
talk on the track
'till my time is up
Then step out my grave
and I'll rise up

like Skyward
I'm rising every day
Outa the cold and
into the rain
Them man are old
always the same
Man I'm laughing
Haven't got the time to complain

I'm killin' it, billin' it,
never be finished with
running round tracks
'till I reach the finish it's
Nothing but love
from the limelight lyricist
more complex
than Egyptian pyramids

always be killin' it
Jump on the beat
I know that you're feelin' in
Energy high in the place all night
There's nothing but love
for the music I'm dealing with.

Maz The set flies by and the crowd are fucking hyped
And when he's back at his decks

I shout:

Oi Joe that set was live!

Joe Sound check was at five.

Maz Joe looks at me for a minute
And I can see he's
making up his mind.

Joe Fuck it we're going into this blind.

Maz What?

And I see Tayo come from the side.
He gives me a wink
as he steps up to the mic.

Tayo's *backing track starts.*

Joe After his opening chorus. You come in. OK?

Maz No way!

Joe *picks up* **Maz** *and puts her on The Stage.* **Tayo** *hands her a mic and comes in with:*

Tayo

You don't even get my way
Never seem to talk that straight
I don't need to care
you weren't there
Just walk away

I don't wanna play no games
Nothing be lost or gained
I don't need to care
you weren't there
Just walk away

Maz

There's pain in my heart
Time gone
grain in the glass
this strain gonna last

balm of the heart
I drink till I can't see the scars
Blacked out from the dark in the past
I'm carving my pain in these bars

We would always laugh so hard
Never knew it was a mask

For your shit
I wished that I'd asked

Wish that I had another chance
You would get blazed and dance
soaked in the rain we'd laugh
Now I'll never see your face
and the pain of this place hits hard

Smoke grade till the feelings fade
And I'm free from the weight of the day
Keep seeing your face, twisted and strange
Deep in my dreams I'm screaming again

I don't eat, or sleep, I sit with the pain
The system's broke, I'm here for the change
Stats gonna point to suicide
So funding cut from the service again.

Tory cunts I'll swerve in your lane
The people's voice is raging again
It's practically murder
Suicide or a burner
You better turn in your grave

Nowhere to go where he's safe
Cause you took the money away
So you better remember my name
'Cause I'm coming for each of you cunts
Mark what I say.

Tayo

You don't even get my way
Never seem to talk that straight
I don't need to care
you weren't there
Just walk away

I don't wanna play no games
Nothing be lost or gained
I don't need to care
you weren't there
Just walk away

Maz I step back from the gassed crowd
And Joe takes me down
To see Darnell
Who's stood at the bar
With a couple of drinks

We stand back and
watch Tayo sing.
And as the alcohol seeps in
I notice something
soulful about him.

I head to the toilet to take a piss
And on the way
I manage to offload a few tickets
To a couple of blokes
When Darnell taps me on the arm
And says

Darnell Is that coke?

Maz And my stomach goes.

No. . it's . . . er . . .

Darnell It's OK. I won't tell. As long as you've got a bump for Darnell?

Maz And my face breaks to a smile.

Darnell I ain't done it for a while. But you know, I'm in the zone.

Maz I sort Darnell a line
on the back of my phone
We get a drink
And link Aaron and Joe

Darnell These two've got real chemistry together.

Joe Trust me. The crowd are gassed.

Darnell I want you both in the studio on Tuesday. You free?

Aaron Yeah

Maz I'll be there.

Darnell I'll catch you then.

Joe Peace.

Darnell *and* **Joe** *exit*

Maz And they're gone.
And it's just us two
And I don't know what to say
Where to go
or what to do.

Aaron I'm starving. Wanna get some food?

Maz So we make a move

to find a chicken shop
And Aaron takes me
to one of –

Aaron My favourite spots.

We transition to a bridge running over the canal in Hackney Wick.

Maz It's this shitty bridge
running over a canal in Hackney Wick
But it's so dark
that I can barely see shit.

I put a beat on my phone.
And we look out across
The frozen water with silent lips
as Aaron eats his three piece meal,
and I eat my chips.

Maz I listened to your tune. The Frozen Lake one. What's it about?

Aaron *considers this.*

Aaron My family, I guess.

Maz Are you close?

Aaron Nah. What about you?

Maz Same.

Aaron (*beat as he remembers the studio*) Sorry that Plots was being a dickhead about your brother.

Maz I'm used to it. Plots just don't like that I'm better than him.

Aaron Does your brother make music too?

Pause

Maz Yeah . . . but nah, he's a chef.

Aaron For real?

Maz Yeah. Got his own restaurant. Michelin star an that.

Aaron Jehz. You get free food?

Maz Always. I'll take you one day. You need to get some new garms though not gonna lie.

Aaron Bro don't start. Darnell wants me to wear this shit. I don't even know why.

Maz *shakes her head. Silence.*

Aaron What you thinking about this music ting then?

Maz *doesn't answer.*

Aaron   Darnell is the real deal you know.

Maz   Yeah he's cool.

Aaron   I think he wants you to feature on the EP. He got some mad plans lined up.

Maz *doesn't respond.*

Aaron   I think your bars are great. Truthful you know.

Maz *is still silent.*

Aaron   Do you only write rap?

Maz   I write Grime. HipHop sometimes too.

Aaron   OK. But, like, do you ever sing?

Maz   Fuck off.

Aaron   I bet you got a nice voice.

Maz   What makes you think that?

Aaron   Dunno. Just think you do.

Maz   Well I don't.

Aaron   You ever tried?

Maz   No.

Aaron   So. Why don't you give a go?

Maz   And he starts to sing. Slow.

The music from **Maz***'s phone rises up in volume and fits perfectly.*

> **Tayo**
>
> *Anxiety*
> *gets the best of me*
> *every time I see*
> *you*

Maz   And he's proper good you know.

> **Tayo**
>
> *And even though*
> *you said you wouldn't go*
> *I know the minutes with you*
> *are few*

Maz   I ain't doin' it.

Aaron Just try it.

> **Tayo**
>
> *I don't even wonder any more*
> *I shut that door a long time ago*
> *I just wish that me and you*
> *that me and you could take it slow.*

Maz You're bare cheesey, bruv.

Aaron Just try it.

Maz No!

> **Tayo**
>
> *Anxiety*
> *gets the best of me*
> *every time I see*
> *you.*

Maz And I don't wanna do it
But there's something about him
The cheesey fuckin' smile on his face
that just makes me feel . . .
I don't even know you know
Just makes me feel OK.

She takes a breath. **Aaron** *smiles.* **Maz** *gives the song a go.* **Tayo** *helps with the lyrics. They grow in confidence together.*

> **Tayo**
>
> *Anxiety*
>
> **Maz**
>
> *gets the best of me*
>
> **Tayo**
>
> *every time I see*
>
> *you.*
>
> **Maz**
>
> *And even though*
>
> **Tayo**
>
> *You said you wouldn't go*
>
> **Maz**
>
> *I know the minutes with you*

Both

Are few.

Tayo

I don't even wonder any more

Both

I shut that door a long time ago

Tayo

I just wish that me and you

that me and you

Both

Could take it slow.

*They transition to **Joe**'s studio and hear the end of a recording of 'Anxiety'. **Joe** is on the buttons and **Darnell** is listening, beaming from ear to ear.*

Joe   Bam! That's the one! We've got it. Yes, yes you two well fucking done.

Aaron   You know she was on at me the other day that she couldn't sing? That was proper good.

Maz   Shut up!

Aaron   I swear! Genuinely proper good.

Joe   He's right you know, Maz. You went in!

Maz   And even though
every fibre in my body
wonders if I should.
I somehow believe him.

Joe   Darnell, what do you think?

Darnell   I like it a lot. The socials are popping off from the rave. Bare people asking when they're gonna see you two again. I reckon we drip feed a couple singles to help boost the profile ahead of the launch. I'm looking to lock in a distributor off the back of it. Keep active on the socials, yeah? Post every day. Pictures, stories, videos of you writing or whatever. Keep it conversational, engage with people, and above all make sure it don't damage your image. We need to get the visuals out too.

Joe   The shoot's lined up for tomorrow. You two got the location yeah? 6AM – it's an early start so don't be late.

*Enter **Michael***

Joe   Yo, Michael, what's going on?

Maz Joe looks between Michael and me and instantly susses the situation.

Joe I'm gonna duck to the station and grab some fags. Aaron, don't forget your bag.

Maz Aaron takes the hint in his tone.

Joe Darnell –

Darnell If you lot need me, bell my phone.

Darnell, **Joe** *and* **Aaron** *exit.*

Maz Then it's just me and Michael alone.

Michael You know there's police looking for you? I got Brenda on the phone going crazy and you didn't show up to your review either! What's going on, Maz? Are you alright?

Maz Why are you even here, Michael?

Michael Look, Maz, if you don't go back tonight I'm gonna have to tell the police where you're shooting that video tomorrow.

Maz Is that psycho still at the house?

Michael Yes, but look . . .

Maz I ain't going back then.

Michael We've got an assessment lined up for Carlos next week. If he's deemed unfit to be –

Maz What so I go back there and wait for him to have this assessment then yeah? And then what? He just stabs me up in the meantime?

Michael I'm trying to move it up as fast as possible.

Maz (*getting emotional*) I can't go back there, Michael. I swear. He screamed at a fuckin' wall! He's actually psycho! Like crazy! It's not . . . It's not fuckin' . . .

Michael Alright. Calm down.

Maz Please don't tell them where I am tomorrow.

Michael Maz I can't lie.

Maz Look I'm doing something good here! Through a brudda you put me in touch with! If you didn't want me to do it you should never have introduced me.

Beat. **Michael** *thinks.*

Michael Debbie got in touch again.

Maz For fuck's sake.

Michael I promised her –

Maz Why you promising her shit.

Michael Because . . . people deserve a second chance, Maz. It's up to you, of course. But she's really changed. Got herself a job at a library. Been working there three years now. She's not touched a drop since –

Maz I don't give a fuck. I never want to see her again.

Beat

Michael Where are you stayin' at the moment?

Maz I'm just about init.

Michael Where?

Maz I'm at a friend's house. On the sofa.

Michael What you doin' for money?

Maz I'm – er –

I can't find a good enough lie
And I can see Michael's
Starting to make up his mind.

Darnell *enters.*

Darnell Sorry. Forgot my bloody jacket.

Darnell *grabs his jacket and goes to leave before he remembers:*

Darnell Oh yeah. Maz, I never gave you your dough either.

Darnell *goes into his bag and pulls out a wad of cash. He takes a few notes and hands them to* **Maz**. **Maz** *is unsure what to do so takes it without giving the game away.*

Darnell There we go. Eighty pound like we agreed. Yeah?

Maz Nice one.

Darnell I'm Darnell. You're Maz's social worker, yeah?

Michael Ah, yeah, sort of. Not any more actually.

Maz He's got a promotion init.

Darnell Congratulations.

Michael Thanks. Alright, look. Let me get this assessment pulled up. If Carlos is as unstable as you say he is, he'll be moved. And once he's gone. Promise me you'll go back.

Maz I promise.

Michael Alright.

Maz And there's something that softens
in his eyes. He half smiles.

Michael Call me if you need anything.

Exit **Michael**.

Maz Thanks for covering for me.

Darnell It's all good. Michael seems cool.

Maz Yeah, he's proper alright. Been there for me for a long time. Do you want your pees back?

Darnell Keep it. (*Beat.*) You got any more of them packs?

Maz Uh, yeah . . . course.

I take a ticket from my bra
And hand it over.

There you are.

Darnell Sweet. I'll see you tomorrow.

Darnell *exits. We transition to outside the studio in Dalston.*

I step outside
Into the early evening light
And look each way up Kingsland High Road.
Trying to figure out where I should go.

Enter **Aaron**

Aaron Yo!

This surprises **Maz**.

Maz What you sayin'? You been waitin' for me?

Aaron Yeah.

Maz Why?

Aaron Dunno. Do you wanna chill for a bit? I ain't got nowhere to go.

Maz Wanna see where I write bars?

I almost choke on the words
as they come out so fast
and I can weirdly feel
the tightness of my bra
around my chest.

Aaron Great.

Maz I take Aaron up the road,
To the dirty white
front of the Rio Cinema.

Aaron Are you sure we should be doing this?

Enter **Patricia**.

Maz Yo, Pat! You alright!

Patricia Yuh no call mi Pat, Maz. Yuh call mi Patricia. An you learn some manners while yuh at it, young lady. What mi tell ya bout breaking in? Come an speak to me inside.

Maz Pat, this is my mate Aaron.

Patricia Call mi Pat again. I dare ya! Call mi Pat again.

Maz *is laughing.*

Maz Sorry. Patricia. This my friend –

Patricia Yeah, yeah. 'yah friend'. Mi know cah'ave the same kind of 'friend' when I was your age, gurl.

Maz We make music.

Patricia Yeah you'll be makin' sweet music tonight, I'm sure. Yuh wanna be sure to check this man inna no stinga, before yuh let his cocky in yuh pum-pum yuh nah. Runnin' around chasing every gally he see's, I know yuh type.

Maz Pat.

Patricia Yuh nah call me Pat. Yuh fi call mi Patricia!

Maz Allow it, Patricia. It's cold out 'ere.

Patricia *pauses. Looks at* **Maz** *with a disapproving look. Then gives in.*

Patricia Yuh nah mi can't say no to you, Maz. Mekin' a mockery outa mi all ah di time!

Maz She says with a smile on her face
And lets us into the bare brick
basement of the Rio Cinema
Which is a maze of tunnels
heading off into separate sections.
Aaron's in awe as he looks down the corridors
that twist off in all different directions.

We transition into the cellar of the Rio Cinema.

Pat brings in some film reels.

Patricia That's all set up for you. Just push di button on di top and it can run. And yuh nah the boss is in. So you have ta be outta here before we close.

Maz No worries, Patricia. Thanks.

Patricia It's alright!

And mek sure if yah gonna be mekin sweet love, to do it quietly. Mi no wanna be hearin' no agony on di street, alright? There's plenty ahweirdo's round 'ere, yuh know. Mi no want them listenin' at the door.

Maz *and* **Aaron** *laugh.*

Maz Got it.

Patricia Me nah joking. Broad day light. An I see ah man outside. Standing right on di street. Just wankin'. Trousers by his ankles. Just . . .

Patricia *does an impression of him wanking.*

Up and down up down. In the middle of the street. Wid everybody watching. So I grab di broom from the store cupboard and I come outside and say, nuh you cani be doin' dat round 'ere! Dis a family place! And he look at me, wide eyed . . . and keeps on wanking, yuh nah! So I say, you dun kno who your messin' wid! Yuh wanna put dat cocky away! And I chase 'im wid mi broom stick. Mek 'im start runnin' up di road wid his trowsers still down by 'is ankles. Still wankin' away. Just running down di road, like Babylon not gonna take 'im away. Cha. Weiirdos around 'ere, I'm tellin' yuh. Weeeiirdos.

Exit **Patricia**. **Aaron** *and* **Maz** *crack up.*

Aaron She's too jokes . . .

Maz Got a heart of gold.

Aaron How do you know her?

Maz Me and Jerome used to sneak into the films upstairs. Then Pat caught us one day and tried to hit Jerome with a bin lid. But when he explained the situation she brought us down here and set this thing up. It's the old one from upstairs.

Aaron What situation?

Maz (*tight on* **Aaron***'s line. Changing the subject.*) What do you want to watch? They're all random foreign films like Kurdish and shit. They're nice to look at though.

Aaron You choose.

Maz He says as he pulls
a bluetooth speaker from his bag.

This one's not bad.

Maz *clicks a button on the projector. A black and white Kurdish film plays.*

Aaron So when you taking me to your brother's restaurant?

Maz *doesn't respond. She's transfixed by the film.* **Aaron** *is sorting out his speaker so he doesn't notice.*

Aaron He needs to cook us up some Michelin Star bangers.

Aaron *starts playing a song. Soft, chilled, HipHop. Instrumental – no lyrics.*

He looks up. **Maz** *is still staring at the film. Silently emotional.*

Aaron What's wrong?

Silence.

Aaron Did I say something?

Maz No it's not you. Sorry. It's the first time I been back here for a while . . .

Drying her eyes. Silence. **Maz** *looks at* **Aaron** *for a bit.*

Maz Why Tayo?

Aaron It's my name.

Maz I thought Aaron was your name?

Aaron Birth name. I mean.

Maz So where did Aaron come from?

Aaron My social worker. When I came to England I didn't speak a word for like six months . . . like I knew the language but I just didn't speak . . . He said I looked like an Aaron so he called me that and it stuck.

Maz No way.

Aaron Apparently my actual name's Tayo. (*Beat.*) I only found that out recently.

Maz How come?

Aaron My mum told me. I haven't spoken to her in fifteen years and she just popped up on Facebook.

Maz Swear down?

Aaron Yeah. She sent me here when I was like seven. Just took me to the airport and put me on the plane. Never saw her again.

Maz A . . . shit man, that's hard.

Aaron She wants me to go back to Nigeria and meet . . . like . . . my family. Half brothers and sisters and shit.

Maz That's crazy. Are you gonna go?

Aaron I don't know. Weird to feel like your whole life you're missing something . . . and then to be told it was just somewhere else, waiting for you to find, this whole time.

Beat.

Maz Oi give me your phone. I wanna play you something.

Maz *plays a song on his phone . . . it's soulful . . . Hip-Hop tempo.*

Aaron What's this?

Maz It's my brother . . . Listen.

Jerome

I'm going home tonight.
I'm going home tonight.
White lines
cross ocean skies
stars shine bright.

I'm going home tonight.
I'm going home tonight.
Darkness lives
on borrowed time
when stars shine bright.

Maz

You was an early riser
always out late
Presence was consistent
Every day at the gate

I never really got it
Why we'd always walk about
Until we came back
and she was shouting down the house

Eyes looking red
stumbling about
Vodka on her breath
discarded on the couch
You were getting vexed
she needs to sort it out
But there was very little chance
Like rainfall in a drought

When she slapped you cross the mouth
I was under the table
You was screamin' loud
Saying she was unstable
We ducked out of the house
as soon as you were able
Lucky that our neighbours
Took us in and we were grateful

Tagging up my labels
On my jacket and that
Tellin' me if I lost it
I wouldn't be getting it back
Maths in the cafe

>   *countin' up the wraps*
>   *I didn't understand*
>   *But I knew you had my back*
>
>   *I wish you didn't feel like*
>   *You had to be my dad*
>   *man of the house at fourteen,*
>   *man that's actually mad*
>   *You raised me to be good*
>   *Told me off for acting bad*
>   *Spent the evenings in your lessons*
>   *That I'm grateful that I had*
>
>   *Never understanding*
>   *why she wasn't there*
>   *hardest pill to swallow*
>   *Is she never even fucking cared*
>   *I know you always told me*
>   *that life ain't fair*
>   *So I keep on moving forward*
>   *Are you proud of me, yeah?*

Maz   What do you think?

Aaron *is moved by the bars. Properly understanding* **Maz** *for the first time. He loves the connection to the tune and joins in the chorus with* **Maz** *and* **Jerome**. *This represents a real connection for* **Maz**. *Perhaps the first real connection she's had since* **Jerome**.

>   **Tayo**
>
>   *I'm going home tonight.*
>   *I'm going home tonight.*
>   *White lines*
>   *cross ocean skies*
>   *stars shining bright.*
>
>   **All**
>
>   *I'm going home tonight.*
>   *I'm going home tonight.*
>   *Darkness lives*
>   *on borrowed time*
>   *when stars shine bright.*

Aaron   Maz . . . they're fucking sick.

Maz *kisses* **Aaron**. **Aaron** *jumps back surprised and stares at* **Maz**, *unsure why he just reacted that way.* **Maz** *is embarrassed. The rejection of something that was so sure, at this time and in this place is just too much.*

Maz   What? Isn't this what you want?

Aaron I dunno . . . Yeah – I was –

Maz You dunno?

Aaron Yeah . . . I like you.

Maz What you like me?

Aaron Yeah.

Maz Go on then.

Maz *takes off her top.*

Maz What so you like me, yeah? Go on then. Kiss me. Fuck me. Go on then. That's what you want init?

Aaron Maz . . . I . . .

Maz Nah? What is it 'cause I'm butters? Is it 'cause I'm a hoodrat? Is it 'cause my mum's a selfish fucking piss head cunt who fucking fucked everything up? Am I not good enough for your Aaron? Nah fuck you!

Maz *can't contain her emotion. She kicks the projector over and runs out.* **Aaron** *grabs his bag and chases after her.*

Aaron Maz!

Maz *can't. She runs out.* **Aaron** *watches her go, unsure what to do. The track comes to an end.* **Aaron** *grabs his bag and decides to chase* **Maz**.

Exit **Aaron**.

Blackout.

Interval.

Act Two

The audience walk back into a music video shoot, with a large production team, immersed in the action as if it's actually happening around them and they are a part of it. The vibe should feel very different – real life and not theatrical. There are cameras set up pointing at the music video's set design which has multiple screens built into it. There are crew members adding the last finishing touches to the set. **Joe** *is chatting to the* **DOP** *and* **Darnell***, sometimes shouting across the space to other people. Making sure everything's going smoothly.*

Tayo *enters having come out of costume and make-up. He goes over and talks to* **Joe** *and* **Darnell***.*

Audience members are asked to stand in positions in front of the set to test shots. The camera crew buzz around them talking with each other. We see the audience members projected on the screen as the crew discuss lighting, shots and design. Then thank them for standing in for the test.

After a little while **Maz** *enters.* **Joe** *comes over and bollocks her for being late. He talks her through the shoot. Then he grabs everyone's attention.*

Joe OK people. We've only got this place for a few more hours so let's make it count. Starting positions please.

The cast and crew move to their starting positions.

Joe Lights.

The lighting changes dramatically.

Camera

Dop Rolling.

Joe Cue music.

Music starts.

ACTION!

Maz, **Aaron** *and the ensemble are positioned in front of the music video's production design. The screens come alive, live streaming everything from different angles as* **Maz** *performs to camera and the audience. The ensemble join her as extras or backing dancers, adding ad libs where appropriate. It feels like a combination of a live performance and a music video created through choreography, live streaming, video design and lighting.*

Maz

> I ain't got time for the fuck boy.
>
> I don't care a about dough
> I got that by the truck boy.

If you step in the club
then watch what you touch boy.

If you're grabbin' up tings
we'll see if you're tough boy.

I'm rough boy, like a diamond
don't need your gifts, man I'll buy them
Rolex, check the timing'
I'll be the queen of this Island

Not a joke ting, no laughter
Bell up my phone, no answer
I'm flexin' about, I'm a dancer
You fishing for me, I'm piranha

Cah!
It's a new chick on the scene
mouthy ting, with the bars supreme.
Count up the pees,
that I made on the streets
If I'm reaching the top
then so does my team

What?
It's the new gal on the block
bars so hot like rocks that you drop
these guys got eyes on spot get clocked
by the team when they roll deep six man up!
What?

I ain't got time for the broke boy

Don't be beggin' from me
man you are a joke boy

Can't fuck with this gal
'cause she on her own boy

Too weak for this game
go play on your phone boy

You slagging me off, I smile
I leave you behind
I'm in front by a mile
all of you man been away for a while
now you're back on the scene
and you're cattin' my style

You're cattin' my words
the words that I spray

> *that are laced with the stories*
> *I live everyday*
> *like what I say?*
> *Start watching this space.*
> *I don't like what I say*
> *Bitch get out my face!*
>
> *Cah!*
> *It's a new chick on the scene*
> *mouthy ting, with the bars supreme.*
> *Count up the pees,*
> *that I made on the streets*
> *If I'm reaching the top*
> *then so does my team*
>
> *What?*
> *It's the new gal on the block*
> *bars so hot like rocks that you drop*
> *these guys got eyes on spot get clocked*
> *by the team when they roll deep six man up!*
> *What?*

The video, lights and sound cut, we revert to how we were before the shoot.

Joe That's a wrap people! Nice one everyone.

Darnell Just got off the phone with Maya Jama's manager – she's confirmed!

Joe Yes Darnell!

Aaron That's actually mad.

Maz Aaron flashes me a grin
Clearly pumped with adrenaline
I ignore him.

Aaron Wait for me yeah?

Maz *doesn't respond.* **Aaron** *exits quickly.* **Darnell** *comes in close.*

Darnell You smacked it today. I'm gonna make you a fuckin' star, Maz, you know that, right?

Maz If you say so.

Darnell Why you doubting yourself?

Maz I dunno.

Darnell Look at me. You are so talented, Maz. There ain't no other female MCs out there doing what you do. But you got something more than that. You got heart. And that ain't something you can teach. What you have is special. Trust me. (*Beat.*) You got another one of them tickets?

Maz Yeah course.

Maz *gets a ticket out of her bra/rucksack/pocket.*

Darnell How are things going with Michael?

Maz It's fine.

Darnell You can talk to me you know.

Maz Just some boy at my yard. He tried to attack me. I've not gone back there since so . . . apparently police are looking for me.

Darnell Shit . . . Maz.

Maz It's cool. Michael's sorting it.

Darnell (*unusually direct and cold*) Well make sure he does. We don't want nothing fucking this up for us, you feel me?

Maz *isn't sure how to take this.*

Maz Yeah . . . I know . . . It won't. You got my money?

Darnell There ain't a cash point round here so I'll get it to you tomorrow.

Maz (*uneasy*) Nah, I need it today.

Darnell Today? No worries. Let me help Joe pack up here and I'll call you later?

Maz I'm so sick of this day
I just want to forget it.
I hear Aaron shout

Enter **Aaron**.

Aaron Maz!

Maz But I'm already out of the exit.

We transition to the top of a carpark nearby.

It's starting to get dark
And I don't have a plan
So I head up the ramp
Of a disused car park

I sit at the top.
And watch the sun drop
Across the concrete
skyline of London's rooftops.

My phone buzzes in my pocket
I take it out and see a mad amount
Of missed calls with bare voicemails on it.

We're let into **Maz**'s *loneliness, the pressure of her life personified in all of the voicemails.*

Michael (*V.O.*) Maz. It's Michael. I need you to go back to the house tonight please. I've got Carlos an assessment booked for Tuesday.

Brenda (*V.O.*) Maz, where are you? I have told you to come home many times now. This is not OK.

Joe (*V.O.*) Easy Maz! We've got the studio booked in for Thursday

Scratch (*V.O.*) Yo Maz! What the fuck man. I need that bread today! This ain't joke you know.

Joe (*V.O.*) I reckon we try that new one Darnell suggested.

Michael (*V.O.*) Tuesday's the earliest I could manage . . . it's only a few days. But I need you back there.

Brenda (*V.O.*) Maz! The police are looking for you. Just come home. Please.

Michael (*V.O.*) Also, I know you said . . . but Debbie got in touch again.

Scratch (*V.O.*) I owe some mad people for this . . . Why you puttin' us man at risk. You fuckin' promised me bro.

Michael (*V.O.*) I think it'd be good if . . . just call me . . . we can talk it through.

Brenda (*V.O.*) Call the house. I'll be here.

Scratch (*V.O.*) Bell me man!

Joe (*V.O.*) Give me a buzz, we can discuss.

Brenda (*V.O.*) Please . . . just . . . give me a call when you get this, alright? We're all here for you, Maz. We just want you to be safe.

Maz *is totally overwhelmed by everything. Enter* **Aaron** *holding a bottle of Cognac.*

Aaron Maz?

Maz *looks up and sees* **Aaron**. *A beat as* **Maz** *takes him in. She looks away.*

Maz What do you want?

Aaron To apologise.

Maz I don't give a fuck.

Aaron We can't carry on like this.

Maz There ain't no 'we'. So it's fine. You do your job and I'll do mine. A couple studio sessions, then the launch and then we'll just do our own thing.

Aaron I'm not doing the launch.

Beat

Maz What?

Aaron I'm going home.

Beat. **Maz** *processes this.*

Aaron   I Face-Timed my mum last night. We got talking for hours. She explained a lot.

Maz   Like what?

Beat.

Aaron   That she had to send me here . . . She tried to find me but couldn't. We think it could be because she was looking for Tayo not Aaron.

Maz   And you believe her?

Aaron   Why would she lie?

Maz *doesn't respond*

Maz   So all of this is . . . fucked. It's for nothing.

Aaron   Doesn't have to be . . . we've got releases. We'll just do the launch when I'm back.

Maz   We'll lose the hype.

Aaron   She's sick. She won't say what with. But she was coughing loads and shit. So I booked the tickets there and then.

Beat

Maz   When you going?

Aaron   Tomorrow night.

Maz   Fuck.

Aaron   I know . . .

Maz   How long for?

Aaron   A week.

Pause. **Maz** *doesn't respond.*

Aaron   Maz. I'm really sorry. For doing this. And for last night . . .

. . . it wasn't cause I don't . . . it's that not that I'm not . . . into you . . . or whatever it's just . . . with everything . . . happening so fast. And I just . . . I feel comfortable around you, like I feel like I get you and you get me. I've never really had that.

Maz *doesn't respond. But she's listening intensely.*

My whole life. I've never known . . . who my family are . . . I could never say, oh that's where I'm from. That's who I am. That's what I might look like when I grow up. . . . I knew I was from Nigeria and I have these hazy images in my head . . . but I can't remember anyone's face or anything. And England is . . . it's great in many ways . . . I would never be doing any of this with my music I don't think . . . but I've never really . . . found anyone who I feel like gets me. I dunno even what me is . . .

Maz *doesn't respond.*

It's just . . . when you did that last night . . . it freaked me out a bit. I don't know why. Maybe with everything going on . . . with my mum . . . and the music and . . . and so I jumped back. And I just wish that I hadn't done that, 'cause I think you're cool and I like you . . . And I feel like I just fucked it up and made you upset . . . I don't ever want to make you feel like that. Like I want to be there for you . . .

Pause. **Maz** *considers this. She looks at him. He's emotional. Staring at her.*

Aaron   I have to go see her, Maz.

Beat

Maz   I get it

Aaron   I'm sorry

Maz   It's cool.

Aaron *offers the Cognac.*

Aaron   I got this. To say sorry.

Maz *takes the bottle, opens it and swigs.*

Maz   Ahh, that tastes like poor man's piss bruv. Why'd you not get Henny?

Aaron   I just spent like £600 on flights. I'm broke. Oi do you want my coat?

Maz   And I suddenly notice
that I'm shivering.

Nah, I'm good. You'll be freezing.

Aaron   Just give me the bottle and I'll be alright.

Maz   We do a little switch.
And I slip into his jacket
which is a perfect fit
even though it's way too big.
I hand him the bottle
and he takes another
swig of the drink.

Looks me in the eyes
and to my surprise he says:

Aaron   Tell me about your mum.

Maz   And maybe it's the drink.
Or maybe it's the way he speaks.
Or maybe it's the way he's looking at me.
Or maybe it's all three of those things

But my chest doesn't feel tight . . . I feel fine

I ain't seen my mum since I went into care. I was nine. She was a piss head. Mum fucked things up for me and Jerome big time.

Aaron You're both doing alright. We're making music. Your brother's got a Michelin Star –

Maz My brother ain't no chef. I made it up.

Aaron Why?

Maz 'cause.

Beat.

Aaron So what does he –

Maz He's dead.

This throws **Aaron**.

Aaron Maz. I . . .

Maz He killed himself

Aaron I'm . . . so sorry.

Silence.

Maz Jerome was my soldier man. My saviour . . . when he was with me he always seemed alright. I guess he just wanted me to think he was a superhero. The man of the house. Whatever the fuck that means . . . Mum was pissed up all the time. Like day and night. So . . . she was no fuckin' use to anyone. Jerome looked after both of us really. It was embarrassing. For him mostly I think. Everyone knew 'cause Plots made a track about her which went round school . . .

Aaron What? Really?

Maz Yeah. Him and Jerome used to go Joe's studio a lot. They used to clash all the time. Both on the track and and like . . . actually fighting. He was only sixteen man. That's my age now, like . . . he shouldn't have had the stress he had. She should have been looking after all of us. Instead of drinkin' vodka like it's fuckin' water.

Pause.

She wants to meet up.

Aaron Do you?

Maz No.

Aaron Why?

Maz How can I forgive her? For pushing him so far that he . . .

Aaron We don't get to choose our family. We can choose our friends, our jobs, our lifestyle. . . . But family, whatever that means . . . it's just the way it is. You gotta do whatever it is that's gonna make you the happiest in the long run, Maz.

Maz   I'm happy on my own.

Silence.

Aaron   Why Maz?

Maz   What do you mean 'why Maz'?

Aaron   Like what does it mean?

Maz   It's my name.

Aaron   Oh I thought it was like a tag?

Maz   No! It's short for . . .

And I stop.

Aaron   What?

Maz   I can't tell him, man.

Aaron   What's it short for?

Maz   . . . Maryam.

Aaron   No way!

Aaron *laughs hard.*

Maz   Shut the fuck up, bruv!

Aaron   That's a proper nice name. I mean it! It was just a surprise.

Maz   I swear if you don't shut up . . . I'm leaving.

Aaron   No you're not.

Maz   He grabs me lightly by the arm
And pulls me in. I lean forward
my face lingers close to his
My stomach flips
a fraction of space between lips
Iris to iris eyes fixed
I can feel the speed of our hearts
beating in time and it's . . .

Beat. **Maz** *is struggling to process how she feels.* **Maz** *turns away and swings the bottle.*

Aaron   Are you OK?

Maz   I'm cool.

Aaron   I didn't mean to . . .

Maz   I said I'm cool.

Aaron *puts his arms around her.*

Aaron   I got you.

Maz   And those three words
hug me tighter
than he ever could.
Even if he tried.

Aaron   Are you alright?

Maz   I'm fine.

Aaron   Do you want to come back to mine?

Exit **Aaron**.

Maz   When I wake the next morning,
head banging, mouth dry,
eyes squinting in sunlight,
Aaron's already gone.

So I gather my things,
put my shoes on
and count the cash
I've made in the last few days
trying to work out
how much more I need
to pay Scratch back.

I'm still short from the ticket
That I ticked to Darnell.
So I give him a bell
But his phone just goes
straight to voicemail.

I need to find some way
To get that dough
So I head to Joe's
But as I walk up the road I hear Scratch go

We transition to a street near **Joe**'s *flat. Enter* **Scratch**.

Scratch   Yo! Where the fuck have you been. Why you ghosting me?

Maz   I'd never do that, cuz.

Scratch   You got the dough?

Maz   Almost.

Maz *hands* **Scratch** *the money. Underscore starts low and grows.*

Scratch   What do you mean almost?

Maz I ticked someone a gram.

Scratch Maz man.

Maz Can't you float me. It's not a lot bro.

Scratch I ain't got enough till I get a reload. They ain't gonna like this man.

Maz Who'd you get it off?

Scratch is staring at the floor
looking more shook
than I've ever seen before.

Scratch Omar.

Enter **Brenda**

Brenda Maz!

Scratch Shit.

Brenda There you are!

Maz Scratch bro.

Scratch Get my fuckin' dough.

Exit **Scratch**.

Maz (*shouting after them*) I didn't know you'd ticked it from them.

Brenda Maz! Where have you been?

Maz Away from you and that fuckin' psycho!

Brenda Carlos has agreed to stay in his room. Please, you need to come home, just one night.

Maz I ain't staying there!

Brenda Please Maz. Otherwise, we'll have no choice but to call the police and put you in a secure placement. You'll have a lot of your freedoms restricted. You won't be able to do the performance. Just come back for tonight and then we can chat about it properly tomorrow OK?

Maz I'm trapped.
If I get nicked I've got no way
Of getting the bread back to Scratch.

Brenda Maz. Come now!

Transition to **Maz**'s *room*.

Maz I let them take me home
and into my bare room.
lie on the not-so-soft bed,
feeling the mattress springs

poke into my skin.
I stare at the ceiling
And drift off to sleep
to the sound of my heart beating.
Aware of this uneasy feeling
that something bad is about
to happen.

A loud bang of some kind

I'm woken up by the sound of wood crackin'.

Enter **Carlos**, *holding a knife.*

Carlos   You ain't gettin' me, babes.

Maz   Carlos, what the fuck are you doin?

Carlos   Protecting myself.

Maz   From what?

Carlos   You're lucky I don't carve off your face after what you've done!

Maz   Carlos what the fuck are you on about, man?

Carlos   Where is it?

Maz   Where's what?

Carlos   My watch!

Maz   Carlos, I'm not being funny but –

Carlos   You've been out sellin' all my shit! Jackin' it while I'm asleep. You and fuckin' Brenda. Takin' the piss!

Maz   Carlos just listen to me, I ain't joking this –

Carlos   I know you want me dead.

Maz   Bro this is all in your head. Carlos! Listen! I don't want no beef, I just wanna get the fuck out of here.

Carlos   What and come back later and get me while I'm asleep? Fuck that! It's either you or it's me!

Carlos *lunges at* **Maz**. *During the fight,* **Maz** *gets cut on the arm which draws blood but it's not serious.* **Carlos** *is looking like he will win the fight and seriously hurt/kill* **Maz**. *He is stopped by a voice of someone in his head.* **Maz** *takes the opportunity and kicks him whilst he's off guard.* **Carlos** *hits his head hard on* **Maz**'s *bed which knocks him out. Enter* **Brenda** *who runs to* **Carlos**' *aid.* **Maz**, *breathless, runs away.*

Brenda   What the ?? What is going on . . . ? Carlos! Carlos. . .! Lord have mercy

Brenda *exits with* **Carlos**.

Maz   As I'm barely able to stand

And all I can do
Is ring the only guy
Who will understand.

Aaron   Maz?

Maz   Aaron. I'm sorry. I don't know why I called. I just . . . Carlos just . . . He had a knife and – My arm's cut and –

Aaron   Slow down. It's alright. I got you.

Maz   And those three words again
hug me tight
before a thought crosses my mind
like a bolt of light

Wait. Weren't you supposed to be flying out tonight?

Aaron   Yeah.

Maz   So where are you?

Aaron   Train station.

Maz   In London?

Aaron   Yeah.

Maz   Are the trains delayed?

Aaron   No.

Maz   So what are you –

Aaron   She died. Last night.

Beat

Maz   I'm so sorry. Come meet me.

Aaron   I can't.

Maz   Aaron. Please. I mean it.
Meet me at your house.
We can talk it out . . .

Aaron?

Aaron   OK. I'm on my way back.

Transition to **Aaron**'s *room.*

Maz   When I arrive at Aaron's flat
He's left the door on the latch
So I let myself in,
make my way down the corridor
and find myself alone
in his dimly lit bedroom.

I take in the bare walls
And the badly packed bag
The empty shelves
With nothing but an old notepad.

Enter **Aaron**

Aaron Maz?

Maz He looks a lot less stable
Than he felt on the rooftop
We've got no words
so we don't say much.
But somehow I feel
That whatever I'm doing
Is just about enough.
And then I do something
That shocks both of us.

Maz *sings a capella. It's nervous and soft.* **Aaron** *can't look at her.*

Maz

*Frozen lake
Ice cold on my face.
Ambition fades from me.*

*Washed on the waves
floats another day
where I can be free.*

*Peace of mind
is hard to find these days.
When what is whole
is made of two.*

*And life seems fine
when we run
from the truth*

*Replace ourselves
with whatever helps
as liquor
takes me through.*

*But that don't help
my sorry self
when all I need
is you.*

Frozen lake

> *Ice cold on my face.*
> *Ambition fades from me.*
> *Washed on the waves*
> *floats another day*
> *where I can be free.*

Maz That night, I stay in his bed
sat upright, straight legged,
with my back to the wall,
cradling his head on my knees,
As he holds my leg tight
And cries silent tears
into the bedsheets.

Aaron *exits*.

Maz I only get what feels like
five minutes of sleep
But when I wake my phone
Says it's half three!
Fuck me. I check my texts
And see that Aaron's said

Aaron Sorry I left. Darnell's going mad, I've gone to the venue early to try calm him down. EP's dropped . . . I'm sorry, I dunno what happened . . .

Maz I quickly flick to Spotify
and type in our names.
But when the album
comes up I feel the colour
drain from my face.

And in a fit of silent rage,
so strong, my body shakes,
I grab my things and make
my way with pace to the place.

Transition to backstage at the gig. **Joe**, **Aaron** *and* **Michael** *are all there.* **Darnell** *is there too looking wired and very stressed. Barely holding it together.*

Maz Yo what the fuck is this?

Joe Maz chill . . .

Maz You fuckin' cut me out you fuckin' snakes! I'm not on a single track!

Darnell We made an executive decision to –

Maz Did you know about this?

Aaron No.

Joe I told you she would react like this.

Maz   So it was your fuckin' idea was it?

Darnell   It was a collective decision.

Joe   Nah, nah, nah don't even . . . You made the decision, not me. Don't bring me into your shit.

Darnell   Fine. I made the decision.

Maz (*goes for* **Darnell**. **Joe** *holds her back.*)   You fuckin' prick! I'll smash your fuckin' face in!

Darnell   You're on the run from an assault charge, Maz.

Maz   What charge?

Darnell   We need to make sure the launch stays clean.

Maz   WHAT FUCKIN' CHARGE?

Michael   Carlos is in hospital. The police want to talk to you about what happened.

Maz   It was self defence! He tried to fuckin' stab me!

Darnell   Whatever happened, they're asking questions. And if this boy wants to press charges it doesn't look good for what we're doing.

Maz   So why didn't you chat to me? I could've told you it ain't nuttin'.

Joe   That's exactly what I said.

Darnell   No one knew where you were. We couldn't get through to you.

Maz   Do I have cunt written across my face? Bell my phone. Text me. WhatsApp. Email. Face-Time. Instagram. TikTok. Snapchat. Facebook fucking Messenger! I'm there! I'm available. Twenty four fucking seven. So don't tell me you couldn't get through! I've been fuckin' bellin' you for my money anyway!

Michael   What money?

Maz   Truth is, you're a fuckin' joke, Darnell!

Darnell   Don't talk to me like that.

Michael   Woah. . . . What's going on?

Maz   You don't know nothing about me? You don't know nothing about my struggle! This is the one good fuckin' thing I had going and this privileged prick fucks it up for me!

Darnell   You ain't the only one who's struggled, you know . . .

Maz   Then you've forgotten your roots fam!

Darnell   I've worked hard to get where I am. None of us need some stupid yout running round fuckin' this up for us.

Maz   You could've just asked about my situation instead of assuming!

Darnell   It's you that's assuming! I've been in your shoes. I know where it ends up! Some stupid girl that thinks this is all a game. It's all parties and gang signs and shottin' coke on the side so it's all 'real'! But what you don't understand is that people work day and fuckin' night to get things goin'! It ain't all music videos and studio sessions you know. It's graft! And that graft is thankless until something happens. I ain't lettin' you fuck this up again! That boy could fuckin' die tonight in hospital. That's you done for murder.

Maz   It was self defence!

Darnell   Press gets a hold of that, you're done.

Michael   They found the knife. All Maz needs to do is explain what happened and it will be dropped.

Maz   Aaron, are you going to do something?

Pause

Maz   Bruv?

Hello? You fuckin' deaf or what? Are you going to Let. This. Happen?!

Aaron   I don't know.

Maz   What do you mean you don't know? We in this together. I got you. You got me . . .

Aaron   You didn't tell me about Carlos –

Maz   It was self defence!

Aaron   Or that you were sellin' drugs . . .

Maz   Aaron . . . please.

Aaron   There's a lot riding on this . . .

Maz   You weren't gonna fuckin' do the show . . . now you're. . . . Oh my days. Everyone's a fuckin' snake.

Enter **Plots**.

Plots   Yo, Maz!

Darnell   Tayo's going on. Plots is supporting.

Maz   You're fuckin' joking right?

Plots   What's happening?

Maz   He cut me out. I'm off the album and I'm not playing tonight.

Plots   What? Darnell what the fuck man?

Darnell   That's the way this game goes. It's ruthless. Are you in or what?

Plots   Bro I've known Maz for time. I know I take the piss and that but I ain't about to snake her out like this

Darnell   Look I've got suttin' cookin' for you. You really want to fuck this up 'cause of her?

Plots   Maz. Listen. You need to call your friend, Scratch. Tell her to get out of the endz for a bit. She should never of got caught up with Omar an' that.

Maz   What? How d'you know about that?

Plots   My boy rang me, said they're gonna run up in her yard.

Maz *is stunned. Then suddenly turns around to leave.*

Aaron   Maz wait!

Maz   Fuck you! And fuck the lot of you! (*To* **Tayo**.) I hope you fuckin' die you cunt!

Maz *exits.*

Darnell   OK! I've just checked in on the influencers. Most of the press are here too. Just missing GRM, but there's still time.

Joe   You ready?

Aaron   I don't think I can do this.

Joe   Look, tonight ain't the end of the road. Just do your thing and we'll sort everything out tomorrow. OK?

Aaron *doesn't respond.*

Joe   I'm gonna go warm them up a bit. You got this.

Joe *exits.*

Aaron   I'm not going on.

Darnell   Tayo, you have to!

Aaron   I can't. . . .

Darnell   This ain't on you.

Aaron   Maz fuckin' hates me.

Darnell   She brought it on herself.

Darnell *gives* **Aaron** *a new shirt. He holds it.*

Darnell   Here. Put this on. You'll look good. I'm gonna head out front and check for GRM. (*He goes to leave.*) You're gonna be incredible, Tayo. Your mum would be so proud.

Darnell *leaves.* **Aaron** *looks at the shirt. Puts it on. Then takes out his phone. He makes a call. We see* **Maz**'s *phone ring. She declines the call.* **Aaron** *leaves a message.*

Aaron Maz . . . I just wanna say . . .

We move to **Joe** *out front at the launch. Hyping the crowd up.*

Joe Alright party people!
You know what time it is, right?
You've heard some of the
wickedest tunes from some
of the realest talent the UK
has to offer tonight.

But we're just getting started.
'cause now we come to the moment
you've all been waiting for.

So raise the volume on the speaker
dim the lights so I can barely see ya!
You lot better get ready you know!
Make some noise

FOR MAN LIKE TAYO!

Piano stars. It's minor. Emotional.

> **Tayo**
>
> *You can't keep fate
> in the palm of your hand
> and all great things
> no matter how tall they stand
> will fall.*
>
> *I've laid my hand
> You better make your move
> Cause we all know
> Betrayal's hard to prove
> at all.*
>
> *I was caught in sinking sand
> starved to death in this baron land.
> I sunk my teeth in the outstretched hand.
> now I'll pay the price*
>
> *Redemption seems so far away
> I'll look back each passing day
> And see it was more than child's play
> I'll give you my life.*

Tayo *begins to transition us to the bridge in Hackney Wick.*

> *Why is nothing smooth?*
> *It left me black and blue*
> *I don't think I can hold on*
> *much more.*
>
> *There's never any doubt*
> *It was me who cut you down*
> *Now there's nothing left of us*
> *At all*
>
> *I was caught in sinking sand*
> *starved to death in this baron land*
> *I sunk my teeth in the outstretched hand*
> *now I'll pay the price*
>
> *Redemption seems so far away*
> *I'll look back each passing day*
> *And see it was more than child's play*
> *I'll give you my life.*

We've arrived at the bridge. The song breaks down to a stripped back section with **Tayo***'s vocals gently over the top – no lyrics. We see* **Maz** *pick up her phone and listen to the rest of* **Aaron***'s message which mixes in with the music –*

Aaron Maz . . . I just wanna say . . . I'm sorry. I really am. I didn't want any of this to happen. I just don't think I'm . . . since everything with my mum . . . I. I didn't want to hurt you. I never wanted that. You're the best thing that's ever happened to me. You were right. About everything. All of it. It's just . . . Bullshit. Isn't it? Nothing's really real. Everyone's just out for themselves. I just. . I think it's better off . . . for you . . . you'd be so much better off . . . If I . . . wasn't around. I'm just causing pain. I'm sorry. You won't see me again.

We see **Maz** *realise what* **Tayo** *is about to do. She tries to call* **Tayo** *back. It goes to voicemail. The song builds. The lighting should be heightened here. Matching the chaos of the music and* **Maz***'s mental state.*

Maz   Aaron? Aaron? Please! Everything's OK! I forgive you. It doesn't matter . . . please just don't . . .

She doesn't have the words. Suddenly the thought drops. She knows where **Tayo** *is.*

Tayo

> *I was caught in sinking sand*
> *starved to death in this baron land*
> *I sunk my teeth in the outstretched hand*
> *And now I'll pay the price*
>
> *Redemption seems so far away*
> *I'll look back each passing day*
> *And see it was more than child's play*
> *I'll give you my life.*

Maz *arrives at the canal over the bridge.* **Aaron** *is stood on the edge. Getting ready to jump.*

Maz Aaron! Wait!

Aaron What are you –

Maz Just come down.

Aaron I can't –

Maz Please.

Aaron I can't cope –

Maz I know.

Aaron What's the point? In any of it?

Maz I don't know. But I'm here. And . . .

Aaron All I cause is pain.

Maz That's not true!

Aaron It is! You. My mum. My family. I'm better off . . . Everyone is better off without me.

Maz I'm not! I'm really, really not! You're the only person I can be around. You get me! And I get you. That's rare . . . I've never . . . I've never had that either. I don't blame you. For what happened. It wasn't your fault. With everything going on I'm not surprised you didn't know what to do. I forgive you. I love you. Aaron. I do. I need you. . . . Please. Please! Just come down.

And for a second
he looks like he's gonna do it.
Then he stops,
His body starts to collapse.
He turns around, looks down
ready to jump off of the wall
onto the safety of the ground
Before he slips back.

And in a split second
He suspends in space
Frozen and framed
By the beauty of this place
His head turned,
panic across his face
As I watch his body fall
Through the glass sheets of ice
cracks snaking on every side
As he sinks away.

Blackout. Silence.

Transition to disused chapel of rest

Michael   Maz. Maz! YO, MAZ.

No reply.

You alright?

Pause. No reply.

I've got some news.

Pause. Nothing.

Carlos's been diagnosed with Paranoid Schizophrenia. All the charges against you have been dropped. He's not going to come back to the house either. So you can stay at home tonight if you like?

Pause. No reply.

Do you remember when you used to come here? When you ran away in the early days?

Pause. Nothing.

I remember the very first time you came here, you know? Man that was so much stress. It was my first fuckin' day! And this nine-year-old girl steals like £300 and runs away. Talk about baptism of fucking fire man. We had half the social workers in Hackney looking for you. Bare police too. I remember I was talking to the brudda who owns the corner shop up there and he said he'd seen a kid come in and buy a Twix with a pinky. I mean for starters, who the fuck buys a Twix. I mean what is it? A biscuit? A chocolate bar? Do I dunk it? Do I eat it straight? Is there like some special thing that I'm missing here or . . .

No reply.

So I came in here and was shouting your name. Lookin' in bushes and that, feeling like a proper idiot. But I couldn't see you nowhere. I'd been looking all damn day for you and I was stressin' 'cause I thought I was gonna lose my job or some shit. Now I realise all you fuckers run away all the time. But back then. Jehz. I thought that was it. I was so stressed, I literally didn't know what to do. So I sat down here and rolled a fag. And then out of nowhere this busker just started playing this song, right over there under that tree.

Underscore of violin starts. It's calming. Simple. Broad. Shouldn't take over the text or get too complex.

I didn't recognise it or nothing but it was kinda . . . beautiful. And in my emotional, stressed out, fucked up state, I just looked out across the pond. And something about it . . . I dunno, maybe the stillness or the water or whatever . . . just made me like . . . I dunno . . . chill. And then, like in a fuckin' cartoon or some shit, this clumsy mother fucker of a swan . . . or maybe it was a goose, I dunno . . . but this clumsy fucking bird just takes off. Waddling across the water like some kind of fat Jesus. But you know. A bird. And I remember thinking. That's a metaphor for my life, fam! All calm and peaceful until you came along and ruined the quiet. And I was so pissed off I pulled out my phone and rang your number. And then instantly shat myself as I heard a phone ring right above my head. And I look up and it's you . . . screw facing me. With a fucking Twix in your mouth. And I looked in your eyes and you just looked so . . . angry and scared and lost and hurt and . . . all the fucking emotions, man. And I dunno, there was something about the image that was just so pure, that all my anger just dropped from me. Until you dashed the Twix in my eye and told me to fuck off and suddenly you weren't so pure no more.

No reply.

You know, Maz. We've been on a journey together. And I like to think I've been there. Through all the shit. And I just want you to know. I'm still here for you init. Anytime, anywhere. I know it must be proper hard to deal with everything right now and things might not make a lot of sense to you but . . . well you don't have to be a superhero init. You just feel things as they come and . . . we'll deal with it.

Maz Was he good? At the launch? Was he good?

Michael He was incredible, Maz. Everyone loved him.

Maz What did the press say?

Michael There weren't no press. Or influencers or nothing.

Maz What do you mean? I thought Darne –

Michael Darnell was a joke. After I figured out you'd been shottin' him coke I asked a friend of mine who works at Universal if he knew him turns out it was all bollocks. The label, Island Records . . . the lot. He was just trying to launch his own career off the back of you two.

Pause. **Maz** *processes this.*

Maz Joe's right. Everything's fucked.

Michael Well . . . Joe's got his own way of making peace with the world. Doesn't mean it's true.

Maz He's right though. Everyone's out for themselves. The system's fucked up. All of it.

Michael Name me a system in the world that isn't. At least we've got one.

Maz I wish we didn't.

Michael What would've happened to you?

Maz I dunno . . . probably no different from Jerome . . .

Michael I'm not sayin' things are perfect. But hating on everything that's let you down ain't gonna bring people back. There's no use just going around shouting about how everything's broken. You either gotta do something to fix it, or make the most of what there is. And if you're angry about things, then let's work to change them.

But right now just concentrate on feeling things as they come in and looking after yourself, OK?

Pause.

Maz How's the job going?

Michael It's good. . . . I'm officially a team leader.

Maz (*with meaning*) Congrats. I'm proud of you.

Michael (*this moves him*) Thanks.

Do you want me to stay? I can keep local if you –

Maz Nah you're alright.

Michael OK. Well let me know how it goes, yeah?

He gets down. So does she.

Maz I will.

Thanks for coming.

Michael Of course. Whatever you need.

They hug. **Michael** *leaves.* **Maz** *is alone for a moment. Enter* **Mum** *unnoticed. She watches* **Maz** *for a moment.*

Mum Maryam?

Maz Y'alright.

Mum Maz . . . I can't believe –
You've grown a lot.

Maz You've aged.

Mum I'm sure I have.

Pause.

Are you OK?

Maz I'm fine. You?

Mum I'm good thank you.

Pause.

It's really nice to see you.

Pause.

I'm so happy that you're willing to give this . . . to give me . . . a . . . erm . . .

Maz   D'you know why I wanted to meet here?

Mum   No.

Maz   Jerome used to bring me here.

Mum   Did he?

Maz   We used to play in that park over there.
Then feed the ducks.
We'd sit just here and look at the water.
And wait until you were sober enough to come home.
One Saturday, I woke up to you and him shouting at each other.
You'd thrown a pan of boiling water at him.
You were so drunk you pretty much missed.
Only got his hand.
He came and got me and took me out, still in my pyjamas.
And he brought me here.
We played on the swings.
Fed the ducks.
Sat and watched the water.
And I saw his hand was all blistered and red.
Bubbling up like it does.
And I said 'I hate Mummy for doing that to you'.
And do you know what he said to me?
He said to me, 'you shouldn't hate Mummy'.
You should only hate bad people.
Mummy isn't a bad person.
She just has a lot of monsters that make her do bad things sometimes.
But inside she's a good person and she loves us very much.
And one day the monsters will go away.
And she won't do bad things anymore.'

Mum   I miss him. So much. Every single day.

Maz   So do I.

Mum   I know you must hate me –

Maz   I don't hate you. I don't love you. But I don't hate you.

Mum   Maz, I'm sorry. I really am.

Maz (*shrugs*)   Can't change the past. Can't change family either. Guess we'll just have to make the most of what we've got.

Mum   I've been watching videos of you on YouTube. Your music. It's really good.

Maz   Thanks.

Mum   You still doing it?

Maz   Not really.

Mum   I heard about your friend . . . Aaron

Maz   Don't.

Mum   Michael said that you saved his life. I'm so . . . you've become everything that Jerome would have wanted. He'd be so proud of you.

Maz   For what?

Mum   For talking him down.

Maz   He still slipped though didn't he?

Mum   That's not your fault. And if you hadn't called the emergency services he might have drowned. Jerome would be so proud.

Maz *doesn't respond. But this lands on her.*

Mum   It's a lovely day. Do you want to go for a walk?

Maz   OK.

Beat

Maz *battles with herself . . .*

Maz   Happy birthday, Debbie. Sorry I . . . didn't get you anything.

Mum   This is perfect, Maryam.

Mum *exits.*

We transition to **Joe**'s *studio.* **Joe** *and* **Aaron** *are rapping/beatboxing.* **Maz** *enters and watches the room. She feels calmer. More grounded, with a greater perspective now. The boys finish up.*

Joe   Oi come on! Let's put it down.

Aaron   Let's get it!

Enter **Plots** – *he see's* **Maz**. *There's a moment.*

Plots   How's your friend doing?

Enter **Scratch** *with her arm in a sling.*

Scratch   Oi I'm telling you, fam, whoever done a shit in there is dutty –

Scratch *clocks* **Plots**.

Scratch   Yo, what's good?

Plots   You're alive then?

Scratch   Just about.

Scratch   Lucky Omar let you off lightly.

Scratch For real.

Plots *goes to leave.*

Joe Oi where you going?

Plots Back to the strip.

Aaron There's nothing out there for you, bro.

Scratch You're just gonna end up like me. Or worse.

Plots (*pointed, about* **Maz**) I'll be calm. It's just me out there. I ain't got no one to let me down.

Joe Look I'm sorry about Darnell. I shouldn't have brought him into this. That was my fault. But we got something special here man. You lot can do some madness together. We got followers, we got the live sessions – we can build the hype ourselves. Don't throw it all away over that guy. You're part of something here. Come run the stream man.

Beat. **Plots** *thinks.*

Plots Come then.

Maz *smiles. This means a lot, even after everything.*

Joe OK let's go.

Scratch Oi, Joe, when we putting my bars down.

Joe After the stream.

Scratch Joe I'm telling you this EP is gonna blow your mind.

Joe Yeah? I can't wait. Yo let's go.

Joe *starts streaming.*

Plots Yes, yes. Welcome back to the livest stream in London people. We got a mad session lined up for you today! But first we got suttin' a little different for you. Let me introduce you to my gal Maz. She's got suttin' to say init. Kill it.

Maz Ready.

Aaron Let's do it.

Music for 'I'm Going Home' starts.

Maz

I'm going home tonight
I'm going home ton–

Maz's *voice cracks. She tries to push through but breaks down unable to continue.*

Joe You alright?

Maz Yeah, I'm cool.

Plots   You sure?

Maz *takes a moment.*

Maz   Yeah. I'm good.

Aaron   You wanna take a break or –

Maz   Nah . . . I . . . er . . . Let's go again.

Aaron   I got you.

Maz   Actually fuck this.
I wanna say suttin'.

Maz *talks directly into the stream.*

This was one of my brother's tunes
His only tune, you know.
Cause he took his own life
At seventeen years old.
For whatever reason
He was drowning in doubt
But for me, he was always
man of the house
Never let me down
But clearly he never saw no way out.

So I'm begging you.
Whatever you do.
Do not let the system beat you.
Do not become another fucking statistic
Because believe it or not
There are people in your life
That will stick with you
Through all of it.
Even if you don't feel there is
There are a million other people
Going through near enough
exactly the same shit.

I don't know who needs to hear this
I didn't know Jerome did.

But you are worth more
than you will ever fucking realise.
Whatever's happened to you
Whoever's let you down
Or fucked you up
Or disappeared without
A chance to say goodbye.
Let them go.

Cause I know that if you don't
There's only one person
who's gonna get hurt
And that's you.

So make your peace.
Find your home.
It might not be in the place you think
But it's out there bro.

Yo, Joe. Run my new tune!

Joe *hits play.*

Maz

Came from the roads got hate from the start
Other guys got praise for their bars
Take stock I pray for a chance
Not afraid of the cold I was raised in the dark

I spit flames bout pain in the past
Lightweight champ make way to the stars
Hybrid dank I fade from the scars
Seen how it is I ain't taking a chance

Oi Maz! Where's she been lately?
On my own tryin' to deal with the pain g
I'm back but now they wanna hate me
Pissed off cause their bredrin's rate me

I'm like Marmite love me or hate me
Leave me or take me no one can break me
Try stop me but they can't make me
blud don't be stupid Maz can't be shakey!!

One time for the fallen soldiers
One time for the bredrins gone
One time for the memories made

Not there but the past lives on

The End.

In conversation with director Maggie Norris

BP *What for you was the attraction of commissioning this show and staging it at The Big House?*

MN   James Meteyard's *Electrolyte*. I saw that show and I was so excited by the music and the way that it was embedded into the story and in gig theatre form. That was the trigger, really. Also, I thought that the themes that he dealt with in *Electrolyte*, which were complex and serious, really suited the form in a way that surprised me. Yeah, so I was profoundly moved by that particular production which I saw in London and at the Edinburgh Festival. That was the starting place. But also, James Meteyard has seen our work over a number of years and he really understands what we're doing. So I thought that he was the perfect fit.

BP *What was the evolution of the piece, from when you commissioned it to when you first put it on at the end of 2021?*

MN   I worked very closely with James on *Redemption* and it was an exciting process as we explored the themes that we wanted to tackle. Male suicide, particularly amongst care leavers, is something that we felt we should be looking at. We wanted to look at two care leavers' experience of suicide that was very different. So we have Maz who is on the run from her care home, whose brother has committed suicide, and we have Tayo who has been put in the system, originally from Nigeria, who tries to commit suicide during the story. Both are desperately searching for their identity and are feeling very lost. Both share a great love of music and although their musical interests are completely different, they are both trying to break into the music industry.

BP *What are other themes you wanted to explore?*

MN   Obviously Maz's relationship with her mother is key to this story and we hear about her in the very first scene, where we also learn that Maz never wants to see her again. We finally meet her in the penultimate scene. When she walks in and their story arc moves towards redemption, we see them come together albeit in a tentative way, and the possibility of a new beginning. The audience were very moved by this scene and a lot of tears were shed (particularly from young people who had difficult relationships with their birth parents) because we had built up to that moment throughout the play.

  We also look at the music industry in *Redemption*, what it's like for someone like Maz to establish herself in what is a male dominated world – to be taken seriously as a young female artist. It was brilliant having Jammz and the Last Skeptik on the creative team, their contribution to the show and its success, through the musical score, cannot be underestimated.

BP *Can you speak a little bit about the character of the social worker, Michael?*

MN   We didn't want to be too critical of the care system because it's an easy target and there are many people working within it who are doing phenomenal work. And that's something that we wanted to highlight in this particular play. Although Maz is frustrated with her situation, she has had very robust support from Michael, who is her old social worker, now moved on to a new job. He has kept a relationship with Maz, however, and that's not uncommon. Some social workers go above and beyond, and it's difficult because there is so much bureaucracy for them to deal with in terms of boundaries and safeguarding and pressure for them to record, in detail, every telephone call or home visit, all discussions day-in, day-out and so on. Social workers have to tread a fine line when making decisions and we wanted to show this. Michael is a character who really cares about this young person and wants to go above and beyond his job to make sure that Maz is safe and well supported.

BP *The lead part of Maz is a big one and a lot of responsibility. What goes into making that casting decision?*

MN Yeah. Maz is a phenomenal part and a huge responsibility for anybody who's playing it. There was really no choice because the young person who I did cast felt so strongly about the part and could really relate to the character, so much so, a form of osmosis happened, she literally absorbed the part! She became Maz. She had also never acted before so that brought a raw energy to her performance that was thrilling.

BP *Could you tell us a bit about the way you used the building?*

MN Maz is on the run. And she doesn't know where to go as she's sleeping rough. We wanted to take the audience on the same journey that Maz was on, never knowing where they were going next. We staged it in our home, which is two small warehouses, a warren of interconnecting big and small spaces. The great thing about *Redemption* is the scenes have very specific locations and I worked closely with James on that. The Rio scene was originally set in a bedroom. But I wanted to tell that love story as it develops in the most romantic place possible. James agreed. The idea of them being in the basement of the cinema, where they could play old films, gave such a beautiful backdrop to the scene. The audience were packed into a tiny room filled with discarded reels and old film posters from a bygone time, the basement of the old Rio. They were part of the scene sitting on cinema seats as the film was projected across the actors' faces. So we were in that moment, in that love story, and hearing the two of them sing, literally a foot away from the front row, was truly beautiful. And also at the end of the scene, when Maz feels rejected by Tayo's reluctance to kiss her, the explosion of her vulnerability through anger in that tiny, tiny space was extremely powerful. I think it's fair to say that many audience members were in shock at the interval.

BP *And in the moment when Tayo pushes her away, there were audible gasps and squeals and people feeling so much for her! Then, at the end, when we went into the chapel, it was not only a new space, but actually a new building . . . Can you speak about that decision?*

MN That was important because in this scene we visit Maz's hiding place as a child and we meet her mother for the first time. It's a momentous scene and a new beginning for Maz. So we go outside and into an abandoned chapel and we find Maz hiding under a pile of rubble amidst broken glass in the place that she went to as a child. The scene was in total darkness until Michael comes in with his torch and locates Maz's face hidden beneath the rubble as she clutches her old doll. That was a moving moment for the audience, because suddenly we saw the child, felt the trauma of a lost seven year old, hiding from an abusive and drunk mother. I think that visual moment told its own story.

BP *Is there anything else that you'd like to add?*

MN I'd quite like to talk about the care home scene. Space – how it affects an audience. So the tiniest space that the audience entered was the bedroom of Maz's care home. We only had room for a bed in the centre, in order to accommodate the audience. When Carlos broke into the room, brandishing a knife and threatening Maz, so close to the audience, we felt her fear. We understood her rage and her explosion of anger at the beginning of the play, because nobody was listening to her or understanding the threat Carlos presented. We had a brilliant sound designer and the crack of the wood when Carlos breaks into her room with the knife was in itself nightmarish, it was SO loud. Having nothing but the bed and Maz in the dimly lit room and then a character that is clearly unstable with a knife breaking in, puts the audience under the same threat as Maz. And that was what we wanted to do. We wanted everybody to step inside Maz's shoes and be terrified in the middle of the night.

Maggie Norris interviewed by Bel Parker
9 August 2022

www.ingramcontent.com/pod-product-compliance
Lightning Source LLC
Chambersburg PA
CBHW050331230426
43663CB00010B/1815